Where lies our hope for ourselves? It lies, I think, in a new and radically different view which we must take of our own professionalism. Just as I argued earlier in this book for the resurgence of hope and humanity in our students that can arise from replacing ability grouping with a fellowship of care, so do I believe that a prognosis of hope for ourselves can be made only if we turn the new professional institution in our midst towards new goals. . . . If unions do not become both advocates and instruments of meaningful teaching evaluation, *then we have lost our last, best chance to establish our credibility as professionals in our own eyes as well as in the estimations of our students and our communities. If* tenure *is not made in part a function of continuing quality instead of wholly a fungus of longevity, then tenure has no hope of survival at all. Both evaluated teaching and dependent tenure are inevitable consequences of professional self-control.*

THE NEW HOOKED ON BOOKS

DANIEL FADER
With
James Duggins, Tom Finn, and Elton McNeil

A BERKLEY MEDALLION BOOK
published by
BERKLEY PUBLISHING CORPORATION

Berkley Publishing Corporation
200 Madison Avenue
New York, N.Y. 10016

SBN 425-03426-7

BERKLEY MEDALLION BOOKS are published by
Berkley Publishing Corporation
200 Madison Avenue
New York, N.Y. 10016

BERKLEY MEDALLION BOOK ® TM 757,375

Printed in the United States of America

Berkley Medallion Edition, NOVEMBER, 1976

SECOND PRINTING

iv

This Book is Dedicated

to

Ivan Ludington

and

Maurice Fader

The Two Kindest Men

I Have Ever Known

Table of Contents

INTRODUCTION

Jim Duggins and Tom Finn are teachers with ten years of experience in the practice of *Hooked on Books* and the philosophy of English in Every Classroom. We met several years ago when they asked me to come to the West Coast to help them introduce my program to teachers in the San Francisco public schools. From that meeting has grown our subsequent friendship and this tenth anniversary edition of *Hooked on Books*.

The purpose of this book is four-fold: First, for the past few years I have been working toward realization of what must precede and accompany the program of *Hooked on Books* in order for it to be potentially as useful in the next decade as it seems to have been in the one just past. In essays whose titles and subjects range from "Remembering Ourselves" through "A Classroom Full of Teachers" to "Toward A Professional Union," I have tried to specify what I believe the appropriate context for the program should be.

Also, I have for some time wanted to expand greatly the section on writing in the original book. The past decade has brought us new information and attitudes, and even some new knowledge about how writing is learned and can be taught. The long essay "On the Teaching of Writing" is meant to be a personal report on what my friends and colleagues and I have learned and done, and hope to do about that difficult subject.

The third purpose of this new edition is to offer a practical environment for the program that expands beyond the two original schools in which it was first established. This is what my co-authors have intended to provide in their new chapters with the self-explanatory titles: "The Elementary Self-Contained Classroom," "Secondary Schools," and "Administering the Program." These three essays reflect their own very extensive experience—successes and failures alike—with the program in the Bay Area of northern California.

Finally, Professors Duggins and Finn have taken on, and completed, the enormous task of providing an entirely new reading list for this edition of *Hooked on Books*. Perhaps the amount of work they have done on "A Thousand Authors" can only be fully appreciated by people who have done similar work themselves, although I suspect that every reader of this book will understand the expense of self necessary to compile a tested and lengthy list of books attractive to young readers.

Those who are familiar with the original text of *Hooked on Books* will find that I have left its substance intact at the heart of this new edition, though I have reduced its extent by curtailing sections such as those on Writing, Team Teaching, and Professionalism—topics which are now the subjects of new and separate chapters. The three most extensive changes in text are omission of my analysis of the original book collection, rendered obsolete by the new Duggins/Finn list of authors; up-dating of the extraordinary Ludington Story, which has its own new chapter in place of the old at the end of the original *Hooked*; and omission of the 26 tables which Professor Elton McNeil had chosen to illustrate the statistical base of the essay which he called "Hooked on Research." As he noted in the original edition, an extensive analysis of more than 130 tables of statistics derived from his research on "Hooked on Books" at the W.J. Maxey Boys Training School, is available upon request from the United States Office of Education.

Chapter I

REMEMBERING OURSELVES

Daniel Fader

Writing now, early in 1976, I have before me a pamphlet entitled "Teaching English at Boys' Training School" which was published early in 1964 by the Bureau of School Services at the University of Michigan. The pamphlet was a first step toward the books called *Hooked on Books* (1966), and *Hooked on Books: Program and Proof* (1968). More than a prototype, "Teaching English" was a statement of my belief in the capacity of imprisoned boys to learn a literacy sufficient to their needs and to their desires. Though the belief may now be widely held, it was not entirely fashionable at the time:

"Juvenile delinquents? Incarcerated boys? Detained girls? Double-talk! They're young criminals, pure and simple. And it doesn't matter what you try to teach them in prison, because they're mostly too dumb or too stubborn to learn. If they weren't, they wouldn't be here in the first place."

The speaker? Head of one of the largest juvenile correctional institutions in the United States. The year was 1966, and the occasion was my visit to his facility at the invitation of his desperate Director of Education who had heard about the success of our experiment at Boys' Training School. The Director and I argued with the Head as much as I could or the Director dared, but we accomplished little in the way of persuasion. I argued that the difference between many boys and girls on the street, and some of those in his

1

prison was a matter of bad luck rather than weak mind, and that young people who had been put away by a world they didn't understand, often had pressing reasons to want to understand that world much better than they did. Literacy was one means to that understanding.

Though my arguments and audience have expanded during the past decade, my beliefs remain essentially unchanged. I believe literacy to be one of the learned responses to its world that makes humanity fully human. I believe that one of the few significant differences between mankind and lower orders of creatures is our sense of our own history: *We remember ourselves.* So far as we know, other creatures—except for genetic imprint—cannot profit from their past as we can. And our past is still primarily conserved in written forms.

Remembering ourselves was once a matter of being told who we were and what we had done. Perhaps for many of us the written word can never rival the oral tradition, whether pure in the epic or compounded in radio and television, for immediate appeal and impact. But the new oral tradition is still an infant, storing little more than present time in its memory. If we are not to be doomed to that fate most terrible for creatures of memory and imagination—continuous reinvention and endless repetition of the past—then literacy embodies our chief hope for ourselves.

I believe too that, beyond sufficient intelligence, the sole requirement upon a student for formal educability—the capacity to learn a useful portion of what the school experience has to offer—is a belief in the future, an anticipation of tomorrow that carries with it a conviction of tomorrow's inevitability. What a strange phrase to bring into question, *tomorrow's inevitability*, for those of us who cannot separate that conviction from our other reflexive life processes. But in our conviction we are immeasurably and often unknowingly fortunate, we who are innocent of the doubt of tomorrow that grows in the poor soil of impoverished days. Because we accept so unquestioningly the idea of consequence as implicit in action, we do not consider that the very meaning of the word is time-derived. If tomorrow is an unreliable concept, can consequence have its full meaning? If consequence is no longer a significant measure for action, then how shall we educate? Certainly in ways profoundly different from those we use now.

What we do now, we hope and intend, is to prepare for the future. Though teachers are sometimes properly accused of preparing their pupils for a world that was (or even for a' world that never was), their intent has always been to offer preparation that anticipates and fulfills tomorrow's needs. But no person, child or adult, who does not know the past, can or will believe in the importance of preparing for the future. Action and consequence are time sequent in a way that demands active remembrance of things past before tomorrow's inevitability can be persuasive. I believe that education as we know it is dependent upon belief in the future, itself dependent upon knowledge of the past. And that knowledge is still largely available only to the skills of literacy.

What report can now be made of the advancement of those skills, during the decade intervening between publication of the first *Hooked on Books* and this tenth anniversary edition? A hopeful report, I think, when it is placed within this context:

Twelve years ago several thousand copies of "Teaching English at Boys' Training School," offered without charge to interested enquirers by the Bureau of School Services, were requested and distributed nationwide with such unprecedented speed that the Bureau's resources were overextended. At the Bureau's request I searched for and found Berkley Books, a paperback publisher interested in marketing *Hooked on Books*, an extended version of the original pamphlet. Two years later, Berkley published the sequel entitled *Hooked on Books: Program and Proof*, in which Elton McNeil and I reported the expenditure of our time and federal dollars to demonstrate this simple thesis: That students who learn to associate both pleasure and necessity with acts of literacy, will learn to read and write.

After more than half-a-million copies of both books, after more than five hundred speeches, seminars, and institutes in forty-two states and three other countries, at least this much now seems sure: The program of *Hooked on Books*, sometimes known as "English in Every Classroom," was projected into a vacuum—the absence of comprehensive, proven schemes for teaching a willing literacy to reluctant learners. It may have spread because it was good or useful or both; it certainly spread because nothing else was available which systematically met the needs of those reluctant learners. The greatest significance of the observation lies neither in the quality of the program nor in the void which it filled. Instead, I think, it lies in the fact of its broadcast spread. Ten years after the first public report upon it was available, the program of *Hooked on Books* or "English in Every Classroom" has spread in some form to every one of our fifty states and at least a dozen other countries. I interpret this to mean that a good many of us who are professionally interested in literacy have taken a very hard look, in the last decade, at our students' motivation as well as at our materials and methods for affecting that motivation. This is the basis for my cautious optimism in reporting upon ten years of *Hooked on Books*.

If optimistic, then why cautious? Because any balanced view of this past decade must weigh a great deal of contrary evidence in assessing our progress toward national literacy:

In the spring of 1975 we had a party at our house that gave me a chance to poll twenty-eight people with a common interest (our fifteen adolescent sons played on the same hockey team), and greatly diverse backgrounds. At some time during a long, convivial evening I asked each of our twenty-eight guests about their primary daily source of local, national, and international news. Twenty-seven of twenty-eight answered in similar terms: "Television . . . TV . . . The six o'clock news . . . Eleven o'clock news." One man cited the radio because he spends a lot of the working day in his car.

I also asked them all if their newspaper, magazine, or book reading habits were different now from their habits of twenty-five years ago. Five men and women said they read as much or more than they did in 1950. Twenty-three said they read less now, and only two claimed to read a newspaper more or less completely every day.

In our community the thirty of us form as broad a cross-section within our age group as anyone is likely to put

4

together. We're fifteen middle-aged couples with thirty-seven children who are, will be, or have been in local public, parochial, and private schools. Several hundred teachers have tried, are trying, or will try to teach our children to read and write. They have gotten, are getting, and will get mighty little help from us.

Oh, we say the right things: "You should read more...Turn off the tube...Have you done your homework?...You can't get anywhere if you can't read and write...Reading is important!" But the one necessary support that teachers could always lean upon before is now gone. Not only are our children unlikely to be more honest or less bigoted than we are, they are also unlikely to learn to read easily or well or pleasurably while we watch television.

Perhaps no teacher ever actually said, or even thought, something like "Reading has a lot of friends out there," but had it been said, or thought, a quarter of a century ago, it would have been a powerful truth. Then we not only said the right things to support the teaching of reading in the schools, we did them, i.e., we praised reading and we read in our children's presence. No, I don't mean we read *to them*, though we did; I mean we read *in front of them*.

If reading ever had a lot of friends out there who provided a base upon which teachers of literacy could build, those friends are disappearing. If reading was one of two equal primary sources of news twenty-five years ago, it appears not to be now. If reading was a widely-advocated and widely-performed leisure time activity then, it probably isn't now. *And yet we express surprise, shock, chagrin, and anger when we rediscover each year that more children read less well than their parents or older siblings did before them.*

In parallel with the loss of the single, irreplaceable support that teachers of literacy must have from their students' families, those teachers have experienced a gain that is equally devastating. In the same quarter-century that has seen the eclipse of reading by television as a primary family leisure-time activity, class size in American elementary and secondary schools has increased significantly. Reliable figures are very difficult to find for at least two reasons: One, at the mid-century mark we apparently cared much less, in a public and published way, than we do now about class size. (Union contracts which specify class size are the obvious, and perhaps also the real reason why we now care in a public way.) And, two, the definition of "classroom teacher" has seldom been interpreted exactly the same way in two communities. Even less frequently has it been rigorously confined to those teachers who bear full responsibility for a class no matter how many special teachers, inside or outside of their classrooms, may be available to help them.

Having admitted that the difficulty of obtaining accurate comparative figures for 1950 and 1975 is considerable, having read what I could find and spoken to school people from every part of this country, I believe that the figure of thirty percent is a restrained estimate of the average rise in class size throughout the United States. Though I think forty percent may be nearer the true figure (from 25 students in 1950 to 35 students in 1975), I accept the conservative estimate that teachers who once had 25 students in their class now have thirty-three.

Given the parallel phenomena of decrease in society's performing (by contrast to its vocal) support for literacy, and increase in class size, perhaps American parents should be surprised only that so many of their children learn to read at all. Perhaps their sole justified anger is anger at themselves and their representatives who have used class size for a quarter-century as the easiest place to save money in budgets for local education.

Chapter II

A CLASSROOM FULL OF TEACHERS

Daniel Fader

If parents have neither taught literacy by example nor resisted the increase in class size that has made good classroom teaching so improbable, then how can teachers fairly be blamed for the diminishing quality of American literacy? Fairly, I believe they cannot be identified as the major cause of that decline. With equal fairness, however, I believe they cannot be found free of this significant blame:

In twenty years of teaching and ten years of active searching, I have not found a single teacher willing to claim that she or he teaches more than half the students in a class that numbers between thirty and thirty-five. Nor do I expect to find such a person, for every experienced teacher knows that no teacher can attend to the needs of that many students as though they were individuals with individual problems, which they are. Every teacher of literacy, by whatever name, understands that increased class size is one of the primary reasons for diminished performance. Knowing this, teachers have been doubly at fault: Once, for not fighting as hard for smaller classes as they have for larger salaries; and, twice, for not reorganizing their classrooms to meet the new reality of more students than one teacher can possibly teach. Here, for example, is the history and anatomy of one classroom reorganization that works:

A man I know whose vocation is production of television programs, acknowledged two sets of TV viewing statistics with responses so different from those I expected that I later wrote down what I could recall of his words and have it before me now. We were sitting in his office waiting for a studio to be available for us. Opening his mail, he found these figures in a public letter from a group interested in children and television, and read them to me: Children have watched an average of 18,000 hours of television by the time they finish high school; television sets are *on* about six hours a day in the average American home.

"Good news for you," I said, "but not so good for me."

"Yes," he said, "I suppose that's true. But in a way it's bad news for both of us."

"You mean because of the reading that doesn't happen while all that passive watching is going on?" Mild sarcasm. Our TV program together was to be about literacy and we had been talking about the relationship of increased television viewing to decreasing standards of reading and writing. "Unless you're worried about their ability to read *TV Guide*, how can all those hours of television be bad news for you?"

I think that his answer was profound, with the deepest implications for his profession as TV producer and mine as teacher: "Because," he said, "television is about people as we know them in their homes, their jobs, their recreation—about people in society. And six hours of TV watching a day has got to be changing society in ways we don't know about and maybe can't even guess. If people don't talk to each other in their homes, if most of what they do when they're together after the workday is to sit and watch, then maybe we're making people so different from what they were that we don't know enough about them even to entertain them. Maybe so many television shows are so bad, and fail so fast, partly because we can't know our audience. Television watching has changed them too much for us to keep up with who they are."

It sounded right to me when he said it, and it still does. Long afterward, I realized how much he'd been telling me about the vocation of teaching as well as the vocation of producing television programs. At first I thought that the most important application of his words, beyond his own

8

world, was to the teaching of literacy: Not knowing who our students are; not understanding that a thousand hours a year before a television set may produce a creature with an intellect basically different from one who spends that time in other ways; not understanding the implications of this difference for the learning and teaching of literacy—we continue to expect a level of performance in reading and writing that our students may be incapable of reaching.

Important as that is, I believe a still more important application of this man's words to teaching can and must be made. If illiteracy is crippling in part because it imprisons humanity within the walls of the present, then social isolation is paralyzing because it imprisons each human being within the walls of himself. Just as visual literacy cannot yet provide the same expansive sense of self-as-inheritor which comes from competence with print, neither can witnessed social intercourse provide the same sense of identity that social participation can give. If six hours a day of television in their homes is making isolated voyeurs of our students, then we must change our style of teaching to meet the needs of a new clientele.

Like so many non-scientific discoveries, the antidote for this new isolation may lie in a revelation which is really a rediscovery. Of all educational institutions or segments of American educational history, the one-room schoolhouse ranks undisputed first in two categories: Most often referred to, and least well understood. When the great strength that it developed to compensate for its great natural weakness is properly understood, I think we may then find ourselves in possession of an antidote equally effective for the slow poisons of social isolation and swollen class size which now infect our schools.

What caused the demise of the one-room schoolhouse with a single teacher in charge of eight or nine grades? The question does not appear to be very interesting because the answer is both easy and obvious: Neighborhoods grew in school-age population to the point where all eligible children could not be accommodated in a single classroom of any encompassable size. The question becomes important for our time, however, when it is rephrased in this way: At what point in the growth of its population did the one-room schoolhouse become an impractical response to the educational needs of the children it was meant to serve? The answer should become exceptionally interesting to us when we realize that the critical point of growth was never defined in terms of how many students a single teacher could teach. Instead, it was always defined in terms of how many students a single classroom could accommodate.

The great natural weakness of the one-room schoolhouse was its expandability. No one asked the local teacher how many students she could teach. The only question she might be asked was how many she could seat. If she had twenty-four in eight grades and a family with six school-age children moved into the neighborhood, she found herself with thirty in eight grades, and no one asked her if she could teach them. So much as I can tell from extensive inquiry, no teacher who taught in a one-room schoolhouse ever experienced the luxury of class size limited by her capacity to meet the educational needs of her students.

Why then is it necessary for teachers' union contracts now to specify class size? And why would anyone write about swollen class size as a poison which infects our schools? Because we have forgotten the great strength that the one-room schoolhouse developed to compensate for its expandable weakness. We have forgotten that the single teacher in the one-room schoolhouse was in fact both a teacher and a supervisor of many teachers who themselves were students in her classroom.

In the hundreds of conversations and interviews I have had with teachers who once taught in those schoolhouses, a common bright thread has woven through their reminiscences. Often against the dark background of remembered vulnerability to the community's habits and mores, teachers have recalled for me their daily sense of well-being that derived from the certainty that no child in their classroom was lost. Representative of those teachers were two women I met on a visit to North Dakota, both of whom had graduated from the same high school almost fifty years ago and gone immediately to teach in one-room schoolhouses.

How had they survived with no training and no

professional support? I asked. Who had helped them when they needed help? Who had given them guidance when they were overwhelmed by their own inexperience? "The children," they both answered. "The children were the ones who made survivors of us." Older children taught younger children, quicker children helped slower children. So long as you could seat them, give them some room to work, and keep them warm in winter, no number was necessarily impossible. Both women said that the difference then between twenty-five and thirty-five students was nothing like the difference that ten children could make in their classrooms now. Yes, it had something to do with the quality of self-discipline taught in the home. But it had much more to do, they thought, with the fact that every child was looked after by at least one other child and maybe more. *No one got lost* inside the classroom and teachers never had to suffer the guilty realization of needful, unattended children.

With that lesson before us as we grew from a rural to an urban nation, what did we learn from the one-room schoolhouse with its multiplicity of teachers? We learned only that one teacher can be made to serve a constantly expanding number of students. We learned only to ask the questions of accommodation, not the questions of quality. How many can you seat? (not how many can you teach?) was for too long the governing measurement for the number of teachers employed in American public education.

But what happened to the second part of the lesson taught by the one-room schoolhouse? What happened to the knowledge that teachers cannot teach large classes without the help of students who are also teachers? What happened to the knowledge that children who can resist or ignore adults are often the same children who cannot deny the attention or withstand the pressure of their peers?

Lost also was the knowledge that all teachers possess from their own experience, the knowledge that understanding more often accompanies the act of teaching than any other act of the human intellect. Knowing that, knowing also that we cannot teach or touch every student ourselves, we have nevertheless failed to use the students in our classes to help the students in our classes.

11

For the past six years I have applied the lessons of peer teaching to my own classrooms. Brought to it by my inability to help more than half the individuals in classes with thirty to forty students; brought to it by my inability to teach all those who wanted to be taught, much less those who didn't; brought to it by certain knowledge that my classes were not going to decrease significantly in size nor my teaching increase significantly in quality; brought to it by the desperation in the teacher that continuously inadequate teaching breeds—I have made every student, in classes of forty or less, responsible for teaching as well as learning. Nothing in my teaching experience has ever worked so invariably or so well.

For me these are the procedures that work best: At the first meeting of the class I announce that this course has a novel and therefore unexpected dimension for each of its students, a requirement I want them to know about and to be prepared to fulfill beginning with the second week of the course. Perhaps the most unexpected part of this new requirement, I tell my students, is that it has everything to do with their fellow students and nothing to do with the materials of the course.

Even at this point, having said so little, I always find my students' interest in what I will say next to be a sad, small comment on the current state of teaching and learning in America. "Everything to do with [your] fellow students" is a phrase they have never before heard applied to a classroom or course requirement. They are so accustomed to thinking of schoolwork in terms of materials to encompass and methods to comprehend *in relation to themselves alone*, that the idea of another dimension to learning has the same immediate attraction for them as serious attribution of a fourth dimension to solid objects has for geometricians. Like them, students can't believe it but they want to.

The scheme, as I explain it, very rapidly acquires believability: "Early next week," I tell them, "I will put each of you in a group with two other students. From the time I tell you who they are, you and I together are responsible for what they learn in this class and each of them in the same way is responsible for you. No one can receive credit for this

12

course or complete it with a grade satisfactory to himself unless the other two people in his group do so as well. You can look at it this way: Either everybody in a group makes it or nobody does."

Their response, of course, is amazement. In fact the surprise is often so great, the requirement so unanticipated, that their first questions are small ones about details rather than large ones about responsibility or ethics; both of those usually come later. They begin most frequently with questions about grouping: How will I divide them into groups of three? Sometimes they also ask why the groups are that size, rather than larger or smaller?

In answer to both questions I explain that I will gather as much information about them from their own mouths and hands as can be had in a single week. Then I will assess that information according to my own mysterious standards and on Monday I will announce groupings based upon my notion of which individuals can work most profitably together. I tell them that much and no more, because the explanation is not only true but usually sufficient to satisfy their immediate curiosity. I also tell them that I will be glad to discuss in detail my methods of grouping when the course is completed. After six years, twenty different classes, and more than six hundred students who have participated in grouping, I can now report that only a very few have asked me about my methods when the course was done. If they ask, this is what I tell them:

With all the oral and written information I could accumulate in that first week—interviews, classroom participation; in-class and out-of-class writing—I ranked you and your classmates from top to bottom according to each person's apparent preparation for the course I intended to teach. Since (for example) there were thirty-six students in your class, I ranked them one through thirty-six, giving the number *one* to the student who seemed to me best able to give help to others in the subject of the course, and the number *thirty-six* to the student apparently most needful of receiving help.

Yes, the judgments were arbitrary, I reply to their most customary accusation, but that becomes irrelevant when you

13

understand the single use I made of the ranking. What I did was to divide the list into three equal segments. Then I made the first group from the students at the top of each segment, proceeding through the three lists until my last group of three was composed of the students at the bottom of each. (If I have a remainder of one when the class total is not divisible by three, I make two groups of two [combining the odd one with a group of three] because I have found that groups of two are not as good as three, but much better than groups of four—primarily because fours tend to break down into two groups of two that waste time in confrontation or, worse yet, into one group of three with a single, isolated outsider either looking on, or looking away. If I have a remainder of two, I am satisfied to leave them as they are.) In the case of your class, the ranking of one through thirty-six divided conveniently into three equal segments of twelve. Those segments numbered one through twelve, thirteen through twenty-four, and twenty-five through thirty-six. Therefore, I made up the first group from students identified by numbers one, thirteen, and twenty-five; the second from numbers two, fourteen, and twenty-six; and I followed that pattern through the twelfth and last group of students numbered twelve, twenty-four, and thirty-six. Then I threw away the list because I had no more use for it. And a month after the course began, I neither knew nor cared to know the place of a single person in that list.

As for the number three—why not two? If I break down remainders of four into two groups of two, why not divide the class into pairs? After a good deal of experimentation with groups ranging from two through five, I think I know why three is best for all levels of education beyond elementary school and probably best for the fifth and sixth grades as well:

Young children usually do very well in groups of two, especially by contrast to how badly they often do in groups of three or more. Perhaps because kindergarten through grades three and four is a time of physical immaturity, children at those years seem to have a fairly primitive social sense. Put three together and too frequently one is either ignored or wishes that he were. But paired children seem to

14

do very well at this level, not only in terms of simple interaction largely uncomplicated by sexuality but also in a kind of useful remnant of the parallel play, now parallel learning, which characterizes their younger years.

Quite the opposite seems to be true of students approaching or in the throes of puberty and menarche. For them, groups of two often intensify private feelings that are diminished by the more varied relationships possible in groups of three. Or, to put the argument for threes more positively, the expansive socialization that usually accompanies increased sexual awareness appears to welcome the more complex grouping. Older students can look after and care for their fellows with a consideration that younger students often cannot express.

I also tell my students that I violate my own method for grouping any time I have individuals of the same sex composing a group of three in a class which has enough males and females to have both sexes in each group. When that happens, I replace one of the original group with the person of the other sex nearest in the list, my purpose being to have all groups of three contain members of both sexes whenever possible. In my own scale of desirable means to accomplish significant teaching objectives, bisexual grouping ranks second only to grouping itself.

If grouping has the potential for bringing attention to every student, what further educational benefits can bisexual grouping confer? Two benefits of very different kinds, one for female students and one for males: For too many teaching years I had a recurrent, unpleasant experience which has been repeated only infrequently since I discovered that bisexual grouping offers a double remedy. The experience always began with the first set of formal papers I gathered from a class after perhaps two weeks of the semester had passed. Of the five best papers, often three and sometimes four and occasionally five were written by people who signed female names. If three, then I was likely to associate a face and a personality with only two of the five best papers—*the other two*. Given Murphy's law, I should have expected what once actually happened: The five best papers in a class of thirty-eight (24 girls, 14 boys) were all written by people who signed female names, only one of which I could fit to a face; the four worst were written by people who signed male names, three of whom I already knew after two weeks of class.

Distressed at what I thought to be unconscious male favoritism on my part, I attempted to confirm my failure by discovering its absence in female teachers. Instead, I was surprised to find that women who were usually open with me and not guarded or self-protective when discussing their teaching, were reluctant to discuss this aspect of their classrooms. Only very slowly, and never without being preceded by a confession of failure on my part, did female colleagues confide in me their similar experiences: After two weeks they too always knew far more faces for male names than for female names on their class rosters. The more I listened, the more I knew that nothing so simple as my male chauvinism could account for an experience duplicated in classrooms taught by female teachers.

It was an irritated and chance observation by a woman teacher that finally put me right in my search: "Boys are so *pushy*! You know what I mean—they've got their hand up before they have any idea of what they're going to say. I'll swear they think of an answer while they're waving their hands in your face."

Pushy! What a perfect word. Pushing their hands not only up but at you, pushing their faces and bodies forward in their eagerness to be recognized, pushing their words out as rapidly as possible . . . while the girls (who know the answers at least as well) sit back, smiling at each other and to themselves at those pushy, pushy boys.

Is aggressiveness inherent in the male human and encouraged by his environment? Do the aggressive, quick-entry and quick-exit games characteristically played by boys and not by girls reflect the boys' bent, society's expectation, or both? Instead of debating the questions, a pursuit too inactive for teachers of pushy boys to afford, let us act upon our certain knowledge and our need: Aggressive male behavior in the classroom is a response which may be both tempered and transmitted by the close interaction of males

16

and females in a small group where each individual is responsible, in a meaningful way, for the learning accomplished by every other member of the group.

Evidence for this statement is the changed nature of my classroom and the classrooms of other teachers who have employed bisexual grouping wherever possible. In this age of measurement, can the report of unmeasured change be persuasive? Whether it can be is a matter for individual decision. That it should be is not doubted by teachers who have seen their students' classroom behavior undergo significant change that originates in bisexual grouping.

In simplest terms, girls seem to talk more while boys talk less. What appears to happen is that girls have an unprecedented number of opportunities to speak when boys become aware of them as people with active intellects and classroom rights that are repressed and abridged by male-aggressive classroom behavior. Such opportunities, frequently taken, first become expectation and then may develop into habit. At the very least, bisexual grouping seems to encourage a considerate classroom relationship between the sexes that more traditional learning arrangements have been unable to promote.

Earlier I stated my belief that bisexual grouping confers two benefits of very different kinds. One is the increased female participation in classroom discussion which results in part from group-modified male aggressiveness; the other is an increased male literacy produced by placing males in an environment shaped by the written competence of female group members. On the average, girls seem to write more easily and more fluently than boys from the time of earliest literacy up through their undergraduate years. As a group, girls have generally scored higher on every test of literacy that I know about, and the difference does not appear to vanish until graduate school.

Not only do I want the early opportunity to notice and to know the female members of my class, but I also want the opportunity for female literacy to influence the work of male students in my class. Both opportunities are made available to me and my students through the device of bisexual

17

grouping. This is especially true of written performance when part of my charge to the groups is phrased in these terms:

"You are responsible for each other in every reasonable way that affects learning outside the classroom and in some ways that affect learning inside the classroom. In both places your first responsibility is to yourself, but now—unlike other classes you have taken—'yourself' has been expanded to include two other people. For example, you will write most of your papers individually after you have discussed the topic collectively. Once the papers have been written, you will have two further responsibilities. The first is to read the papers of the two people in your group to see if they make good sense; the second is to see if they are well-written. Unconvincing rhetoric and bad grammar; inaccurate spelling; poor punctuation, paragraphing, and capitalization—all are as much your responsibility in the papers of your group fellows as they are in your own.

"Your task is not to *make* changes in the two papers you read; instead, it is to *suggest* changes and to *explain* why you have suggested them. As important as it is for people to see examples of good practice, it is even more important for them to understand why those examples are good. Your primary and perhaps most difficult continuing assignment in this course is to *explain* the rhetorical and grammatical suggestions you make so that they are understandable and therefore useful to your peers."

One of the most common positive responses my students have made to this demand, has been the clarification of their own practices that results from the need for explaining them to others. Which is another way of saying what a student told me about the change in his own self-test for competence: "I used to know I was ready [for an examination]" he said, "when I could answer every question I could think of. Now, after being with my group for a whole semester, I don't know I'm ready until I can *explain* every answer." For six years I've been collecting such student opinions about grouping and I intend to end this section by giving students the last word. But before I do, I want to look briefly at another and far more popular form of grouping

18

which is pandemic in North American schools. I refer of course to ability grouping which, by any name (tracking, streaming), is the single most destructive arrangement of human beings into groups ever invented by other well-meaning human beings.

Some angry teachers, hoping as I do to dismantle the structure of ability grouping, deny any claim that it was ever well-meant. They cannot find a trace of good intention in an act which formally separated more and less able students into groups that have come to know themselves even as they are known—as "promising" and "unpromising," as "continuing" and "terminal," and ultimately (in their own eyes) as hopeful and hopeless.

In view of what it has spawned, perhaps tracking is now inconceivable in its former role as a method of helping teachers to pay more attention to good and bad students alike. "Speak to the students!" my angry friends say. Ask them, and not the well-intentioned arbiters of their fate, how it is to look about the classroom, day after day, and to see your own dulled hope for yourself reflected in the eyes of your classmates? What can be so good, they ask, that it can counter-balance something so bad?

The answer to the question, of course, is *nothing*. Nothing at all can be so profitable in the segregation of the more able from the less able that it redeems the cost of hope's destruction. That tracking or ability grouping was wrong-headed to begin with, every teacher who ever taught or studied in a one-room schoolhouse must have known. Now, in retrospect, after the incalculable damage of a half-century when able children have learned that they need look after no one but themselves while less able children have learned that they are not worth looking after, many teachers are shocked and frightened at the depth of community alienation directed at American schools. But who can be truly surprised that the vast numbers of children taught to regard themselves as an inferior species, have become adults and parents who do not value compulsory education and do not teach their children to value it?

A damage more subtle, if not less destructive, is done to the privileged participants in this system of ability grouping.

By contrast to their able counterparts, both in one-room schoolhouses and in the intellectually unsegregated systems which briefly took their place, privileged students now suffer from a progressive attenuation and atrophy of their humanity. So marked is this debilitating disease, so weakened are they by their unremitting attention to themselves, that they are genuinely startled at classroom demands upon their humanity rather than upon their understanding or memory. And it is this same ceaseless self-attention that causes them to become the manipulative parents who obtain the best schedules and best teachers for their own children, no matter what the cost may be to other students or to the system itself.

Who are the worst people we have in our classrooms? Not the worst students, but the worst people? What a painful commentary upon ourselves as educators, is the response that repeatedly confuses the quality of being a human being with the quality of being a student. In hundreds of instances I have asked the question about worst people and received answers in terms of worst students. The point of my enquiries has been to emphasize ability grouping as a prime cause for more able students to lose a part of their social humanity, their ability to attend to human needs not originally their own. What teacher has not had enough experience of moderate brightness coupled with immoderate self-interest in her students, the precise coupling that makes them again and again the worst people in her classroom?

Where the homogeneous classroom is made heterogeneous, where ability grouping is replaced by the kind of group work I have advocated in this section—in those circumstances it is possible to treat the parallel diseases of swollen classes, monstrous egos, and deflated hope with the contagious cure of responsibility-for-learning genuinely shared between teacher and students. Where such a cure is invoked and unremittingly pursued, words such as these from my own students can become a representative summary of both prognosis and results:
1. "When you have to explain why something's wrong or something's right, you really have to understand."
2. "I never realized how different people think about words.

20

You know, it's one thing when a teacher says 'change this and this.' But it's something else when somebody in your own class, your own age, says it."

3. "I got so used to thinking about people as smart or not smart that I forgot how everybody learns things different and knows different things. I thought _____ was kind of dumb at first and I wished he wasn't in our group. But now I think maybe he taught me more than I taught him. Not about poetry or writing, but about getting along. You know what I mean?"

4. "I've always liked school...but I never looked after anybody else and nobody ever looked after me. This was really something. The three of us are going to take another class together next semester so we can do the same thing."

5. "I never thought that three people could write one paper. But we did, both ways. I mean, when we had to do three separate papers that fitted together, and even when we had to turn in one paper that all three of us had written. That really taught me something about different styles. Before that, I don't think I knew what *style* meant."

6. "When you told us we were responsible for the grammar in each other's papers, I about gave up right there. Why? Because to tell you the truth, _____ and _____ weren't too good at punctuation and things like that. Then, when I saw I could explain it so they understood and did it better - wow! that was really something. I'll tell you a funny thing. I think I could even be an English teacher, maybe...."

7. "It was good to have three people because then you could say what you really meant and not worry about it being too heavy. I mean, if it's only two of you, then maybe you wouldn't say just what you were thinking because it might be wrong or it might hurt and there wouldn't be anybody to balance it."

8. "It's a great way to get to know people. We're going to try to live together in the dorm next year. You know, we're friends, and we wouldn't have been if we hadn't worked together."

9. "It was like having three pairs of eyes instead of one."

Chapter III

ON THE TEACHING OF WRITING

Daniel Fader

Of the public events which have had the most profound influence upon American education since the end of the Second World War, a chronological ordering might begin with the GI Bill, the advent of the Television Era, and the 1954 Supreme Court decision which began desegregation of Southern schools, continue through Sputnik, the war in Vietnam, and the revolution exported from Berkeley, then conclude with the movement for women's liberation and the use of busing to begin desegregation of Northern schools. These eight events, seen in a lengthening perspective, now seem to me to fall into two distinct categories. Standing by itself, enormous and uncomprehended in its implications, is the advent of the Television Era. Standing together, the remaining seven form a second group educationally less significant in its entirety than the single, pandemic fact of television.

In spite of identifying the seven together as less significant, I do not mean to underestimate their social impact. For the emphasis in the statement derives from their effect upon education, rather than their effect upon the social texture of our lives. Each of the seven has not only exerted a force more immediate than television upon my own life, but the individual power of each has been relatively clear to me. By contrast, slowly, even yet dimly, I am just beginning to perceive what television has meant and may mean to my profession.

One of the most striking examples of its effect upon the lives of students and teachers may be inferred from an old collegiate dilemma which has recently taken on a new dimension demanding a new response. The old dilemma is the question of what to do about the literacy of undergraduate students at all levels of collegiate education in North America. The new dimension is the dissatisfaction now expressed throughout every department and program of humanities, sciences, and engineering faculties; throughout graduate and professional schools; throughout the entire range of employers, both part and full time; and throughout the student population itself—at the deficient quality of undergraduate literacy. One recent response to this new dimension of dissatisfaction (so broadly expressed as to have become different in kind rather than different only in degree), is a radical proposal for the certification of undergraduate literacy, which now awaits formal action of the faculty in the College of Literature, Science, and the Arts at the University of Michigan.

The context for this proposal is a complete internal review of the graduation requirements of the College which was undertaken in 1973 and completed in 1975. As part of the review, many open hearings were held in which students and faculty offered opinions upon the graduation requirements and suggestions for their improvement. According to members of the Graduation Requirements Commission and other faculty members who attended many of the hearings, their greatest surprise was the breadth and vehemence of faculty opinion about the composition requirement—one semester of English composition taken in the first year of residence. Or, more accurately, their greatest surprise was the breadth and vehemence of faculty distress at the quality of student literacy.

No, said one observer, he was not so much surprised at the expressed dissatisfaction as he was at its widespread, *conscious* existence in the faculty. For the first time in his long career in this and other schools, he said, he had actually heard teaching scientists declare that undergraduate literacy had to be everybody's business because nobody's students could read or write well enough to satisfy even themselves,

23

much less their teachers. *That*, he said, from the mouths of chemists, physicists, mathematicians, biologists, and statisticians, not to mention the social scientists and humanists, was a mouthful. *That* also forms the context for the proposal reproduced in full at the end of this chapter,* a proposal which begins with the following paragraph:

According to testimony taken by the Graduation Requirements Commission, many [College] faculty have perceived a significant decline in the quality of their students' literacy during the past two decades. When asked to characterize the nature of that decline, our colleagues often used descriptive terms and phrases summarized in the word "unpracticed." Faculty members repeatedly told the [Commission] that many of their students appear to be unaccustomed to the demands of literacy, that they seem to be unfamiliar with both perceptive reading and careful composition.

The proposal goes on to attribute this unpracticed literacy to the demands of a lifetime of three hours a day of television "in homes where television provides six hours of daily visual diversion", and to secondary school English classes in which "very little English composition is assigned or completed" because of the great increase in class size that has coincided with the advent of the Television Era. Having thereby attempted to identify the primary causes of the disease, it then proposes a remedy that may be relevant to the problems of teaching writing with which this chapter will be concerned:

A. The Graduation Requirement in English Composition shall have two parts:

1. Part One shall be election ... of two courses, in two of the first three semesters after matriculation, which are numbered below three hundred and chosen from those offered for certification in English Composition by any unit in the College.

2. Part Two shall be election...of one course in the major field in either semester of the junior year or first semester of the senior year, which is numbered three hundred or above and chosen from those offered for certification by any unit in the College.

B. The Graduation Requirement in English Composition shall have been fulfilled when three different instructors teaching three separate courses, two taken in the first three semesters after matriculation and a third taken in the major field in the fifth, sixth, or seventh semesters, have declared themselves reasonably satisfied with the quality of a student's English composition.

At the heart of this requirement is the concept of certification in literacy awarded by teachers of all subjects, rather than credit for literacy given by teachers of English. Certification is here distinct from credit, because the former is to be obtained as the result of work in any subject while the latter can be obtained only by work done in English composition.

I have two reasons for quoting from this proposal to a college faculty in a book intended primarily for teachers of literacy in elementary and secondary schools. The first reason must be apparent to anyone familiar with the two basic concepts upon which the original Hooked on Books program was built: *Saturation* referred to the distribution of paperbound books, magazines, and newspapers throughout the curriculum, while *Diffusion* referred to the requirement that every teacher become "an intermediary between the student and functional literacy. In order that the student may come to view writing as a (necessary and useful) means to all ends, all ends which he pursues in a scholastic context must insist upon writing as a means through which they can be approached. In short, every teacher becomes a teacher of English and English is taught in every classroom."

Only little more than a decade after proposing English in Every Classroom for the faculty of a boys' training school, and soon thereafter to the faculty of an urban junior high school, I find myself proposing it once again to the faculty of an undergraduate college. My sense of cyclical history has never been stronger than when I attended hearings on the graduation requirement of English composition, then meetings on my proposal with the dean and various other teachers/administrators—in each case to hear ideas that I had advocated a decade earlier now recycled into a form intended to fit the collegiate privileged as well as imprisoned boys and impoverished adolescents.

The second reason for including this proposal in the new *Hooked on Books* is to obtain emphasis by contrast, in this instance the contrast between a proposition that was believable in the mid-sixties and a proposition (the same one) that is unbelievable now. I quote that proposition from the opening paragraph on the teaching of writing in the 1968 edition:

> One of the most interesting yearly statistics made available to many university faculties is the number of incoming freshmen chosen from the top ten percent of their high school classes. The number has recently grown so large at some universities, that their faculties are now more concerned about good students who are excluded than about poor students who may still be admitted. Though this improvement in quality in the entering class has been nowhere more marked than in Freshman English, the promised land of no Freshman English course is not yet at hand. In spite of the notable increase in intelligence and accomplishment which characterizes the average freshman, he still writes miserably when he enters the university. Because of his wholly inadequate preparation in composition, he must take an English course designed to teach him how to write at least well enough to survive four years of college. There can be little doubt that, at many schools, Freshman English is successful in realizing this aim.

What an index to an era, happily now passing, those sexist pronouns are! Both context and substance are as anachronistic as the form: In the mid-sixties, members of the English Department at the University of Michigan could propose to their colleagues throughout the College that the time had come to require of all undergraduate students a single semester of work in English composition. The proposal was remarkable then in a way exactly opposed to the way that it would be remarkable now. Such a proposal in many colleges and universities of the mid-seventies would be an admission of failed hope and exasperbated need, for it would be a return to an English requirement that had been dropped from the curriculum a decade before. It would, in 1976, be both regressive and realistic.

In 1966, at the University of Michigan, the proposal was made and welcomed in recognition of the increasing intellectual quality of our entering students: "They are better prepared than they ever were," we said to each other in our department and subsequently to our colleagues in the College. "Because the schools are doing a better job, we need to do less to remediate or polish their compositional skills." Proceeding to reduce a two-semester composition requirement to a single semester, we believed and acted upon an analysis that was a delusion mounted on a chimera, both about to plunge over the edge of ten years of declining SAT verbal scores.

What sent us so wrong? Three reasons, I think, two being of relatively small importance to this section on writing: One, we were tired of spending 40% of our department's budget on Freshman English; two, the great increase of applicants to all colleges had allowed us to raise our entrance standards even higher than they had been. The third reason, however, is critical to the teaching of writing in our time: We who teach and who place such a premium on knowledge, confusing it often with information, persistently praised our students in the early and mid-sixties with adjectives like "knowledgeable" and statements like, "They know so much more than we (I) did at the same age (stage)." What we never fully comprehended was how they had gained that information and what price they had paid for it.

My argument must now be transparent: That the level of worldly information so frequently remarked and sometimes

27

admired in the young, is a level often now attained by life-long membership in the Television Era, a membership purchased at the expense of literacy. My department's response ten years ago to one manifestation of that membership was thoroughly appropriate in the context of the many schools that had and would abolish Freshman Composition entirely or in part. Appropriate or not, the response was profoundly mistaken and has done its part to produce the outcry from employers, professional schools, students, and *finally* from faculty that has caused me to construct the proposal for an English Composition Board and a certification program reproduced at the end of this chapter.

It is a bitter irony that, in the words of the first editions of *Hooked on Books*, "the promised land of no Freshman English course" may now be at hand. Once we hoped for it because we believed that its inevitable coming would be sign and symbol of rampant national literacy. How little we realized that the promised land would be populated by an insatiable race of television sets which, aided and abetted by overcrowded classrooms, would nourish itself by consuming the literacy of the young.

What to do? As I have indicated in the previous chapter, we must begin by disposing of the twin myths of our students' predisposition toward literacy and our own ability to teach literacy effectively to a class of 35 students, whether or not that class is multiplied by five such groups in a day. Once we are impelled by the sense of loss of self that loss of the past implies, once we understand the full poverty of the imagination that afflicts those who have no need to supply their own images to complete the television experience—by contrast to three other common sources of recreation in the home: radio, reading, music—then perhaps we will be brave enough or wise enough to seek the help we need to ensure that our students survive a changing culture in possession of themselves.

In order that our students may learn to write, thereby to know the self-possession that written language gives, the help we need help to give is just that help our students need help to receive: Even as we cannot give attention in sufficient

28

quantity to each of our students, not only because of their numbers but also because of their need, they cannot beneficially receive our attention, not only because of their numbers but also because they have grown accustomed to the absence of attention given or received in the new familial structure engendered by six hours of daily television in the average home. No one, I think, can now know the full meaning of this extraordinary influence upon our North American culture, but anyone can know what this social change means and has meant to the teaching of writing in our schools.

What anyone can know is that every successful writing program of the past twenty-five years (*success* defined as programs in extensive use that significantly increased both the quantity and quality of literacy for almost all of their participants), has had *great frequency of examined performance* as its primary component: You write a lot though you don't ever write much for any single assignment, and everything you write receives some sort of response from the instructor. Which is, of course, why almost all such programs, no matter how well conceived, have failed either to enjoy long life at their place of origin or to replicate themselves frequently beyond their original environs.

With the oppressive burden of class size increased by forty percent in twenty-five years, teachers have been unable consistently to attend to frequent writing performance even where they and their students may have been so inclined. Student literacy, spread thin between the twin poles of declining faculty attention and vanishing familial persuasion, now requires what no teacher alone can supply, what few families appear willing or able to provide, and what is still available without stint in the classroom: unavoidable, unremitting pressure for performance. In this case, *peer pressure* is its name.

Having discussed grouping—the most powerful, available, and unutilized source of peer pressure—in Part II of this essay, I mean now to apply its principles and usages to the teaching of writing. The first of its benefits is at once its greatest and most controversial: where students are placed in groups of two through perhaps the fourth grade and in threes thereafter, readers with eyes that are not teachers' eyes are available to attend to every word written by every student in every class.

No one denies that the predominant reason for so little writing assigned or performed in later elementary and all secondary grades, is the impossible number of responses required of teachers of today's impossibly large classes. But reason does not require that the presence of such classes must dictate the absence of much writing. Instead, reason would note the functional illiteracy of so many North American high school graduates, the improbability of dramatic reduction in class size, and then reason would determine to make use of the single unused resource it has immediately available: *peer attention*. If reason would so conclude, then why have I characterized the benefit of peer attention as both great and "controversial"? The following four paragraphs, quoted from the section on "Writing" in *Hooked on Books: Program and Proof* (1968), provide the basis for an explanation:

Team teaching is an old phrase which this plan hopes to invest with new meaning. In return for lightened classroom responsibility, each English teacher acts as a resource person and a guide for his colleagues in the diffusion of English throughout every classroom in the school. He assists each member of his team to set up a writing schedule which produces at least one piece of writing every other day in all subjects other than English. Writing in mathematics class about processes of arithmetic or practical applications of algebra; writing in shop or art classes about particular skills and necessary procedures; writing in science classes about the physical nature of his environment—all these occasions serve not only to make the student master of a significant portion of his verbal world, but to reinforce his special knowledge of that particular subject. Since in this view of the English curriculum the frequency of written exercises is far more important than their length, they vary from a few sentences to an occasional page. They are never unpleasantly long, they are not always read, and their grammar and rhetoric are not corrected by the subject instructor unless he strongly desires to do so.

First, let me explain the unusual practice of requiring students to write papers that no instructor will read. The purpose of written exercises in all divisions of the curriculum is not so much to get students to write correctly as it is simply to get them to write. The radical aspect of this approach to teaching writing does not lie in some Utopian notion of making prose stylists of all public school students. The real innovation is that it depends far less upon the teacher and far more upon the student than do more traditional methods of teaching writing. Instead of a few papers covered with his own corrections, the teacher has many papers at least partially covered with students' prose. Of the five sets of papers received in every two-week period by instructors in subjects other than English, one set per week is read and commented upon for content by the class instructor, one set every two weeks is passed on by him to the students' English teacher who corrects grammar and rhetoric, and one set per week is filed *unread* in the students' folders. This treatment of one set of papers each week in every classroom recognizes and encourages the idea that the practice of writing may be distinguished from its performance. It offers the student opportunity to condition himself for performance by allowing him time to exercise his writing muscles. Filing one set of papers each week without either reading or correcting them serves as a constant reminder to English teacher and subject teacher alike of the real purpose of these continuing exercises—to develop the student's prose-writing muscles to the point where he can use them without fear of aches and strains. Until that point is reached, practice will be far more beneficial to the student than correction.

The idea of unread papers has long been rejected in American education on the basis that "children must have some tangible evidence that their efforts are appreciated or they won't work." Translation of this unchallengeable truth into the notion that everything a student writes must be read, or otherwise he won't write, is a tribute to the human capacity for the illogical. And whoever thought that "appreciation" and "reward" could be equated with papers covered by red-pencil corrections?

The unsurprising fact is that a child can be taught to practice writing, both in the classroom (brief papers) and outside of it (the journal), just as he can be taught to practice a musical instrument or an individual sport. Just as in music and sports, the key to practice in writing is expectation. Our experience at both the Garnet-Patterson and Maxey schools has been that even the worst students take some pleasure in the idea of uncorrected writing when they have been conditioned to expect and value their freedom to practice.

Nothing else in the introduction and installation of English in Every Classroom generated so much controversy—so much emphatic agreement and disagreement alike—among the faculties of the two original schools as the practice of student papers written but unread. "If we don't read, they won't write" was the rallying cry of the dissidents, a cry repeated again and again by many other teachers in the ensuing ten years. In spite of their beliefs, based solely on surmise, both faculties eventually capitulated to the assault of their own observations: students wrote; teachers didn't read all that students wrote; students kept on writing. No evidence to the contrary has been generated during the intervening decade.

In spite of the very widespread use in literacy programs of *practice*, i.e., unattended writing (especially in journals), many teachers who were uncomfortable with the concept as it was first advocated in *Hooked on Books*, are distressed for similar reasons by the concept of peer attention to writing that I am proposing here. Their expressed reason—how can one or two students who don't write well help another who writes even less well?—lies at the surface of a pool of discomfort fed by their own concept of their roles as teachers. Unlike teachers in one-room schoolhouses, who

32

were unhappy when children were not teaching other children, many contemporary teachers appear to believe that they are neglectful of their students if they *and they alone* do not attend to all their students' work. Which, of course, can only lead in the future to the same place it has led in the past—to less work being done by each student as every teacher has become responsible for an increasing number of students.

The use of grouping to teach writing has been wonderfully effective at every level at which it has been attempted during the past six years by my colleagues and acquaintances, my former students who have become or returned to being teachers, and by myself. Among the great variety of practices and techniques we have all developed to suit ourselves and our students, three have seemed to be especially useful:

1. The Signature

It is an interesting if ambiguous fact that our signatures vary, often in an experimental way, through the years of our childhood and into our early maturity. No one can doubt that, in part, they are a reflection of how we feel about ourselves and the world in which they are our mark. Though most adults are aware to some degree that signatures are revealing of self—witness the inevitable comment on signatures unusually florid or cramped—they often forget (especially adults who become teachers) that children are extraordinarily aware of this revelation, and are as likely to be fascinated by their own signature as they are by their reflection in a mirror. Unlike older people, children and young adults view their signatures as flexible extensions of themselves, not lightly to be employed.

Taking advantage of this protective sense of self-extension, I have all members of a group sign their full names (no initials; too little of the self is involved in a few capital letters) to every paper submitted by the group. Whether one page or three, whether one paper or three—no matter who

33

and how many the individual producers may be, the group acknowledges with its signatures that it take responsibility for each person's production.

Before defining just what that *responsibility* is, let me first define *production*: Often I tell my groups of three that I want a single page (or two or three pages) written together by all three members of the group and I don't want to be able easily to identify the place where one person's writing ends and another's begins. At other times I ask for separate three (or two or one) page papers, each signed by all members of the group. Or I ask for paragraphs or sentences, telling my students that I want these brief writings to be as stylistically anonymous as possible. At the very least, I tell them, that means three papers (paragraphs, sentences) which communicate in similar ways with roughly equal clarity.

Speaking of production, who gets credit for the writing that the group produces? Or, to put the question in a way nearer if not dearer to our teaching hearts—how do you derive a fair grade for individuals when the work of the class/course/subject is done by groups? First, I postpone individual grades for as long as I possibly can in order to convince the groups that I really mean what I've said: Each person is responsible in a clear and limited way for the work of the other person(s) in her group, and that is her first responsibility. Second, only the *primary* work of the course (as well as the majority of it) is done in groups. I assign enough individual work to provide me with a sufficient basis to know my students individually as well as in collective relationships. Third, the definition I use of "responsibility" helps me to discriminate between and among individuals:

2. Limited Responsibility

One of the evanescent fears that some teachers have about group work, a fear in the same class as their concern that "they won't write if I don't read," derives from the belief that the better students in the group will do the work of the worse.

34

In fact, in my experience of grouping, this is both always and never the case: It is, in the beginning, a highly probable mode of group work. The good students are impatient or intolerant or both, and therefore do more than their fair share. By contrast, after a few weeks of making intense and extensive demands upon the group, teachers almost invariably find that a new mode sets in: Good students, being generally the more apt survivors, discover that overwork and survival are not synonymous. If they've been doing too much, they rapidly and permanently right the balance.

Second and third forces also prevail here to give just proportions to the collaborative work of the group. The second force is the pride of less able students. If imperceptible in the classroom before grouping, their pride in their work—a phenomenon of peer pressure that usually eludes the best efforts of teachers—often develops remarkably beneath the bright light of peer evaluation. Again and again I have seen and been told about the least able students who insist upon doing and saying it their way: "It sounds right to me and it looks right to me and I don't care what you say, I'm going to leave it that way!" Even if it isn't right, that kind of commitment is hard to find and even harder to create in its absence.

The third force that helps to distribute work fairly among the group's members, is the recognition of individual standards and methods of accomplishment that is often the greatest benefit and surprise of group work to the more able student. A pluralistic basis for judgment—one which fits personal effort rather than impersonal criteria—can be a great discovery to students accustomed to meeting the intensified competition of a single standard. In the words of the student whom I quoted at the conclusion of Chapter One: "I got so used to thinking about people as smart or not smart that I forgot how everybody learns things different and knows different things." Of all the revelations that group work brings to the individuals who participate in it, none is more important than that.

Each student is guaranteed living space within the group by the governing definition of *responsibility* which I am careful to make as explicit as I can at the same time that I form groups within the class. Like the device of the signature, this definition of limited responsibility has been exceptionally effective in bringing my students to full participation in their groups. Because I find it so vital to the success of my scheme, I have written it as well as I can and I read it to my classes: "You are not responsible for *making* changes of any kind in your partners' written work. You are only responsible for *suggesting* changes and for *explaining* the changes you suggest. In our group work, the explanation you make is more important than the suggestion you give. Without it your partners will learn no more from you than they have from other teachers who were satisfied simply to tell them what to do. And I will consider your explanations to have been insufficient when your partners' independent work—the work they do without your help—is less satisfactory than their group work done with you. Remember, suggestion and explanation *both* are your responsibility in group work."

3. Reading Aloud

If in some unimaginably flattened world I were limited to a two-dimensional writing program, the two I would choose would be great frequency of brief writings over a long period of time and rehabilitation of the individual voice. Whereas the first is a dimension common to many programs, therefore easily discovered if rarely explored, the second is the Atlantis of modern rhetoric—sunk so nearly without a trace that the name itself has almost no meaningful reference.

One of the persistent memories that has led me to believe in the existence of the individual voice and in the possibility of its rehabilitation, is the memory of a special kind of learning that once occurred in the one-room schoolhouses of North America. Many adults, both those who are school people and those who are not, have recalled that they learned enormously—some have identified it as the single greatest source of their classroom learning—from listening to children in their own and other grades recite their lessons, and from reciting those lessons themselves. In recalling those days when voices were more valued than silence in the classroom, a woman who does not teach put words to the most interesting and significant memory I've heard: "If I didn't learn anything else, I learned that what I said was alright." What an extraordinary lesson, and how completely it has vanished!

"Listen to yourselves," I tell my students. "The single most reliable source of language you have is your own voice. Listen to it, write what it speaks, and you are likely to have made your meaning as clear as you need to make it."

Only an educational establishment that has confused the historical fact of vernacular and literary *languages* with the more recent fact of spoken and written *styles* could have so abused and disvalued the human voice as we have done. Having observed that very few published writers write as they speak; having observed that differences in metaphorical language and absolute accuracy are likely to favor the more considered written tongue—teachers have therefore concluded that the spoken sentence is not a reliable guide to the sentence that should be committed to the page. In so concluding, they have effectively taken from their students the one guide to successful written communication that many of them possessed.

In my own experience as a teacher of writing, nothing has rivalled or even approached the following instruction for immediately obtaining clearer prose from students who write sentences and paragraphs that obscure rather than clarify their intended meanings: "Give me no sentences that you have not spoken aloud before giving them to me. If they do not sound right to you, they won't read right to me."

Grouping has allowed me to add not only two pairs of eyes to the writer's one, but also two mouths and two pairs of ears. Now I can tell my students that they should give me work that they have read aloud to themselves and to their partners in the group. Furthermore, I now tell them that I expect them to read aloud their partners' work as well as their own, and I expect them to read it in their partners' presence. If it is salutary to hear your written words in your own mouth, it is startling to hear them in somebody else's mouth—especially somebody like you. No other treatment that I know about has so much power to provoke attention to meaning, or so much power to elicit clarifying change.

Just as I am embarrassed for my colleagues who do not read well aloud, believing that part of their responsibility as teachers of language and literature is to make the qualities of their discipline available to the ears as well as to the eyes of their students, and believing further that every teacher can train herself or himself to fulfill that responsibility, I am chagrined for my students who do not believe in their own voices. Because I am convinced that their own voices are themselves a standard for clarity which must be rehabilitated and reinstated in schoolroom usage, I subject them to their own voices in three different situations: In addition to reading their own papers and their partners' papers to themselves and to each other, each group is responsible for several readings to the class of prose and poetry. According to their testimony and my observation, preparing and delivering a classroom reading with two other people is relatively simple and pleasant when compared with doing the same thing yourself.

More important than the pressure of performance, in part relieved by sharing it with two other performers, is the reflection of self that intimacy with other selves provides. To teach writing by using classroom groups of twos or threes is to employ the effective opposite of school- or system-wide ability grouping, because it teaches human beings to know themselves by the help they give and are worth giving rather than to know themselves by their isolation or by their concentration upon themselves.

*A Proposal to the Faculty for an English Composition Board

According to testimony taken by the Graduation Requirements Commission (GRC), many LS&A faculty have perceived a significant decline in the quality of their students' literacy during the past two decades. When asked to characterize the nature of that decline, our colleagues often used descriptive terms and phrases summarized in the word "unpracticed." Faculty members repeatedly told the GRC that many of their students appear to be unaccustomed to the demands of literacy, that they seem to be unfamiliar with both perceptive reading and careful composition.

We who have a professional interest in language competence, a category which includes all whose teaching depends upon their students' ability to read and write, may speculate that two phenomena of the last quarter-century are largely responsible for diminishing undergraduate literacy. First, various surveys have found that high school graduates in North America have watched approximately 18,000 hours of television by the time they complete the twelfth grade. Even more important than the average of 1,000 hours a year, nearly three hours a day, may be the further finding that these same high school graduates have watched three hours of television each day in households where the television set was *on* for twice that length of time.

One of the many conclusions significant for undergraduate literacy that can be drawn from these numbers is an implied absence of the *predisposition toward literacy* that we expected and found in our students in the era that preceded television. After having fed their visual appetites for eighteen years, students often come to college both indisposed toward and unpracticed in the use of written language. Perhaps they are impersonally persuaded that they should read, but they do not appear to be personally convinced that reading is a pleasurable or profitable private activity suitable to their own instruction and entertainment. Their literacy has suffered because one of the primary uses of leisure time in the home has changed, in the last twenty-five years, from print reading to television watching. Literacy is neither much practiced nor praised by example in homes where television provides six hours of daily visual diversion.

The second phenomenon of the last quarter-century which may be suspected of contributing to our students' diminished literacy is the precipitate rise in class size during that period in American schools. Though reliable statistics are rare, the most accurate approximation of growth is probably forty percent—from twenty-five students in the average secondary classroom in 1950 to thirty-five in 1975. Which, as any teacher of English composition can testify, is a lot of papers, especially when thirty-five is multiplied by five to give the number of students comprising the average secondary "teaching load" in the United States. Even Atlas might have shrugged and faltered beneath such a burden.

Since English teachers in secondary schools are neither more gigantic nor less heroic than their elementary or collegiate counterparts, very little English composition is assigned or completed in those grades. Whereas the first six years of school are meant to establish a substantial base for literacy, the second six are critical for confirming a practiced rhetoric. Having done remarkably little writing throughout their secondary schooling, having come from homes where literacy is often praised but seldom pursued—our students come to us neither well disposed toward nor well practiced in literacy.

In an attempt to provide the framework for a solution to the problem of our students' declining literacy, the GRC made proposals confirmed by the faculty in three articles reprinted at the end of this document.* As a first response toward satisfaction of these requirements, Dean Frye has asked me to be chairman of the English Composition Board (ECB) and has asked Professor Jay Robinson, Chairman of the English Department, to serve as a member of the Board. During the first two weeks of May, Professor Robinson and I attended three meetings at which Dean Frye was the host and to which all department chairmen and program directors or their designates were invited. At these meetings I asked for and received advice about the proper philosophy, duties, and membership of the ECB. As a result of those and further consultations (discussions with colleagues in various departments as well as a meeting in June with the combined Executive and Curriculum Committees of the College), with cooperation and concurrence from Professor Robinson, I now make the following recommendations. They are intended both to expand the substance and fulfill the spirit of the English Composition Requirements passed by the LS&A faculty in 1975.

I. The Requirement
   A. That the Graduation Requirement in English Composition shall have two parts:
      1. Part One shall be election and specification of two courses, in two of the first three semesters after matriculation, which are numbered below three hundred and chosen from those offered for certification in English composition by any unit in the College.
      2. Part Two shall be election and specification of one course in the major field in either semester of the junior year or first semester of the senior year, which is numbered three hundred or above and chosen from those offered for certification by any unit in the College.
   B. That the Graduation Requirement in English Composition shall have been fulfilled when three different instructors teaching three separate courses, two taken in the first three semesters after matriculation and a third taken in the major field in the fifth, sixth, or seventh semesters, have declared themselves reasonably satisfied with the quality of a student's English composition. OR that the ECB, acting in place of the instructor at the instructor's invitation in any or all of the certification courses, has declared itself reasonably satisfied in each instance with the quality of English composition of students recommended to it for help.
   C. That transfer students must invariably satisfy Part Two of the Graduation Requirement in English Composition, and will be subjected to or exempted from some or all of Part One at the judgment of the ECB.
II. The Board
   A. That the English Composition Board be composed of five faculty members, two from the Department of English and three from other departments or programs within the College. That the Chairman of the Board be from the Department of

41

English; that the second member of the Board from English be the department chairman.

B. That the Board be an agent of the College faculty, responsible to every unit in the College but the responsibility of none. That its budget be provided by the Dean and its chairman appointed by the Dean for a three-year term. That the chairman's work for the ECB be considered half of his or her teaching responsibility.

C. That the Board be responsible for offering immediate, intensive instruction in English composition to all students who may present themselves or may be recommended by their instructors as needful of special help.

D. That the Board's tutorial work be accomplished by both faculty members and graduate student teaching assistants (GSTAs) who have special interest and competence in teaching English composition. That the ECB pay an appropriate portion of the salaries of both its faculty members and the GSTAs; that the Board supervise and train where necessary the GSTAs who teach for it.

E. That the Board provide assistance and guidance in the transaction of teaching composition to any faculty member who may request such help in planning or offering a course which carries with it potential certification in English composition.

    1. Specification: since a student may elect several courses in one semester which offer certification in English composition, the student must specify at the time of election the course to be counted toward fulfilling the requirement.

Daniel Fader
Professor of English

*GRC proposals confirmed by vote of the faculty:
IV. 8   Every freshman be required to take one course in

English composition unless upon *adequate evidence,* the student is excused by the English Composition Board.

IV. 9 Any student in the College may turn to the ECB for additional help in learning to write effectively, and any member of the faculty may call upon the Board to assist some or all of the students taking a particular course. The ECB shall oversee a variety of efforts to improve the quality of undergraduate writing. The Board will also encourage the establishment of other courses—in the Department of English, other departments, among freshmen seminars—that emphasize writing but focus on other subjects and may, on its recommendation, be counted as substitutes for the required course in composition.

IV. 10 The English Composition Board, named by the Dean and the Executive Committee, shall be chaired by a member of the Department of English with experience in teaching English composition, and should consist of two or three additional faculty members at least one of whom is also from the Department of English and at least one of whom is from another department. The Board should select and regularly meet with a group of teaching fellows assigned to it and whose number will be determined by the Dean. For full-time members of the faculty, membership on the Board should be considered the equivalent of teaching one course.

Chapter IV

HOOKED ON BOOKS

Daniel Fader

A. One for the Street

This is a hard story to tell right. In fact, it's a hard story to tell at all:

The principal and I had been to lunch. As we stepped out of our air-conditioned car into 90 degrees of September heat, he said he'd only be a minute and walked across the narrow street into the shade of a very small, two-story, flat-roofed house. My vision was blurred by the reflected heat, but I could see a pretty young girl in the window. They talked, she smiled and showed him something that I couldn't see, and then he came back across the street.

"Pretty little thing," I said. "How come she's not in school?"

"She's working," he said, shortly, and I let it go. But it wasn't gone for good, because when we got back to his office he turned to me and asked, "Did you see what she showed me?"

"No," I said. "You were in the way."

"It was one of our paperbacks. Judith Scott's *The Art of Being a Girl*."

"Well?" I said, when he didn't say any more. There was a point to what he had told me, but I didn't know what it was.

"Like I said, she's working today." When he saw that I didn't know the language, he told me straight. She was thirteen years old and she worked two days a week as a prostitute to help support herself and her family. The other three days she came to school. It was something, he said, to see how the students treated her. Especially the boys. The girls, so far as he could tell, treated her like any other girl. But not the boys. They *never* fooled with her and they cooled any new stud who pawed her ground. They were good to her, he said, and that was the only way to put it. They were considerate. They knew how it was with her and they didn't try to make it worse.

That's all there is to the story, but I can't get it up and it won't go down. It's not that I haven't know thirteen-year-old prostitutes before. I just never knew one who read *The Art of Being a Girl* while waiting for business, and I never knew any junior high school boys who knew enough to be kind to her. But it's more than that.

Maybe it's the pap we feed them. Maybe it's the peeled and overripe bananas we feed them in the schools, when they've got the teeth to bite through tough fiber and scaly skins. How can we offer them Dick and Jane and the castrated classics when fourteen-year-old Dick protects the peace of thirteen-year-old Jane on Mondays, Wednesdays and Fridays, and purchases a piece of the same Jane on Tuesdays and Thursdays? How can we get them to believe that we're for real when we spend our hours from eight to three eluding them in a ground fog of words, and they spend their time from three to eight plus Saturdays, Sundays and holidays bumping and scraping against **HOW IT IS?** We can't. We're not for real; they know it, and they've put us down.

Who are the unreachables? Who are the unteachables? Do they have any reality other than in the blind eyes of the beholder? Is their existence a function of our failures as teachers rather than their failures as students? How does a boy make it all the way down to the bottom tenth grade class in a large high school in a very large city when, with emphasis in his voice and excitement in his face, he can tell one of his classmates, "I don't care if you seen the movie. You *got* to read the book!" Where were we when the intelligent, upper-middle class boy got so traumatized in his California public schools that he had to be put into a very special reading class staffed by psychologists from the University of California at Los Angeles? Summoned by the teacher from his seat in a rear row, he began to walk directly toward the front of the room; suddenly he stopped, backed up a few steps, turned about and walked around the periphery of the room to reach his teacher. What had stopped him? An open book lying on a desk halfway toward the front of the room. Who knows what horrors it symbolized for him, after ten years of scarifying failure in the public schools?

Has anybody told you all about the desperate children, no longer children but unable to become adults, who inhabited the Job Corps camps? What did they want? A job, a trade, a way to buy a decent piece of the world they never made. We'll give them the currency of a vocation, we said, and they'll be able to buy that place in society. But how do you teach a boy to become a man who drives big rigs or repairs cars and trucks or cooks in a restaurant kitchen, if the boy can't read? You can't hold a job as first or twenty-first cook if you can't read the recipes. Put paperback books in their Job Corps classrooms; the immediate and overwhelming favorite became *30 Days to a More Powerful Vocabulary*. They knew where they hurt the worst.

If this book appears to be speaking only of children in poorer public and penal institutions, then its appearance is deceiving. For the kind of poverty that identifies the child who is the true subject of this book is a poverty of experience—a poverty which can afflict lives lived at $100,000 a year just as readily as it curses the $1,000 a year existence. The poorest adults in the world are those limited to their own experience, those who do not read. This book is about every child who may become such an adult.

B. Inside the Schools

Before poverty became a good thing to some who have never known it (and to some who have), I spent a day as University Accreditation Visitor in the English classrooms of Poverty-Level High School. Though I don't know the average family income in P.-L.H.S., I do know that only about 5 percent of its graduates get any formal education beyond high school. Since we all know that one test for the quality of poverty is the quantity of education, I know enough to recognize a Poverty-Level High School when I see one. I tell part of its story now because that story is a prelude to the program for teaching reading and writing which occupies these pages.

One of the two most striking features of P.-L.H.S. was its undefeated principal and undiscouraged teachers. Having read neither widely nor deeply in the lore of the poor, they did not understand that "educationally unaspiring" means "essentially uneducable." Instead of conducting a holding operation, with the principal as warden and the faculty as guards, this high school was actually convening its classes on the assumption that students who are not going on to college can profit from their education. If this appears to be a commonplace assumption, then the following evidence may place it in a clearer light:

In the many secondary schools I have visited where some students go on to college and some do not, I have often asked the principal or the head of the English Department to send me to the teacher who does the best job with noncontinuing students (an awkward phrase for an awkward situation). I have invariably been directed to the teacher who keeps the best order in the classroom. *Discipline* is clearly the criterion of success, and if the price is the student's pleasure and enthusiasm—well, order comes high. In this case, so high that nothing is valued beyond it and classes in such schools (they are legion) are convened with the tacit understanding that little will be taught and less will be learned. The optimistic working assumption at P.-L.H.S.

47

was remarkable by comparison.

The second of the school's striking characteristics was as negative as the first was positive: In spite of the good feeling between teachers and pupils, and in spite of the pervasive notion that both occupied the classroom for some useful reason, very little teaching or learning occurred in the English classes. The discovery was especially disturbing because the children were happy in the corridors, respectful to their teachers, apparently clean, rested, and well fed . . . were, in fact, everything but successful learners. And the English faculty was pleasant, enthusiastic, reasonably knowledgeable . . . everything but successful teachers. The mystery embodied in the mutual frustration of teacher and pupil at P.-L.H.S. was one of the major causes of the research and development that have gone into the experiment called *English in Every Classroom*.

Four o'clock came and our team had been at the school for seven hours. The first hour had been spent listening to the principal tell us something about the school, the middle hour had been sacrificed to eating Home Economics Class meat loaf, and the last hour had been spent telling the faculty about our day's observations. In between were four hours of class visiting, two or three classes per hour; then, as Accreditation Visitors from the University of Michigan, each of us was to write a report to the university's Bureau of School Services appraising the quality of the school's instruction in our special subject.

As we drove back to Ann Arbor, I tried to formulate the report I would write. To write that the school was doing very badly in English seemed somehow unfair, but the day's inescapable truth was that they were doing very badly indeed. And yet, by comparison with the Highly Recommended High School (more than 50 percent going on to college and most performing well) which I had visited during the preceding semester, P.-L.H.S. deserved to be praised. In H.R.H.S., the English classes for students not going on to college were travesties, mocking the very cause they were meant to serve. Instead of freeing and augmenting the student's store of language, English classes there served an inhibiting function.

It was shocking to see the apparent change in the English teachers between the time they dismissed a class of academic students and convened a class of general students. Stevenson could have created Henry Jekyll and Edward Hyde from the schizophrenic model embodied in the average H.R.H.S. English teacher. Dr. Jekyll in the academic classroom changed to Mr. Hyde when dealing with the "other" students. Creative, compelling teachers of students who were going on to college, altered their countenances and personalities in a matter of minutes to become little better than jailers of students who could not respond so easily or so well to the language and literature their teachers valued. I had seen the same sorry scene enacted in a dozen schools. Today, in P.-L.H.S., the feeling had been very different, and yet the results had been largely the same. No easy report phrases took shape in my head.

My companion on the journey back to Ann Arbor was Ray Kehoe, Associate Director of the Bureau of School Services. When I had told him of my day at the school, he told me of a problem he faced which might have something to do with the day's experiences. In the name of the Bureau he had accepted a commission that had become unexpectedly difficult to fulfill. On the surface it appeared to be simple enough: Engage members of the Bureau and of the University faculties to construct a curriculum for the W.J. Maxey Boys' Training School, then being built in Whitmore Lake, Michigan. But only the appearance was simple; among other difficulties, he had been unable to find anyone to write an English program for a school full of noncontinuing students. Would I be interested? We were both surprised, I think, when I accepted the commission.

A few days later I met with Bureau officials and the two men who were responsible for organizing the new school. Bud Maxey and Stanley Black were to be director of the entire facility and supervisor of instruction, respectively. We were to come to know each other very well in the next three years, but at that point we were strangers. To ease the moment of meeting, Ray Kehoe said something about my familiarity with juvenile delinquency. No adult, he said, could shoot pool like that and not have led a misspent youth.

We all laughed, but the damage was done. I left the meeting confirmed in the belief that my experiences as a pool hustler and high school stayaway would make it easier for me to write a program for boys who were more of the same.

That belief was foolish, and it cost me months of mistaken research. My original assumption was that language training was a matter of discovering and effecting techniques for making lasting changes in performance. Like so many other would-be innovators, I looked more closely at myself than at my subjects. I had a mild case of juvenile delinquency; I had only to remember myself and I would have a point of departure for writing a program. Now I know how wrongheaded that assumption was, but the realization was long in coming.

My kind of delinquent was the product of a hopeful society. No matter whom or what we hustled, bashed, or lifted, we did not view the past as desperate or the future as hopeless. Shooting pool, gambling, fighting, staying out of school or breaking into it—all were temporary accommodations to a world that was going to be *much better when we grew up*. That was our credo, and we held to it in spite of everything.

Misled by irrelevant memories, I visited elementary schools, junior high schools, senior high schools, juvenile homes, and training schools. During the first three months of school visiting I caught only occasional glimmers of light that would not fit under the bushel I had built for them. But as weeks of traveling and questioning wore on, the occasional glimmers became intrusive beams with deep shadows. In the shadows were all the faces in all the classrooms where language, though the apparent subject of the class meeting, had obviously gone out of style. If I saw one, I saw a hundred teachers addressing themselves to four students (usually girls) in a class of forty empty faces with vacant eyes. Better than any written evidence, those eyes and faces testified to the irrelevance of what was happening in English classes.

Their teachers told me that gaining the attention of those blank eyes became more difficult with each year, and that holding their attention was impossible. As I returned from daily school visits and tried to write about what I had seen, I began to realize how much I knew about the teachers, their methods and their materials, and how little I knew about their students.

How could I set up a school program when I knew so little about the people it was meant to serve?

I began again. This time I went to the students. What's wrong with your English class, I asked, that causes you to turn it off the way you do? You're out to lunch during your English class, I said, and I want to know why. They told me why: They told me that it didn't make any difference about them. That the teacher didn't like them so they didn't like the teacher. She didn't talk about anything that mattered ("Sentence diagraming? Shoot! What do I care about that?") and she didn't talk like she *wanted* you to understand. And never nothing to read that was any good, even if you wanted to read. What difference does it make anyway?

What difference does it make? The words are repeated so often that they become part of the litany with which the burial service for school is conducted. For the student not going on to college, school is dying and the English class is dead. We must exhume the body for examination.

Listening to students rather than to teachers had given me a new starting point: Who or what was responsible for the murder of the English class? Could it be revived? Was revival important? Could English in a school context ever matter to the student who saw no purpose in schooling and little hope in anything else? With six more weeks and sixty schools behind me, no closer to the right answers and wondering if there were any, I began school visiting again. But this time I began with one firm piece of information.

Children are rarely indirect or misleading about what they feel. Unlike adults, children seldom learn to mask, postpone, or abrogate the effect of any cause that moves them. Just as the living language is never wrong, so are children always accurate in reflecting things as they really are for them. Therefore I knew there was no use identifying the children as causes of what was wrong in the English class. They may be all that they shouldn't be, but they *are*, and must be met where they are before they can be led to where

51

they *should be* (i.e., where *we* are).

If not to the children—their lack of manners, their lack of interest, their deficient home environment etc., etc., etc.—then where to attribute the cause? Where else but to their teachers and the materials and methods they use? One advantage of identifying the source of the trouble in this way is that here at least it may be remediable. Remedying children is something else again; adult logic has a way of being persuasive only to adults, and lines of communication between teachers and parents are practically nonexistent.

The first step seemed to be to find out what teachers were doing in *all* classrooms, with the purpose of translating the successes of math, science, and social studies into the English curriculum. My first efforts in that direction turned out to be my last, for visits to a dozen schools and conversations with some forty teachers led me to understand that the failure of the English teacher was only one part of the failure of the schools to meet the needs of the unpromising student. Programs in all areas were no more hopeful than the students themselves.

Having eliminated the children as cause and the successes of other subjects as remedy, I returned to the person, the materials, and the methods of the English teacher.

C. The English Teacher

In my next round of school visits, and in discussions with teachers outside the school environment, I remarked again and again that one of the most serious deficiencies of the English teacher is her exclusivity. Why, I asked, do only English teachers teach English? What a silly question, I was told. Only English teachers teach English because only English teachers are qualified to teach English. *Everyone* knows that. If *everyone* knows that, I replied, then surely *everyone* must also know that English teachers have failed to teach their subject, no matter how it is defined, to hordes of students for a very long time. And *everyone* must also know that a child without a functioning and willing literacy—the minimal responsibility of the English teacher—cannot successfully be taught any other subject in the academic curriculum.

Surely if *everyone* knows all this, then *surely no one* can expect the English teacher alone to teach English. But that is exactly what everyone seems to expect. We're history teachers (or math or science or shop or music or...), they told me, and we have enough to do to teach history, let alone English. Or—we do *our* jobs; why can't the English teachers do theirs? Whatever the posture of friend or antagonist, the result was that the English teacher was exclusive indeed. Her responsibility was the student's literacy, and the responsibility was entirely hers. After all, I was told several hundred times, no one asks the English teacher to teach history (math, science, *et al.*). Why should teachers of other subjects be asked to teach English?

Because the reasons seem very compelling for having *all* classroom teachers teach English, the first part of this program, originally intended to promote literacy at the Maxey Boys' Training School, is based upon the idea of **DIFFUSION**, which describes the expansion of responsibility for teaching reading and writing to each teacher in every classroom. First among the compelling reasons for making such a change in customary practice is the failure of that practice.

It is a remarkable fact that I met not a single principal or teacher who cared to argue that students who were not going on to college were being adequately prepared in the English language. This silence is all the most significant when contrasted with the sound of success which accompanies any discussion with the same people on the subject of college preparation. Turn conversation from the general to the academic student and high school English teachers rightfully expect to be praised. Their expectations are very different, however, when they talk about their less malleable clay.

A second and equally powerful reason exists for making *English in Every Classroom* the philosophical and operative basis of a new program in literacy. That reason is the nature of the students themselves. "Practical" is the adjective recurring most often in language used by secondary school teachers to describe their nonacademic pupils. The word seems to have a wide variety of meanings, at least some of which are pejorative. But where it is used with a favorable meaning, it seems to refer to the unusual (in middle-class terms) need of such students to perceive and to be able to judge the immediate relationship between cause and effect before they can be successfully motivated. Satisfaction of this need is the lever most frequently employed by this program to raise the "practical" student toward literacy.

Put yourself in his place: What lesson would you learn if your English teacher were the only teacher who consistently required something more of your literacy than a minimal display? You would learn exactly what generations of "practical" students have come to know so well: that the English teacher can be effectively ignored, for only she really cares about your use of language. Since school language is not easy for you—one reliable criterion of the intellectual difference between general and academic students—and since it is apparently unimportant for all the other teachers who shape the bulk of your school day, why should it be a big thing for you? Leave your mind in the corridor as you walk into your English class; put your brains out to lunch and your eyes out the window for forty minutes a day and you've got it made. Why strain yourself when nobody but the English teacher seems to care?

Now change the situation: Every day in every major subject classroom you enter, you're required to read and write as though reading and writing really mattered to every one of your teachers. "Everywhere you turn there's writing!" was the exasperated comment of one District of Columbia schoolgirl after the program had been in action for six months in her junior high. Her exasperation was her teacher's hope. Being a "practical" child, she had learned that the coolest survive longest. Before English had assaulted her in every classroom, she had managed to freeze it into quiescence. Now she was losing her cool, and her teachers were being warmed by the thaw.

D. The Materials and Methods of the English Teacher

The title of this section is an index to the prejudices of the author. "Methods and Materials" is the customary phrase; its implications for teacher and student have been very unpleasant indeed.

Having asked one thousand English teachers and instructors in other subjects why only English teachers teach English, I had exhausted half my stock of questions. The second half of this meager armory was, "Why do you use the materials and methods you use to teach English?" Responses were as various as the responders; all could be summed in the following fashion:

1—For methods: "The methods I use are those I have found through experience to be successful."

2—For materials: "The materials I use are those made available to me by the system"; or "I use the materials I use because those are the materials I've got to use"; or "I use these materials because these are the materials I've built my lesson plans on"; or "Ask the principal [supervisor, superintendent]. Don't ask me. They order the stuff. I just use it"; or "These are the best materials available. We have the newest and the best, and we're proud of them."

The one response I never heard, however, was this one: "I use these materials because they are effective with my students. They like the textbooks and other materials I use, and they learn well from them."

This missing response is illuminated by the phrase, "methods and materials." The order of the words reflects their order of appearance in the field of education. According to this order, methods do not rise out of materials; rather they *are,* and the practices they produce lead to the types of materials selected for use in English classes. But if not from the materials, then whence do methods come? From the needs of students? Hardly, since not even the most optimistic teacher claims much language success with the general student. From the needs of the abstract subject called "English"? Far more likely, and far more likely therefore to result in the painfully limited human success such methods have known.

The argument for their inevitable failure goes something like this:

A subject taught for its own sake, rather than for its utility in meeting real life situations, may or may not be engaging, depending upon the teacher's and the student's ability to understand and enjoy its content. On the student's part, at least, this enjoyment is directly related not only to his capacity for perceiving and enjoying abstraction, but also to his capacity to apply abstractions once he has mastered them. This may show itself in his ability to turn abstract grammar into good speech, or it may be nothing more exotic than mastering the difference between spelling and defining words in lists and using them in sentences. For instance, English teachers are all too familiar with the child who can spell words in a list correctly, but who cannot spell them when required to use them in sentences. Perhaps even more relevant to my argument is the legion of children who can define words by rote but who can only use them meaningfully in self-defining sentences.

The point is this: Pages of grammar rules and sentence diagrams, lists of words to be defined and words to be spelled—these have become part of materials which arose from archaic methods long proved ineffective. Furthermore, and far worse, precedence of methods over materials inevitably caused undervaluation of the materials selected. The implicit, underlying assumption *must* be that the materials don't really matter very much if the methods are efficient. What other assumption could conceivably account for the books, the incredible books at present in use in the schools?

But what happens when materials used in classes for the general student are selected to meet the practical needs of the student rather than the more abstract needs of the subject? In English, for example, rhetoric takes precedence over grammar, and utility becomes more important than beauty. When such criteria become the new basis for selection of materials, a radical change is inevitable. For example, such extremes of the same language as Shakespeare and the daily newspaper are found to have much in common. In terms of the student's practical needs, the newspaper takes precedence. Because it begins more nearly where he is, it may prove to be the bridge across which he crawls, stumbles, and finally walks, erect, to where he should be. If he finds Shakespeare at the other end of the bridge, then the simple, inelegant newspaper, magazine, or paperback book has become a legitimate and necessary means to attaining a complex, eloquent end.

When the goal of the English class is redefined in terms of rhetorical ease and willing expression, the ancient methods of the schools become as irrelevant to the subject as they have generally been to the student. Ease in understanding newspapers and pleasure in reading magazines cause both to replace the grammar texts and workbooks of time-dishonored usage. Instead of a student who spells according to inert rules, we may now have a student who spells by the active image of words which have a thousand times impinged on his reading consciousness.

Because the reasons seem as compelling as those for asking teachers *in every classroom* to teach English, the second part of this program is based on the principle of **SATURATION**, meaning the replacement, whenever possible and in whatever classroom, of customary texts and workbooks with newspapers, magazines, and paperbound books. The object of this is to stir the sensibility of the practical child. Even as he learns to be reticent in a world of words he cannot fathom, so he may learn to be receptive in a world of words he can understand. Because he finds newspapers, magazines, and paperbound books in every classroom, and because he *can* and *will* read them, he may yet be brought to compromise with a verbal world he cannot avoid.

E. Preface to the Program

Hogman was sweating and so was I. The morning was hot

and we had hundreds of paperbound books to unload from the rear of my Volkswagen sedan. Why hadn't we boxed them before putting them into the car? Why my car? Why me at all—a teacher of English literature, a lover not a mover of books? We talked as we waited for some cartons.

"That a mighty tiny sheen," he said.

"Mighty tiny," I said, looking at the pile of books filling up the rear.

"Them's tiny books," he said, asking me to talk.

"We get any of yours?" I asked. The principal of the school and I had spent two hours in Cottage Unit A searching the boys' rooms for books. Those we had found were now sprawled in the back of the car. Hogman had come with us from the cottage, where he had helped to collect the books and load them into the car.

"Had all them James Bondys, but I done read 'em a couple times."

"We get anything you weren't done with?"

"I reckon."

"What?"

"The chuck what makes hisself into a splib."

"Black Like Me?"

"That one."

I reached back and shuffled through the pile until I found one of the many reclaimed copies of Griffin's book. "Here. Bring it back when you're done."

He ducked his chin and half turned his big body away from me. Then he took the book and slipped it into his back pocket. We were both sweating through our shirts, but he didn't have to be back in Ann Arbor to give a two o'clock lecture. I was thinking about that lecture when Hogman turned toward me, a broad smile on his face, and said kind of low and chuckly, "Like reading, man. You know—it ain't so bad."

You know, it ain't. The program for teaching English outlined in this book, is based upon the idea that reading ain't so bad and it's time more people learned how good it is. Since everybody agrees that people never learn better than when they're children, this book describes a school program suitable in some measure to all children in all American school systems from kindergarten through twelfth grade. Though suitable to all, this program is particularly concerned with the student whom educators have identified as "general," meaning all too often that the school system has few specific programs to satisfy his educational needs. This is the same student who can sometimes be identified as disadvantaged and can more often be characterized as impoverished. He is disadvantaged if he is poor, but he may be impoverished and be rich. He is impoverished if he does not read with pleasure, because if he does not read with pleasure then he is unlikely to read at all.

Big Bill, Superduck, Hogman, Lester—all were students in the W.J. Maxey Boys' Training School at Whitmore Lake, Michigan, a few miles north of Ann Arbor. Their routes to the school were as varied as the faces of poverty; but if their pasts were various, their futures were alike: they would return to Maxey or to another penal institution, whether state or federal, juvenile or adult. They spoke of Jacktown (Jackson, Michigan, State Penitentiary) like an old and reliable acquaintance. They were boys, they were old men, they were tough, they couldn't fight their way out of a Girl Scout meeting. Sometime during the first weeks of my work at the school I said to one of the physical education teachers, "You must get some pretty fair athletes out here." I'll never forget his answer:

"These boys ain't good at nothing. If they was, they wouldn't be here."

I watched them fight. He was right—they didn't have anything but hate going for them. Awkward right-handed leads from flat-footed stances; long, looping punches that landed, when they landed at all, on shoulders and tops of heads. More than one teacher and cottage supervisor told me that he'd just as soon let them fight because they seldom hurt each other. Basketball, football, softball—sadball. They were society's losers. The hate they had as their sometime ally was as likely to be directed against themselves as against others. "Man, what's the use?" The words were engraved on their lips.

On this hot September morning, the principal and I were holding a shakedown. Criminals' cells and delinquents' rooms have, in the history of penal institutions, been shaken down for everything from money and drugs, to knives, guns, files, and blunt instruments, but this may have been the first time they were shaken down for books. The supervisor went ahead of us, unlocking the doors; Hogman followed, pushing the cart. We knew we'd find books, but we never thought it would be like this. Books were everywhere: on their shelves, their desks, their beds, their washstands. Their teachers said they were reading; the books they carried with them, stuffed in their pockets, said they were reading; the number of books missing from the library said they were reading... but here, suddenly, was evidence we couldn't question. It was a perversely happy two hours for both of us, faced as we were with the stolen evidence of our program's success.

That program, as it has been developed and tested, is described in this book. The children and young adults for whom it is intended usually need to perceive an immediate relationship between cause and effect before they can be successfully motivated. Their questions about literature are often put in terms of "What does it mean to me?" which is only a more specific version of their "Why should I?" in answer to the demands of reading and writing. The purpose of the program called *English in Every Classroom* is to help those who teach such students to give them useful and satisfying answers.

This approach to learning is designed to provide general students with *motivation* for reading and writing, at the same time giving them appropriate materials with which to practice and reinforce their literacy. Its potential significance to education lies in its systematic expansion of what good English teachers have done, or tried to do, or wanted to do in schools and classrooms everywhere: convince their colleagues in all subjects that English must be taught by each teacher in every classroom with materials that *invite* students to learn.

All aspects of this curriculum proceed upon the assumption that the chief problem in teaching reading and writing is not intellect but motivation. The program further assumes that a student's desire to learn makes learning

60

probable.

Members of the Departments of English and Psychology and of the School of Education at the University of Michigan were engaged for four years in shaping and testing a curriculum for the teaching of English in the W.J. Maxey Boys' Training School at Whitmore Lake, Michigan. The English program at the Maxey School, which was also implemented under experimental conditions in the Garnet-Patterson Junior High School in Washington, D. C., and is now in use in some form in all fifty states and at least a dozen foreign countries, is the source of methods for teaching English described in these pages. Incredible as it may seem, this is apparently the first schoolwide approach to the language problems of the general student. Equally revealing is a discovery made by psychologists who tested the program: Within the varied and subtle spectrum of devices invented and validated for testing literacy, almost no work at all has been done in the vast area of testing *attitudes* toward reading and writing. The implications of this discovery are remarkable:

In the modern history of education, attitudes of readers and writers toward the processes of reading and writing have been regarded—when they have been considered at all—as no more important than the attitude of any mechanical object to the work it performs. Who would ask if a computer likes its work or if a can opener likes the act of opening or the can it opens? Judging by their policies, American educators believe that most children are well disposed toward reading and writing and that they will so continue, independently of the methods and materials used to teach them. No alternate explanation is available. Either the reader/writer is like a mechanical device, to be rated in terms of the relation between input and output (performance), or educators have believed that attitude does not really matter very much after all. One apparent resolution of this unhappy choice was offered me by the former chairman of one of Michigan's largest and most successful (very large percentage of graduates doing well in college) high school English departments: "Reading and writing are *necessary*, don't you see. If we get the performance up, we know we've got a child

61

with the right attitude."

This is the same man who gave me information he felt I would be glad to have in my role as Accreditation Visitor in English for the university: *His* staff of English teachers was so cooperative and sensible that he had been called upon only once to ban their use of a book—*The Catcher in the Rye*. But of course we *both* understood about *that*. Though in fact we both did understand about *that*, we both did not understand about attitude. Attitude follows performance only where children are performance-oriented, and even with such children the attitude may not be the one that educators intend to foster. When reading and writing are merely means to the end of school success, what happens to performance-oriented children when that success has been attained? To put the question another way, what happens when the performing child becomes the school-graduated (performance-certified) adult? Any librarian or bookseller will tell you that the average modern adult avoids bookstores and libraries as though they were leprosaria. Had the goal of modern, performance-oriented education been the creation of unwilling readers and writers, it could not have succeeded more completely. All the supporting evidence is bottom-rooted in front of television screens across the nation.

If this is true of the performance-oriented child, what of the child whose environment and training aim him elsewhere? I am using "performance-oriented" to describe the child, usually middle class, who is taught that time-saving, orderliness, and self-control, all elementary in the process of gratification deferment, will lead him to eventual joy. But what of the child, usually lower class, whose ethics make "live for tomorrow" a joke today? His causes must have very immediate effects, and the devil (who has a school text in his hand) take the foremost. What of this child, to whom "performance orientation" generally has meant mediocrity or failure? At least one part of the answer is clear: We must first re-evaluate our goals as educators before we can hope better to profit our students. In the case both of performance- and other-oriented children, we must admit that performance orientation is not now—and probably never has been—enough. We must take careful and unremitting aim at the child's *attitude* before we can expect to see any lasting effect upon his performance. The plan for teaching English which is introduced here takes the child's attitude as its primary, and sometimes its sole, object.

F. English in Every Classroom

"English in Every Classroom" is an approach to learning based on the dual concepts of SATURATION and DIFFUSION. The first of these key concepts, SATURATION, proposes to so surround the student with newspapers, magazines, and paperbound books that he comes to perceive them as pleasurable means to necessary ends. The advantages inherent in selecting such materials for classroom use are very great. First, and most important, all newspapers, most magazines, and the great majority of paperbound books are written in the knowledge that commercial disaster is the reward for creating paragraphs that people *should* read. With the choice a clear one between market success and business failure, publishers, editors, and writers know that survival depends on producing words that people *will* read. This program advances the radical notion that students are people and should be treated accordingly.

A second and perhaps equally important advantage in saturating the student's school environment with newspapers, magazines, and paperbound books is their relationship to the world outside the school building. No one believes that we are training children from any social level to be performers in school; everyone believes that students come to the schools to learn skills they will need when they leave school, no matter at what level they leave. And yet, instead of importing materials from that world for teaching the literacy that world requires, we ignore such materials as unworthy of the better world we teachers are dedicated to creating. This program yields to none in its desire to help make a better world. It is equally strong, however, in its desire to educate students to deal with the world as it is. No literature better represents that world than the various periodicals and softbound books which supply the basic materials for the SATURATION program.

The third advantage of these materials is closely related to the second. Not only do newspapers, magazines and paperbound books *enable* the student to deal with the world as it is, but they *invite* him to do so. All educators are only too familiar with the school-text syndrome, that disease whose symptoms are uneducated students and unread materials. School texts often go unread just because they are school texts and apparently have very little to do with the nonschool world. One certain way to break the syndrome is to remove the proximate causes—in this case traditional school texts—and substitute newspapers, magazines, and paperbound books.

A warning to those who follow the foregoing advice: You'll have at least three unhappy types on your hands when you remove traditional school texts and substitute paperbound materials. Least important will be the parents who want to see their children with traditional texts because paperbound books (or magazines or newspapers) "don't look right. They were never used in *my* day in school!" Yes, you may reply, and look what we turned out.

Most important of the unhappy types will be the teachers who won't change "and nobody's going to make me." Whether they act from the pressure of invincible ignorance or forty (or four) years of lesson plans, they will prove to be immovable and should be fired. But since removal is the prerogative of employers whose staff members take responsibility for their products—a description in no way applicable to the business of education—such teachers must be ignored. In my experience, they are very much in the minority and the harm they do can be greatly mitigated by their colleagues.

Last among those who will be predictably unhappy at the change in texts will be certain students. These are the ones who have built up a careful and relatively complete system of defenses against the varied apparatus of the school world. We see the worst of them in Maxey and in a few of the big-city public schools where parts of the program have been installed. They are immediately recognizable by their anger, which is very funny in a bizarre way. They are angry because they have been given paperbound books, magazines and newspapers instead of the customary texts. "Where are the *real* textbooks?" they ask. What they are really asking is— "Where are the recognizable symbols of a world we know how to resist? Make us comfortable with the old texts, and we'll be able to fight back because we'll recognize the enemy."

The fourth and final asset of softbound materials reflects a new sort of hope. Though it's not exactly what I had in mind when I first advocated replacing classic school texts with paperbound material, it is an asset which can hardly be overlooked. Its spokesman is a former English teacher who, in the best tradition of a peculiar profession, has been rewarded for excellence in teaching by being removed from the classroom to the position of administrator. He speaks here in the reduced voice of a principal:

"If you couldn't say anything else for newspapers and magazines for teaching our kind of student, you'd have to say that they get a mighty important message across to him. Maybe the most important. No matter how bad he feels about his world, he has only to read a newspaper or magazine to know that somebody else has got it worse."

SATURATION applies in principle not only to the selection and distribution of periodicals and softbound texts throughout the curriculum, but to the explosion of writing in the student's school environment. This explosion is based upon the practice of DIFFUSION, the second of the two key concepts in the design of *English in Every Classroom* and the concept implied in its name. Whereas SATURATION refers to the materials used in every classroom to induce the child to enter the doorway of literacy, DIFFUSION refers to the responsibility of every teacher in every classroom to make the house of literacy attractive. In discharging this responsibility, every teacher becomes an intermediary between the student and functional literacy. In order that the student may come to view writing as a means to all ends, all ends which he pursues in a scholastic context must insist upon writing as the means through which they can be approached. In short, every teacher becomes a teacher of English, and English is taught in every classroom.

The teaching of English should be viewed as the primary responsibility of the English teacher and as a secondary responsibility of every other teacher with whom the student has regular classroom contact. This division of responsibility, with its resultant diffusion of reading and writing throughout the entire curriculum, should have a number of salutary effects, most important being communication to the student of the sense that reading and writing can be as natural to her existence as walking and talking. Her previous experience has assured her that only English teachers demand constant proof of her literacy; she can hardly avoid assuming that reading and writing are special functions reserved for special occasions, in this case the English class, and that they have no normal relationship to the rest of her world. It is to dispel that damaging illusion that this recommendation is made.

Implementation of the practice of shared responsibility for the student's training in English proved not only relatively easy in the Maxey Boys' Training School and the Garnet-Patterson Junior High School, but also unexpectedly pleasant for the faculties involved. When I first met with the full faculties of the Maxey and Garnet-Patterson schools for three-day training seminars, I was uncomfortably aware on both occasions of how cold a welcome my program might receive. For it proposes an approach to the teaching of reading and writing which challenges two of the dearest and most ancient misconceptions of the profession. These are the myths, customarily paired for strength, of the teacher as individualist and the classroom as castle. Together they have done more harm to the profession of teaching than any other combination of ideas or events. The myth of the teacher as individualist serves as an example; because of it and the mental set it represents, meaningful cooperation among teachers is essentially nonexistent. Each teacher is so concerned with perpetuating the values and conditions of his own preparation, so concerned with protecting his feudal rights as a free man, that he effectively isolates himself from his peers. Teachers have *no* peer group in the functional sense of that term. They may attend professional classes, taking courses during the academic year and during the summer, but they tend to be speakers and auditors of monologues rather than participants in dialogues. *They do not profit from each other* because they are the true inheritors of the modern theory of compartmentalized education, a theory which declares each man sufficient unto his subject and each subject sufficient unto itself. General practitioners are as little respected and as meagerly rewarded in teaching as they are in medicine.

The inevitable corollary to the idea of teacher as individualist is the theory of classroom as castle. Without the second, the first could hardly be as destructive as it is. Part of our feudal inheritance is the notion that a man's home is his castle. Sanctified by law and custom, this theory has become a practice imitated in the schools. Like most imitations, the shape of the thing has undergone subtle change. Whereas in the home a man has the freedom *to* order his life and raise his family, in the classroom this tradition has been interpreted as freedom *from*. Rather than exercising freedom *to* experiment and freedom *to* criticize (both self and colleagues), teachers distinguish themselves by a process of in-gathering which frees them *from* all criticism to a degree foreign to any other profession. I would be the last to deny that public criticism—often reflecting only ignorance and prejudice—has given teachers one very good reason for insulating themselves from further shocks. But the insulation has become a burden rather than a protection. Teachers now suffer most from their inability to hear each other.

The program I proposed to the faculties of both schools asked them to hear and to help each other. Within this program, each English teacher at Maxey and at Garnet-Patterson became both leader and servant of a team of teachers and every teacher except the physical education instructors became a team member. Teams were formed as much as possible by grouping an English teacher with the other instructors of that teacher's pupils. Where, because of the varied curriculum in the public school (foreign language instruction, for example), such grouping was not completely feasible, teachers of subjects other than English were assigned to the team which taught the majority of their students. Teams met weekly in the Garnet-Patterson School and less often at Maxey after the teachers had put three years of work into the program. These meetings were meant to be supplemented by and—as in the Maxey School—eventually replaced by the personal interaction of the English teacher with individual members of her team. In order that the English teacher may have sufficient time to devote to coordination of team effort, she is assigned one class less than the school's normal teaching load. Where an English Department chairman is designated, she is relieved of a second class in order to coordinate team teaching efforts and materials distribution throughout the school.

I should like to emphasize here that this approach to the teaching of English does not envision making English teachers of instructors trained in other specialties. It recognizes that only in the best of all possible worlds will instructors of all subjects perceive the dependence of their disciplines upon the verbal adequacy of their students, and take appropriate steps to insure that adequacy. Meanwhile, until such a millennium is upon us, this program is built upon the expectation that only English teachers will correct the grammar and rhetoric of student papers, but that all teachers will be encouraged to make simple corrections where the necessity for such corrections may be apparent to them. Since this procedure depends on the good will of the subject instructors who help to effect it, they must not be made to feel uneasy about their own mastery of the language. Much effort was expended in both schools to make teachers of other subjects understand that they could regard their role, if they wished, as that of passive intermediary between their students, on the one hand, and functional literacy on the other. In making this point clear, great emphasis was placed upon the *quantitative* importance of these written exercises.

The speed and thoroughness with which teams formed and began their work at both the penal and public schools was attributed to a surprisingly narrow range of causes by teachers and supervisors at both institutions. Foremost in this very brief list was the feeling of growing failure and lessening hope which pervades the faculty of every school with a considerable percentage of students who terminate their education at the end of high school (if the system can manage to keep them that long). In many public schools I have visited, the song of success has ended in a dirge: We believe we are reasonably successful in the first three grades with most of our children; we know we are doing moderately well with our bright students at almost all levels and better than that in our college-preparatory and advanced placement work. But our results with the general student vary from bad to shocking. We need help. Where can we get it? We need help. . . .

The other reason for the speedy inauguration of this program at both the Maxey and Garnet-Patterson schools is the schoolwide, nationwide awareness that the greatest failure in the education of the general student lies in his language preparation. He is so difficult to teach, say teachers from other subject areas, because he is so difficult to communicate with. Stripped of its social implications, this complaint often reduces itself to the basic problem of literacy. The student who can't or won't read or write or listen well cannot be educated in any subject in the school curriculum. Because he is essentially unreachable in every teacher's classroom, and because teachers in every classroom recognize his language deficiencies as a great part of his problem, the majority of his teachers are ready to aid the English teacher in giving the student language to deal with his world. That readiness, born of frustration on the part of *all* the teachers, has played a very large part in leveling the customary barriers that might have impeded the progress of *English in Every Classroom*.

In concluding this section on the teaching of literacy as a responsibility of the entire school faculty, let me quote from comments made about the program by those who have been asked to teach within it:

"I haven't got time to teach English and math. You'd better tell me which I'm supposed to do."

"Their vocabulary seems to have about doubled. They really go for those dictionaries."

"I've noticed a big improvement in their history spelling. I don't know if it's due to the program or not."

"I find that the pupils show much greater freedom of

expression than they did at the beginning. The papers most recently written are much more interesting to read than the earlier papers."

"I've taught for a long time and I know you can't get kids to write if you don't correct their papers. Their parents would complain too."

"Every member of my team has said how much better our students are writing. It's important to the students that all of their teachers are working on their writing together. They like that."

"It makes the child aware of the consolidated efforts of the teachers."

"It gives the English teacher opportunities to evaluate her own effectiveness by the quality of work done by the child in other classrooms."

"I like the democratic way we plan."

"It's a wonderful method of teaching."

"It stinks."

G. The Journal

Of the many and varied encouragements and inducements to writing within the scope of *English in Every Classroom*, none has been more consistently successful than the journal. The journal has been used in schools, before. English teachers and teachers of other subjects have occasionally turned to it as a support for more formal writing assignments. I have seen journals in public schools used for continuing book reports in English classes, for observations upon municipal government in civics classes, and as diaries in social studies classes. Wherever they have been included within the school program, they seem to have pleased teacher and student alike. Taking their own inclinations and their students' pleasure as a guide, the faculties at Maxey and Garnet-Patterson used the journal with a breadth and freedom not found in other schools.

In addition to the two paperbound books from the library

that each entering student was allowed to choose for his own, and the paperbound dictionary he was given to keep, he also received from his English teacher at the beginning of the school year a spiral notebook. This was identified as his journal, an appropriate name for a notebook intended for daily use by every student. When he was given his journal, the student was told that quantity of production would be the only criterion for judging his writing. Content, style, grammar, rhetoric—all are insignificant compared to quantity. This journal, the student was told, has only one reason for existence: to provide you with a field upon which you can practice your writing. You will be required to write a minimum number of pages each week (two pages a week at Maxey and Garnet-Patterson), and you will be asked each Thursday to turn in your journal to your English teacher who will return it on Friday. Your teacher will read your journal only if you invite her to read it. Under no circumstances, however, will your journal be corrected. It will be assessed for quantity, nothing else.

The use of the journal in the Garnet-Patterson Junior High School differed in one important way from its use at the Maxey School. Journals were given a cursory reading by teachers in the public school. This was very different from the procedure of the training school, where the fact that the journal was never read by teachers, except by specific invitation, was one of its most attractive aspects from the boys' point of view. Journals could remain unread in the training school because a penal institution, no matter how progressive and enlightened, is still a closed system designed to remove offenders from society. Each member of the training school staff teaches and counsels there because he understands that vituperation and obscenity are methods by which disturbed children may free themselves from some of the frustration and fear that shackle them to illiteracy. In the public schools, however, this problem must be handled very differently because of the public nature of all the students' school language, spoken or written. The simple expedient of telling the students that their notebooks will be glanced at each week, though neither read carefully nor corrected, largely solves the problem of preventing the use of publicly unacceptable words and ideas.

The quantitative view of writing has, as a necessary corollary, the permissive handling of journal entries by the teacher. Whether written inside or outside of class, whether legible or barely intelligible, whether a sentence, a paragraph or a page—each entry is another building block in the structure of the student's literacy. If the teacher can bring herself to regard the journal in this way, she will be equally satisfied with prose that is original and prose that is copied from a newspaper, a magazine, or a book. And both she and her students will be more than satisfied with work which is evaluated by no one. If this permissiveness in the nature of the entry is closely coupled with an unvarying weekly check on the amount of production, then the formula for success in much of human enterprise—a little license with accompanying obligation—can make the journal an exceptionally useful teaching tool.

Teachers in the program found that varying the pace of the journal's use by varying its place was an especially successful teaching strategem. One teacher alternated weekly periods of using the journal in the classroom for brief writing assignments with having his students write outside of class. He found that he got a good deal of personal writing outside of class, but that the diarist receded into the background when students were called upon to write their journals in class. Furthermore, he discovered that he got surprisingly creative production when he reserved the last ten minutes of the hour rather than the first ten for journal writing.

In the early stages of the program at the Maxey School, a disappointingly small number of boys wrote more than the required minimum of two pages in their journals. We had half expected that the journal would be used by many as a kind of private stamping ground where they could work over their enemies, work out their fears, and work at the habit of writing. We were wrong; two years later, we knew why: The journal became all we had expected it to be, and more, but instead of taking its anticipated and immediate place as a cause of change in student attitudes, it became a result of that change. As language took on real value, as speed with a dictionary and ability to write for the school newspaper and literary magazine became means for achieving peer esteem, the average weekly production in the journal increased slowly but surely. A page a day, once highly remarkable, became more usual, and five pages a day became the average output of one young man, who confided to his teacher that he'd written that much in the first fifteen days just to see if the school would really give him another notebook when he filled the first one. It would and did; he filled eight notebooks before he left the school.

Among the many creative uses found for the journal, one of the most interesting was the "good listening" device employed by one of the English teachers. The more she spoke with her students, the more she had come to believe that though they appeared to understand what she was saying—and, when asked, would claim that they did—they did not in fact usually understand her spoken directions. With this realization came the inspiration to employ the journal as a dictation workbook in which "listening good" became a challenging pursuit. A few days of this practice every two weeks became a popular pastime with her students as they concentrated upon reproducing exactly what she was saying. She thought that the interest in her exact words which this exercise fostered carried over into closer attention to her words when interpretation rather than mere transcription was the requirement.

A discussion of the journal would not be complete without the story of Lester. Lester came to the penal school by the surest of several possible routes; he got himself born Black. Having managed that, he proceeded to increase his chances greatly by growing up in his mother's care in Detroit's Black ghetto. Get born Black, get raised by your mother on Detroit's East Side, and you've done about all you can to make it to a training school. The rest is a matter of luck.

Lester had the luck, all of it bad. If you're a White boy from a rural area, just drag race your car, badmouth the sheriff, and WHAM! B.T.S. But if you're a Black or White boy from Detroit, you've got to go some to make the scene at Maxey. Lester went some. When he arrived at the school, he was sixteen years old and a habitual criminal. He had to be, to get one of the places reserved for Wayne County boys.

During his stay in the reception center at Whitmore Lake, Lester underwent testing designed to produce a sufficient paper identity for juvenile penal authorities to classify and assign him to one of five available programs throughout the state. The sum of the testing was that Lester was passive, that he would like to be in a school program, and that he functioned on a fourth-grade level at the age of sixteen. With that identity, Lester came to Maxey.

Perhaps the experience he remembers most clearly from his first day in class at B.T.S. is the large spiral notebook he was given and the accompanying directions for its use. He remembers being told that he would be expected to write at least two pages a week in that notebook, and that under no circumstances would anyone correct what he wrote.

"Suppose I can't think of two pages worth?" Lester may have asked the question. Someone always did.

"Then copy from a newspaper or a magazine or a book."

"Copy?!!!" The boys were always shocked and incredulous. In school, COPY was the dirtiest four-letter word they knew. Punch your teacher in the nose. Break the windows and destroy the books. What can happen to you? Suspension? Probation? But whatever you do, and by all that's damned and dumb, *don't copy!* Because for that you get thrown out. They'd rather scrawl almost any other four-letter word on the walls of the toilet or locker room. But COPY! That's a word right out of the darkness. And a teacher just said to_____(it's hard to bring yourself even to say the word).

But they *do* copy. They copy and they copy and they copy. Then they copy some more. The modern, no-holds-barred record for copying at B.T.S. was forty-five pages in the first week. Teachers were grateful, however, if they got two. One youngster, who had never read it before, was fascinated by *Time* magazine. For six weeks he copied from the same well-worn issue. His teacher was delighted. Not only had he written more in that brief period than he had written before in his life, but his conversation was full of the things he was reading. During that period he passed from truculent reserve to something like participation in his English and social studies classes.

A few boys with remarkable stamina copied the bulk of their journal work throughout the entire academic year. Most got tired of copying, however, especially when no teacher renewed its attraction by forbidding it. Most go naturally to the next stage of journal usage, the diary. For almost all the boys this second stage was also the final stage of their journal development. Like the majority of his fellows, Lester filled his journal with the thoughts and happenings of his daily life. Unlike his peers, most of whom wrote little more than the prescribed two pages each week, Lester wrote and wrote and wrote. Fourth-grade attainment on a test validated upon White middle-class children by White middle-class adults would have meant nothing to him. He liked to write; he discovered he liked to write by writing.

What Lester wrote at first gave his teacher bad dreams, for he filled his pages with the sickness of an adolescent tortured by every confusion and every desire—magnified unbearably by intelligence and incarceration. One obscene word repeated eight times on each line for seven full pages is an index to the depth from which Lester viewed the world above him. He was striking out with the only weapon he had. With patience and understanding, the only weapons *she* had, his English teacher waited. And waited and waited and waited. Neither she nor any of us could have said exactly what it was she waited for. But we all knew that Lester had to get that sickness up and out before anything good could come from him.

Then, before class on a Thursday morning (the journals were collected each Thursday and returned the next day after having been checked for quantity), Lester brought his journal to his teacher and told her to read it. She reported that her knees got weak and she felt suddenly queasy as she tried to guess what he had spilled onto the page. "Lester," she began, "I don't think that I ... uh ... well, that I should...." She had intended to say that she would read it later or that evening or next year ... but she knew he meant *now* and she

75

had to read it *now*. She remembers the sensation of narrowing her eyes against the shock as she opened the notebook.

It was a poem. A nice, inconsequential piece of verse carefully divided into four stanzas of four lines each and painstakingly rhymed on alternate lines. Some sixth sense reserved for teachers in a bad spot told her not to ask him why he wanted her to read a poem she recognized as having been copied from a daily newspaper. Instead, she praised it. And she praised poetry. And she praised the writing of poetry. Her praise included the people who write poetry because they find it helps them to say what they mean. She was fishing, and he was watching her like a hawk waiting for the right catch before he swooped. She was running out of words and ideas when he suddenly reached inside his shirt and drew out a sheaf of papers covered with his own handwriting.

It was poetry. Some of it. Some was just doggerel verse. And some was nothing at all. But Lester had been trying to write poetry for months, not quite knowing how, not knowing whether or to whom to show it, failing often, giving way to emotions he couldn't control and couldn't express, and, occasionally, succeeding. His teacher praised it as much as she dared. Now that he had come out into the open, she had to be careful to give him no cause, including effusiveness, to return to heavy cover.

Lester brought in new poems before every English class. The poem copied from the newspaper, his own sheaf of poems finally revealed, the teacher who didn't snigger or patronize—all had combined to break the wall Lester had been building for all his sixteen years. The breach became a spillway down which Lester poured.

"Miss Farnell, can I publish my poems?"

Put yourself behind the teacher's desk. What do you reply? Lester didn't mean that he wanted to publish a book. He only wanted to make a mimeographed booklet—a sheaf of papers prefaced by a title and his name—for distribution within the school itself. Certainly a booklet like that should be easy enough to make, even in a training school? Yes, and easy to distribute. But impossible to recall, once distributed.

Lester was in the midst of the most significant change-process of his life. The changes were so radical that they hardly seemed real. A relatively few months of accomplishment—perhaps the first unqualified success of his life—had begun a process powerful enough to change a passive, effeminate, obnoxious boy into an aggressive, masculine, obnoxious boy. But the process was reversible. And the fearful vision that haunted his teacher was the reception those poems might receive in the school.

For what is a poet in a training school? He walks with a certain lightness of foot, you can hear him swish as he passes, and, baby, in a training school that is VERY BAD. So bad that we would have given a great deal to spare Lester the experience. He had been promised an answer to his request on the following day. Our collective decision to publish the poems was based, finally, on the simplest of reasons—none of us had the strength to say no. But our "yes" was weak and worried. The poems were mimeographed and distributed throughout the school. We held our breath.

Of all our private predictions, varying from hot disaster to cold indifference, none dared to be as hopeful as reality. None of us, barricaded within the assumptions of our middle-class worlds, foresaw the eminence that poetry would bring to Lester at B.T.S. And we were even less capable of foreseeing the value that Lester's writing would give to poetry at B.T.S. One type of book we had omitted completely from our original paperback library was the poetry anthology and the book of poems by a single author. If we were collectively certain of anything, it was that these boys had never willingly read poetry in their lives and were unlikely to begin at B.T.S. We now think somewhat less of collective certainty. Lester's poems were published. Lester was lionized. And we were overwhelmed by the discovery of thirty-five poets in the Maxey School population.

Lester published two further collections before he completed his stay at Maxey. With each publication, the group's view of Lester and poetry (and Lester's view of himself) changed profoundly. Lester saw something in himself to value, and his peers saw something in poetry. Even after Lester was long gone from Maxey, the librarian was still having trouble meeting the demand for books of poetry.

What began as an improbable story ends as an impossible fantasy. As Lester underwent the dramatic change from a passive to an aggressive human being, from a local laugh to a local leader, his aspirations changed as well. To him, the world of the W.J. Maxey Boys' Training School at Whitmore Lake became even smaller than it was. Lester wanted to copyright his extensive production of poetry. Acting upon the advice of his English teacher, Lester wrote to Congressman Weston Vivian, Democrat, then representing Michigan's Second District, of which Whitmore Lake is a part. Lester sent along his poems with a letter inquiring about copyright. Mr. Vivian's response was predictable—if you still believe in the Age of Miracles. All this remarkable Congressman did was to read one of Lester's poems into the *Congressional Record*, get Vice President Humphrey's autograph on a copy of that edition of the *Record*, fly to Detroit, motor to Whitmore Lake, and present the autographed copy to Lester at an assembly of the entire school. No one will ever be able to assess accurately what Mr. Vivian's visit did directly for Lester's ego, vicariously for those of his fellow students, and incidentally for the causes of poetry and literacy at Maxey.

Because improbability is boundless, Lester's story has a sequel. After his release from B.T.S., Lester called his teacher regularly to report on his activities. A few months after his release I walked into the school library one afternoon to find her staring vacantly past the spinners full of paperbound books.

"Lester called this morning." I could barely hear the words.

"What's wrong?" Nobody makes it, I thought. Not even Lester.

"He says he just got a five hundred dollar check from a publisher for his poems."

It was true. Improbable. Impossible. Nevertheless true. Another B.T.S. alumnus who keeps in touch with his former teachers came to visit the school sometime after Lester's telephone call. He was able to verify the story with the best kind of evidence—he had *seen* the check. It was no surprise to him, he said. "When that cat come from Washing Town," he told us, "everybody *know* Lester going to be *the man*."

H. Newspapers, Magazines, Paperbound Books

No student is likely to learn to write if she believes that writing is an affliction visited upon defenseless students solely by English teachers; nor is she likely to learn to read unless reading is made a part of her entire curricular environment. Therefore this program requires that *all* teachers base a significant part of their course content and a portion of their written exercises upon textbooks designed to *invite* reading. These textbooks are the newspapers, magazines, and paperbound books which import the nonschool world into the classroom.

An acceptable text in this program is one which is not an anthology and does not have hard covers, for the hardbound text and the anthology have a number of serious defects in common. To the unsuccessful student both are symbols of a world of scholastic failure, and both to some degree are causes of that failure. No hard-bound text was ever thrust into a child's pocket, and no anthology was ever "read" in any meaningful sense of the word by anybody. The student fed a steady diet of highly selected collections is not being encouraged to read so much as she is being trained to survey, to mine, and to collect shining nuggets of precious literature. The discrimination she is taught by reading a typical school anthology is greater than it need be, while the actual quantity and continuity of her reading is less than it should be. The use of such an anthology often testifies to a lack of effort or imagination, or both, on the part of the educator, and the surrender of inspiration to convenience. Furthermore, the anthology shares with all other large, hardcover books in the desk-top-and-locker disease which so often afflicts these less portable and digestible texts when they are given to poor and mediocre students. Such books were obviously not made to give companionship to immature students; recognizing this, these students usually give them the minimal attention they appear to deserve.

In emphasizing the importance of softcover, easily portable texts, I wish to point out two of their greatest advantages. First, the traditional, limited sense of "text" should be expanded to include any appropriate paperbound book and periodical now being published. Certainly the attention given by educators to *what* a student reads has proved, by its exaggerated emphasis upon "quality," damaging in the extreme to *how much* she reads. Generations of students, nurtured solely on anthologized and authorized classics, have become the parents of children who, like their parents, lack the reading habit because the typical school program neither stimulates nor breeds a desire to read in the average student. In teaching all children, but most especially in teaching the environmentally disadvantaged child, attention should be refocused upon the *quantity* of supervised reading they can accomplish. This argument makes the strongest case for materials which are from the world outside the school and classroom. The greatest possible use should be made of newspapers and magazines in every class in all curricula, and softcover books should be preferred to hardbound texts wherever choice is possible.

The second great advantage of softcover, easily portable texts lies in the invitation to possession and casual reading inherent in their very form. In many less fortunate children, the need to possess is unusually strong. Softbound books and magazines are an ideal means of satisfying this need, for the full possession of them involves more than mere ownership. The physical possession of books and magazines is the most likely method of encouraging a child to read, especially when reading materials closely resemble those with which he is at least vaguely familiar outside the classroom.

Speaking of portability and possession, one of the most remarkable facts to come to our attention during the history of *English in Every Classroom* at B.T.S. was the attrition of library books that we came to identify in our records as the "walkaway factor." The Maxey School attempted to rehabilitate its wards within a minimum security program. Among many other implications, minimum security means that anybody who really wants out can find a way. One result of such a policy is that many of the boys made genuine progress toward personal responsibility in their brief period of incarceration. Another result of minimum security, however, was that a significant number of boys became "walkaways." Their motives were various, their plans nonexistent, their futures alike (almost all were returned to the school), but their companions on the road bore a certain resemblance to each other. Though a boy might leave everything else behind, including his friends, he took along some or all of the paperbound books in his possession at the time. Which, said the librarian, was not the worst way to lose books.

If paperbacks are a bargain, newspapers are a wholesale delight. The most telling recommendation of the newspaper, repeated in many forms by English teachers who taught from it at least three times a week for periods varying from three months to three years, was that it was *warmly welcomed* by their students. Again and again teachers said that the newspaper "gives me something to do all the time; I don't have to worry about how I'm going to hold their attention." As any teacher knows who has had to deal with reluctant readers (as which of us has not?), the first step is the most important in moving them toward literacy. Once they willingly take that initial step toward reading, their literacy will be as functional as the fingers that turn the pages.

Occasionally the overture toward reading is played in strident tones, as it was in an English class of eight boys at the Maxey School. The teacher had planned the class around the newspaper. The boys had written a paragraph summary of a lead story on the front page, begun a letter responding to a controversy in the "Letters to the Editor" column, and answered a series of questions about a number of brief articles in the sports pages. They had been subjected to the newspaper for almost an entire hour when the teacher told them that the class was over and the time had come to pass in the newspaper. Their rising growl of protest had brought me quickly down the hall from the library. The sight and sound of eight sixteen- and seventeen-year-old "nonreaders" complaining loudly because their English class was over for the day was so unexpected that I stood in the doorway, confused and uncertain, until I saw the smile on the teacher's face. As he said afterward, he knew he should do something beside grin at me, but nothing else seemed to fit his feelings.

The newspaper is no more the answer to a teacher's prayer than any other inanimate teaching tool. But it is a superior tool when coupled with the animating force of the teacher's confident use, because it contains within its pages something to engage and reward the interest of every student. Like all novel devices, however, it must be protected from overexposure. The best protection we discovered was to alternate its use with the magazine. The average we strove for in the English classes of the Maxey and Garnet-Patterson schools was to use newspapers three times a week and magazines twice. This pattern can be varied, of course. Most important, however, is the recognition that any tool may have its cutting edge made dull through overuse.

A question often asked is, "Is it better to use a local newspaper or one with a nationwide circulation?" Since the purpose of using the newspaper in the classroom is to place before the student materials which are likely to *invite* her to literacy, a local paper is easily the better choice. *The New York Times*, for example, may be in every way superior to the local rag dominated by an editor-publisher who may be a moral dwarf and a grammar school dropout. Limited though he may be, he nevertheless fills his paper with local news of every description. Because of this, the reluctant reader is very likely to find his product more attractive than any big-city journal, no matter how famous.

The choice between local papers is not so easy, implying as it does a selection likely to create ill will if the school system purchases any considerable number of papers. In such cases, the use of more than one newspaper can be a boon, since two newspapers offer opportunities for comparative study of everything from style to accuracy.

Practical arguments can be cited for using either the morning or the evening paper. The evening paper is useful because of the time it allows teachers to review it for teaching purposes. The morning paper is equally useful for the fresher news it contains. Whether published in the morning or evening, however, the newspaper communicates a sense of vitality and immediate excitement equaled by no other public writing of our time. It is just that sense of excitement which has been so sadly missing from the texts of our public schools.

Because the magazine captures the reader's attention in a way quite different from the newspaper, it is an excellent complement to the paper's use in the classroom. Whereas the newspaper does very little to make itself visually attractive, hoping instead that the topicality of its contents will lure the reader, the magazine can afford to stress form and color because of its longer life and the more leisurely reading pace it invites. Magazines proved extremely successful teaching devices at the Maxey and Garnet-Patterson schools.

How many magazines and newspapers are enough? After a great deal of experimentation, we discovered that one set of papers per day for each English teacher is a very workable arrangement. The size of the set should equal the number of students in the English teacher's largest class, plus one for the teacher. In a public school with 840 students, for example, all of whom are taking English every day in classes of thirty-five, with teachers handling four classes each, six full-time English teachers would be required. Each of these teachers would receive thirty-five papers each morning for her students plus one for herself, a total of 216 papers a day. These papers would be used by the English teacher three times a week in each of her four classes; they would be available to the members of her team for use at all other times. In practice this means that the papers are in use in English classes for about half the teaching periods of the week and may be employed for an equal period of time in all other subjects combined.

Magazines can be ordered by a somewhat similar formula. For each magazine that the school decides to use, the number of copies should equal the number of students in the school's largest homeroom class. Distribution through the school was the responsibility of the English chairman in the junior high school and of a selected teacher in the training school where no chairman was appointed. Both employed approximately the same methods: Teachers were asked to reserve those magazines they knew they would want to use on particular days in ensuing weeks. During the week before the reserved magazines were to be used, a list of magazines with unreserved days was circulated throughout the school. When magazines arrived at the school, they were held out of circulation for one or two days to allow all teachers to become familiar with their contents. At the end of that period, a final list of available magazines was circulated throughout the school.

The formula for minimal usage—at least twice a week in the English and social studies classroom, at least once a week in every other classroom—guarantees a considerable classroom reading of magazines within the program. But no formula can guarantee *meaningful* usage of materials, no matter how reasonable the formula and how attractive the materials. The success of magazines within the plan of *English in Every Classroom* is due entirely to the discovery by teachers in every classroom that magazines are good for learning and good for teaching. As with newspapers, magazines are in constant use because students will learn from them and teachers can teach from them. No higher recommendation is possible for any textbook.

Speaking of guarantees and recommendations, all recommendations for the adoption of paperbound materials as substitutes for conventional texts carry guarantees of failure if such changes are not made within a program which also makes meaningful changes in the methods of teaching English. No child, no matter how disadvantaged, is so imperceptive that the mere substitution of one format for another will permanently raise his opinion of the essential processes of the classroom. Before very long even the slowest will recognize that he has been had again, and newspapers, magazines, and paperbound books will come to symbolize for him the same irrelevance and frustration that he has always known in school.

I. The School Library

A Philosophy of Use

The concept of the school library requires the same sort of basic reconsideration that this program advocates for the teaching of reading and writing. Many observers have remarked the depressing lack of visual appeal and the even more disturbing absence of reading activity in public school libraries. Most depressing of all, however, are the schools so overcrowded that they have no room for a library. The following recommendations are aimed particularly at alleviating these three problems of space, visual appeal, and reading activity:

Where change is most badly needed is in the ideas of economy which dictate the selection of books and methods of display. For what reason other than economy of space are books displayed with their spines out? The spine of a book, with its Dewey decimal notations, is no more attractive than any other spine with such markings would be. And yet we expect the partly literate student, who relates to very little through words, to relate to books through words printed on their spines. This is the same person, remember, who is *always* attracted to pictures, whether found in comic books or on the television screen. Why then do we not make the most of her tastes and predispositions, give up the false economy which shelves large numbers of unread books, and attract her to books through bright pictures on their covers? Let us replace the typically drab, unread books of our school libraries—libraries full of books with pictureless, unopened covers—with paperbound books that attract children (just as they attract adults) by the bright covers that commercial artists and advertising experts have made so inviting.

School librarians should take a useful lesson from operators of paperbound bookstores, who have learned to let their merchandise sell itself by arranging their stores so that customers are surrounded by colorful and highly descriptive paper covers. But what of the expense of purchasing paperbound books to begin with, and of maintaining a steady supply to replace the easily tattered, broken, and lost paperback? What of the expense? Two questions must be asked in return: What is more expensive than the waste of human intellect implied in a library of unread books? And what sort of destruction is more admirable than that of the book tattered and finally broken beyond repair in the hands of eager readers? We have had too little such destruction; the time has come for our school libraries to invite it.

Perhaps nothing more clearly reveals some school librarians' antiquated and insular view of the world than the relatively small use made of paperbound books in many school libraries. "Why don't you have more paperbacks in your library?" I have asked the question of hundreds of librarians in many sections of this country. In general, where they have not pleaded simple poverty—a plea difficult to defend once the Federal Government discovered that social action could be influenced through the schools—they have in effect pleaded simple prejudice. Exceptions to this generalization are still painfully few. Public school libraries are disaster areas, and librarians who do not display books attractively must share the blame with teachers who do not make reading pleasurable.

The simple prejudice of so many librarians is best illustrated by the widespread notions that paperbacks are too perishable, and that visual appeal is relatively unimportant. Both ideas are dead and should be given the interment their ancient bones deserve. For years we used paperbacks and nothing but paperbacks at the Maxey School. For 280 boys our library had 2,200 titles and 7,500 volumes including titles in class-size sets available to all teachers. No group of boys anywhere was more capable of destruction or more willing to destroy. Yet we failed utterly in what appeared to be one of our simplest testing objectives: To determine the average life expectancy of a paperbound book when that book is circulated repeatedly among hands unaccustomed to giving or receiving gentleness. As far as we could tell, our books seemed likely to last forever. Read heavily, handled incessantly, they proved virtually indestructible—not, mind you, because they couldn't easily be ripped or destroyed, but because they became something of value to the boys and were treated accordingly.

So much for the outmoded notion of financial disaster through the destruction of the books. But another bogeyman hides in the dust of unread library books—a kind of high-minded drawing back on the part of school libraries from the successful vending practices of commercial booksellers. How can school libraries refuse to use every means at their disposal to attract *their* clientele—the students? In this case, the means available are the expensive, graphic covers of the paperbound trade. Any magazine or paperback publisher will tell you how much good covers mean to his sales, and how happy he is to pay well for them. Do we dare refuse any advantage available to us in the battle to win children to the world of books? One of the clearest advantages is the cover of the paperbound book—an advantage proved effective in bookstores across the nation.

If reading activity follows visual appeal as effect follows cause, what about space problems of shelving books with their covers showing? The answer lies in the wall racks and free-standing spinners traditionally used to promote paperback sales in corner drugstores and other places where space is at a premium. The problem of library space has another interesting solution—the combination classroom and library advocated by this program. In order for the library to become an organic part of the English curriculum, it should be available as a classroom to all teachers and should be designated as the meeting place once each week for every English class. Where no better room is available, as is so often the case in the old and seriously overcrowded buildings where the disadvantaged child finds his education, a larger classroom can be easily adapted to the minimal space requirements of revolving wire racks for paperbound books.

Fundamental to the malaise from which conventional school libraries suffer is the universal assumption that students will use them because they are there. Were this assumption applied to other human activities, ranging from toilet-training to the use of tools, only catastrophe would result. Regarding the library as something less than an irresistible attraction to students is a useful first step in revitalizing it. Implicit in this approach is an objective review of its lending procedures. Instead of placing the responsibility for first (and, too often, last) acquaintance upon the student and/or the teacher, the responsibility should be put where it rightfully belongs—upon the books themselves. *Give* each child a paperbound book or two to begin her school year. Let her understand that she may have any other paperbound book in the library by the simple expedient of trading a book she has for a book she wants. Then *schedule* her twice each week for the opportunity of book borrowing, and if our experience at the Maxey and Garnet-Patterson schools has been any guide—stand back and enjoy the sight of children reading.

Selecting the Books

Just what selection procedures create the best paperback library? The youngest boy at B.T.S. was twelve, the oldest eighteen; the average boy read as well as a fourth-grader, and most were in junior high before they came to the Maxey School. Almost all had lived materially disadvantaged lives; almost all had come from culturally impoverished worlds. At the age of twelve they knew more about physical man— from sex of some kinds to violence of all kinds—than any child should and most adults ever will. At the age of eighteen they knew less about the world outside the neighborhoods in which they had lived (all alike; moving often is easier than paying the rent) than middle-class children half their age. Everybody knows *about* them. But who *knows* them? And who knows what kind of books they might read?

Haunted by the specter of our own ignorance, we took refuge in a copy of *Paperbound Books in Print*. We tore the title list into six equal sections, one section for each English teacher. In his section, each teacher placed a check beside each book he thought the boys would like to read, and two checks beside each book he thought the boys would like to read and he would like to teach. Then he exchanged sections with another teacher and, using crosses instead of checks, did the same with the second section he received. Next, each teacher found a section he hadn't yet read and no third reader had marked; this section he marked with small circles in the same way. Finally, each teacher took the last section in his possession, made a list of the books with three kinds of marks beside them, and a list of the ones that had at least one of those marks twice. When the last step had been performed, we had our library list. In addition, we had a list of books the teachers would like to have in class-size sets for teaching purposes.

Now for appeal to the final authority—the boys. First we had to arrange for the books to be obtained with the privilege of returning them. We knew that our list was intelligent, democratic, inclusive, unique. What we didn't know was whether it contained books the boys would read. If we spent the little money we had on books that would go unread, we might just as well have stocked our school library with all the hardbound books that nobody ever reads anyway and saved ourselves a good deal of trouble. Out of our need came the best experience we were to have at the Maxey School. We discovered the wise charity of Ivan Ludington Sr. and his Ludington News Company of Detroit.

The letter I wrote him was something less than a masterpiece. Only college presidents and skid-row bums are really good at begging. But the answer I got would have made a president proud and a bum delirious. Two days after I mailed the letter the phone in my office rang. Ivan Ludington speaking—what did I need and where did I need it? He would be glad to come to Ann Arbor to make arrangements. No, I would come to Detroit. Somehow that seemed to be the least I could do. It was. It was also the most I could do. Mr. Ludington supplied the school for six years with all the paperbound books and magazines we requested—absolutely free of any charge. The numbers were upwards of 25,000 paperbacks and 50,000 magazines. Combine these figures with the equally remarkable generosity of that excellent paper, *The Detroit News* (one hundred copies a day, seven days a week), and the principle of saturation is vividly illustrated. But more about the Ludington story later.

Those of us who participated in selecting the original 1,200 titles for the Maxey paperback library will never again have to be reminded of how little we know about the students we teach. None of us will forget the untouched 700 titles that decorated our gleaming drugstore spinners while the boys read and reread the 500 they liked.

My private prediction for our list was that some 200 books might go unread, largely because they seemed to me to be either too difficult or too passive for a sixteen-year-old boy with a ninety I.Q. who reads at a fourth-grade level. But I had no doubt whatever that the remaining thousand were books the boys would read if we could display them attractively within an effective language program. I could hardly have been more mistaken. Not only was I one hundred percent wrong in my estimate of the number of successful books on our list, but seventy-five of the books I had thought would be ignored proved to be popular with the boys.

Our highly eclectic list represented books so attractive to young people that the average boy at B.T.S., who arrived with a reading rate of no books per lifetime, was reading one library book every two days by the time he left. And that *average* included all the boys—those who never read anything as well as those who read a book a day. However, it does not include the large number of paperbound books used as texts, or the immense number of newspapers and magazines devoured by newly awakened appetites.

Speaking of newly awakened appetites, what do *you* do at a basketball game? Play or watch, you say? Well, that's only because you haven't recently discovered the world of paperbound books. Sam Sublett, director of the Boys Training School at St. Charles, Illinois, tells the following story:

After days of grapevine publicity, a shipment of paperback books, along with their spinner racks, arrived at St. Charles. By Friday morning they were ready for distribution and by Friday afternoon the boys had them out. Only one condition for their presentation to the school was set by Charles Levy, president of the Charles Levy Circulation Company, who had followed in the Chicago area the lead of Ivan Ludington in Detroit. "I'll give you all the books and magazines you want and your boys can read," he said, "if you'll promise me to handle them as though they were expendable. Get them out of the rack pockets and into the kids' pockets as soon as you can, and, if you can, keep them there." By Friday afternoon, Mr. Sublett and his staff had kept the first part of their bargain.

Friday evening's game was not just another horserace, reports Mr. Sublett. The teams were evenly matched and hot. He and other staff members were held spellbound by a real contest. Midway through the second quarter, up on his feet and yelling, Sam suddenly had that lonely feeling. Only then—for the first time since the game began—did he look around him instead of in front of him. "How," he asks now, "do you tell anybody who wasn't there that *half* those kids were reading paperbound books while a red-hot ballgame was burning up the gym they were reading in?"

Some of those same boys were among the twelve who signed the waiting list for Joseph Kane's *Facts about the Presidents*. Of all books, why that one? And *twelve* boys? One of the staff said it: "Before, we couldn't get twelve volunteers to sign up for anything short of a breakout."

Warming up the cold list of a thousand paperbacks were the sparks of light and heat given off by rubbing children against books. On a Monday morning, just before the first class of the week, an English teacher is about to close the door to his room as a seventeen-year-old runs past to a classroom farther down the hall. The boy turns, pulls out of his shirt Dick Gregory's *From the Back of the Bus*, waves it at the teacher, and shouts, "I bought it, man, I bought it! Bought four more while I was home. Didn't steal none!" Bought or stolen, those five books were the first that boy had ever owned. Home for a weekend as part of the school's rehabilitation program, he had been able to think of no better use for his time and money than to spend both on paperback books from the corner drugstore. Even if he had stolen them, this would certainly have been the first time he had stolen *books*.

Or the Case of the Bonds Going Out of Stock. The boys wanted the James Bond books. What's more, they wanted them loudly and often. Our usual enthusiastic response to their desire to read books we didn't have, was considerably tempered in this case, by the covers of the Ian Fleming novels, and by our limited knowledge of what went on between those covers. Most of us had seen *Goldfinger*, but few of us had read any of Bond's adventures. My own response had been to suspect the usual book-movie relationship, i.e., if Pussy Galore was a character in the *movie*, how much cleaning up had the producer done to make the author's work acceptable on the screen? That suspicion, plus the undressed covers, had kept the Bond books out of our library.

Like all other censors, self-appointed or otherwise, I was unequal to the job. When it occurred to me—as the howl for Bond grew—that I might at least read the books I was banning, I read them all as a kind of penance. I was embarrassed by their contents; I was embarrassed by the discovery, for instance, that *Goldfinger* is far sexier to see than to read. Henry Miller at the age of ten could have spotted Fleming-Bond two red lights and three double beds, and won the race in a crawl. We asked for a dozen copies of every Bond adventure that Ivan Ludington had in stock.

The books were delivered to the librarian one morning just as she was going into the hall to help a teacher separate a couple of featherweight battlers. Ten boys from the same class were in the library at the time. The bell for change of class had just rung, and the boys were at the door, preparing to leave, when the teacher with them told them to remain inside the library until the fight in the hall was under control. In the confusion that followed, the ten boys were left alone in the library. The librarian says she was gone long enough to walk fifteen feet from her door, see that the situation needed a man, and turn back to get the male teacher who had been in the library with his class. When she saw him coming, she returned immediately to the library. She could not have been gone more than three minutes. As she entered the library, the ten boys were leaving by the other door to go to their next class. She called to the last one to shut the door, and remembers how he jumped when she called his name.

Not until half an hour later, when she began to catalogue the Bond books, did she realize why he had been so startled. In the brief time she had been out of the room, eighty of the 007 adventure stories had disappeared. A little arithmetic led her to the realization that each boy had taken one complete set of the eight titles she had received. Though impressed by such a feat of distribution, and pleased by so evident and massive a desire to read, she felt that the least she could do was to catalogue the books before they were stolen. When she entered their classroom, the boys were upset only because she had discovered the larceny so soon. Nobody had gotten to do any reading. Leaving questions of crime and punishment to philosophers and psychologists, the librarian promised the boys they could each borrow two of Fleming's books if they'd come in at the end of the day when she had the books catalogued. Her final comment was that she had made the promise because their disappointment was so real. They had taken the books because they wanted to read them.

Sometimes, however, wanting a thing and getting it can be frustrated by the ancient problem of "face." Who can look tough with a book by Ann Landers sticking out of his hip pocket? One young man solved the problem to his own satisfaction by informing the librarian, as he borrowed *Ann Landers Talks to Teenagers About Sex*, that he was only bothering with it "because this here guy axed me to get it for him."

The same guy who axed him to get Ann Landers would also be likely to axe him to return for Ralph and Shirley Benner's *Sex and the Teenager;* Maxine Davis' two books, *Sex and the Adolescent* and *Sexual Responsibility in Marriage*; or Evelyn Duvall's pair on *The Art of Dating* and *Facts of Life and Love for Teenagers*. If that weren't enough, and it wouldn't be, he would return (with a different story) for Winston Ehrmann's *Premarital Dating Behavior,* Havelock Ellis' *On Life and Sex*, Aron Krich's *Facts of Love and Marriage for Young People*, and Rhoda Lorand's *Love, Sex and the Teenager*. Being sensitive to our students' tastes, we began to get the impression that implications of sex in a title would guarantee the popularity of any book.

At Maxey, one of the funniest and most meaningful examples of this guarantee involved *The Scarlet Letter*. On a Friday morning, an English teacher watched one of his poorest readers choose Hawthorne's novel from the rack. Knowing how difficult the boy would find the book, and fearing that he would be discouraged by the experience, the teacher suggested that perhaps he had mistaken *The Scarlet Letter* for something else. "Ain't this the one about a whore?" asked the boy. "And don't that big 'A' stand for whore?" When the teacher had to admit that this description was more or less correct, the boy had heard enough. If it was a book about a whore, it was a book for him.

Three days later, on Monday, the same boy came to his English teacher with *The Scarlet Letter* in hand and two sheets of notebook paper. On those two sheets, front and back, were all the words—and their definitions—the boy hadn't known in the first eleven pages of the book. He had clearly spent the weekend with Hawthorne and the dictionary, and he was looking for praise—which he got, lavishly. His English teacher was amazed; the two sheets of notebook paper represented at least six hours of work. According to the teacher, this was a boy who may not have spent six hours reading since he was nine years old, and had no apparent idea of how to use a dictionary when he came to the Maxey School. Motivated by Hawthorne's whore, he fought his way through the entire book. He produced no more lists but he kept at the book (between other novels) for months; during that time, and long after, his conversations with his English teacher were full of his view of what was happening to Hester Prynne. Proceeding as slowly as he did through the story of her life, she took on dimensions of reality for him which authors dream of imparting to their readers and teachers despair of conveying to their students. His valediction on Hawthorne's heroine may not have been couched in the author's own phrases, but it conveyed an understanding of the book that no one could improve upon: "That woman," he announced as he returned the book, "she weren't no whore."

94

One implication of this boy's experience is especially interesting. Hawthorne's vocabulary is difficult for *college* students. I have taught *The Scarlet Letter* to freshmen and sophomores at two universities where more than half the students come from the top 10 percent of their high school class. I have often followed the first reading assignment of the introductory chapter with a ten-minute written quiz asking for definitions of ten words chosen from the first three pages of that chapter. Each time, I caution the students to "read the introductory chapter *carefully*." Every student is allowed to use his textbook and any notes he may have prepared. Only the dictionary is forbidden. Full credit is given for the barest suggestion of knowledge, *e.g., bark:* some kind of boat; *truculency:* meanness; and even *prolix:* says a lot. But no matter how ominously I emphasized the word "carefully" in the assignment, and no matter how undemanding my standards of definition, no more than one-fifth of the students in any of the classes managed to define as many as five of the ten words.

My ringing, rhetorical, unfair question as I return the quizzes at the next meeting of those unfortunate classes is always, "How can you claim to have *read* anything when you don't even know what the words mean?" The question is unfair because I know perfectly well that they could read with great understanding without knowing what all the words mean. The quiz is merely one method of forcing a slower and more careful reading practice upon students convinced that fast reading is the best reading.

But what has this to do with a juvenile delinquent struggling through *The Scarlet Letter?* Just this: Semiliterate readers do not need semiliterate books. The simplistic language of much of the life-leeched literature inflicted upon the average schoolchild is not justifiable from any standpoint. Bright, average, dull—however one classifies the child—she is immeasurably better off with books that are too difficult for her than books that are too simple. But this generalization involves a whole theory of education. All I want to emphasize here is what teachers have observed at the Maxey and Garnet-Patterson schools, and what I have experienced as a teacher of students of a considerably different type—"reading" is a peculiarly personal interaction between a reader and a book, an interaction differing in each case as widely as readers may differ from each other in breadth of experience and quality of mind. But *in no case* does this interaction demand an understanding of every word by the reader. In fact, the threshold of understanding—of meaningful interaction—is surprisingly low, and even in many complex books can be pleasurably crossed by many simple readers.

J. A Guide for Teachers of Subjects Other Than English

This program for teaching reading and writing depends upon you, the instructor whose professional responsibility lies outside the area customarily defined as "English." Making an English program dependent upon teachers of other subjects may at first seem unlikely to succeed. After all, what do *you* know about teaching English? But a second look demonstrates that while the program is unusual in its dependence upon teachers of other subjects, it is likely to succeed for at least two very good reasons: All teachers care enough about their own students and about their own subjects to recognize the potential benefits to both of willingness and competence in English throughout the student body.

We are all familiar with the complaint that teaching partly literate students *anything* is doubly difficult because they can neither sufficiently understand oral directions nor adequately interpret written instructions. Though the complaint is often heard, it has never been directly answered. Instead, it has been referred again and again to the English teacher, the one person who has the least chance of finding the answer precisely because she *is* the English teacher, instructor in the one subject in which the partly literate child has always experienced his worst failures. Given full support by her colleagues, the English teacher may be able to help the nonliterate child. Working by herself, she has amply demonstrated that she cannot do enough. The purpose of this plan, therefore, is to help the non-English teacher to help the student. In so doing, every teacher will be helping each child to become a better student in the teacher's own subject area.

The basic assumption upon which this program is built is the nonliterate child's desperate need for language competence. The child who cannot understand oral and written directions becomes the adult who cannot hold any job above the level of the simplest manual labor or household drudgery; in a technocracy characterized by decreasing individual labor, such jobs become more and more difficult to find. Furthermore, and equally important, since partly literate children cannot depend upon a language they cannot use, they must depend upon other means of expression – force, for example—which they are sure they can use. Perhaps if we can give them language, they will give up some of the wordless violence which they use as a megaphone to communicate with a world which they cannot reach in any other way.

Too much emphasis cannot be placed upon the claim that making all instructors in the school teachers of English will be profitable to all subjects in the curriculum. What subject, after all, does not depend upon language for teaching and for learning? In what subject would both teacher and student not be greatly helped if they could understand each other's conversation and if the student could be relied upon to comprehend written directions? The answer of course is that no subject is independent of language; the obvious conclusion, therefore, is that all subjects should teach what all depend upon for their existence.

The role of the teacher in subject areas other than English is clear, for the minimal demands of the program are remarkably simple; by contrast, its maximal possibilities are unknown and lie entirely in the individual teacher's hands. This approach to teaching and learning is hampered by no absolute precedents, no irrevocable traditions, and no unchallengeable methods. The flexible methods it advocates are easily encompassed in the following summary:

97

1. Reading

a. Use of Popular Magazines and Newspapers

Part of the program to create a new learning environment for partly literate students is the use of familiar reading materials imported from the nonschool world in which learning—especially language learning—was never forced upon them. Since popular magazines and newspapers are not part of the school world that such students often view with hostility, these materials greatly recommended themselves for use in this approach.

In addition to the appeal of novelty which periodical texts possess, they have another and more important justification: they are easy to handle and easy to read. Each teacher should plan part of her teaching program around newspapers and magazines; they contain matter relevant to every course in the curriculum.

b. Use of Paperbound Books

Part of the effort of English teachers to make reading more enjoyable for their students should be very extensive use of paperbound books in their teaching procedures. Since other courses may not primarily be reading courses, other teachers cannot be expected to use these books in the same manner. Instead, the program asks that all other teachers carefully research the materials in their disciplines in the effort to discover and use any paperbound books and magazines having special application to their subject area. Paperback books should be available throughout the school.

The library created as a result of and as an aid to this program is modeled upon a paperbound bookstore. It is designed to make a wide selection of easily handled, attractively covered books available to the student on a barter basis. If these are books that the students read with pleasure, then they become a vehicle to promote learning with an ease seldom found through the use of other texts. Recognizing this, teachers in subject areas other than English should thoroughly explore possibilities of using the library and of suggesting additions to its collection which will benefit their own teaching.

c. Use of Written Directions

The third aspect of this reading program in classrooms other than English urges frequent use of written directives. People very often learn to read when they have to. Or to put it another way, when reading seems necessary to survival, then it becomes a process to master rather than an intrusion to resist. Few students ever really cared whether Jack went up the hill or Jill fell down, but all of them want to accomplish something someone will praise, even if that someone is a teacher. If the road to accomplishment is paved with written directions, that road should be made neither too long nor too difficult so that a student may find pleasure in traveling it.

2. Writing

a. Scheduled Writing in the Classroom

Just as no one ever learned to read except by reading, certainly no one ever learned to write except by writing. Making the act of writing a normal, inescapable part of the student's school environment is one of the chief aims of this plan. One thing we are certain of: The average public school student has always identified writing as part of "English" and therefore easily avoidable because the English class was the only one in which writing played any noticeable role.

Changing this attitude is crucial to increasing the student's ability to write.

Making the act of writing a standard part of every classroom assumes that each teacher will follow a uniform plan. In this case, the plan requires that every teacher in every humanities and sciences classroom collect five *in-class* writing assignments from each student every two weeks. This plan neither prescribes nor is vitally concerned with the length or content of these papers. It assumes that the repetitive act of writing is the only essential element, and prefers to count papers rather than words. It also realizes, however, that the process of making writing an unavoidable part of classes in which writing has been unimportant before, may at first be difficult for teachers newly involved. Therefore, the plan is based upon small groups of instructors centered about an English teacher whose responsibility is to make the new program as easy as possible for the teachers in her group and as profitable as possible for the students.

In addition to acting as a consultant to her colleagues, the English teacher also handles one of the five sets of papers received biweekly by each teacher in her group. The remaining sets of papers should be handled by the subject instructor himself. Two should be read for content; the other two should be filed *unread* in the student's folder. This latter procedure, unusual in any system of education, is based upon the analogy of exercise: Just as the music teacher does not listen to all the exercises practiced by the music student, so should the writing teacher not read all the exercises of her students. This method allows the student to get the practice he needs without overburdening the teacher.

b. Unscheduled Writing in the Classroom

Writing practice of this sort should be a natural outgrowth of learning procedures within the classroom and a natural complement to planned written exercises. Implementation will require improvisation on the part of the teacher. When a student requires a new tool, or asks a complex question, the teacher's reaction should be to ask for the request or the question in writing, just as the child's superior may do in the world of daily employment outside of and beyond the school.

For teachers of industrial arts, home economics, music, and art, student writing is very much less a natural part of the teaching method than it is in some of the other subjects in the curriculum. This new program in English will find a different place in each of their classes. To begin with, it merely asks tolerant support of an effort that touches each of us as teachers—an effort to bring language competence to children who need it as badly as they need good food and steady affection.

This teacher's guide for instructors in subjects other than English would be incomplete without at least one example of how the program of *English in Every Classroom* has been adopted and modified by the needs and capabilities of an independent system. By "independent system" I mean a school or group of schools committed neither to the whole program nor committed as a whole to any part of the program. This description fits Detroit's Northwestern High School, which made full use of the reading room concept (as it is described in the chapter entitled "The Ludington Story") and of an interesting adaptation of the classroom program.

When Northwestern inaugurated a limited curriculum change known as the "Integrated Curriculum in English and Biology," reasons for that change were included in a descriptive paper written by Mrs. Ruby Gillis, the school's reading coordinator:

At Northwestern High School there are several basic problems we must face with our incoming 10B students:

(1) Many of them read far below grade level. Of the 750 in-coming 10B students, 397 were reading two or more years below grade level.
(2) Failure rate in general biology is extremely high.

Part of this is attributable to reading levels.
(3) Students lack a sense of identity within the school. They feel lost in an institution of 2,500 students. Time for orientation is limited, making it difficult to reach students individually.
(4) Many of our discipline problems occur with 10B students.
(5) Generally their basic reading skills are very poor. Reading, writing, and study habits are especially bad. There is not enough time to work with these students in the current forty-minute period to help them overcome their disabilities in time to make a success of their high school career.
(6) Most of these students will not stay after school hours for enrichment courses or special remedial help.

These six clear reasons for undertaking a new type of teaching relationship led to the enunciation of six equally clear purposes for the teachers and students involved:

(1) To integrate the reading and writing activities in the English and science classes
(2) To provide the slow student with motivation for writing and reading
(3) To provide the student with varied and appropriate materials
(4) To provide an additional class period to give the students specific help in reading skills under the guidance of a person trained in the teaching of reading
(5) To give the student a sense of identity through the block time approach
(6) To provide an opportunity for a team of teachers to work closely with a class group.

According to Mrs. Gillis' description, the integrated curriculum was organized on a "tri-class" basis with 10B students who average a fifth-grade reading level. "These students are programmed into three classes: English, reading and biology. They meet five days a week for English and biology" and on four of those days they meet in a reading class which intervenes between the two subjects. "The reading class centers on subject material (largely science) and basic reading skills. All teachers involved work together to plan the curriculum.... The Reading Coordinator is responsible for coordinating the material as well as [guiding] the English and science teachers in reading techniques."

In her description of the project, Mrs. Gillis observed that "the program in its initial stages has been highly successful. We have been able to get a variety of paperback materials in science. Through our paperback reading room program each student has been supplied with a dictionary. The *Detroit News* gives us newspapers twice weekly." She continued by saying that the "team approach is excellent" and "teacher enthusiasm is high." Noting that each instructor seemed to feel an unusual sense of responsibility for these students beyond the confines of the teacher's classroom, she felt that more time than a weekly planning session might be required to direct the program.

Finally, and perhaps most important, Mrs. Gillis observed that this daily, three-hour group experience promoted a sense of unity and identity within the class groups: "Attendance and punctuality [are] better than average. [This is] very noticeable in the Reading Class which students think of as a *Science Reading Lab*. This takes away any stigma of remedial reading."

K. The English Classroom

Imagine the scene: eleven delinquent boys sitting in an English classroom, each reading intensely in his own copy of the same paperbound book. *Goldfinger? Black Like Me? West Side Story?* What else could generate such attention from a group like that? A dictionary.

Breast, whore, lesbian, prostitute, vagina, copulation,

103

intercourse, etc., etc., etc.—the boys find them all. The dictionary is any fifty-cent paperbound lexicon. After a few days of use it opens automatically to a page with one of the "good" words on it. A boy raises his head to ask of nobody, "How you spell that U-word?"

"What word?"

"You know, man. That good word."

"You mean U-terrace?"

"Yeah. What's a U-terrace?"

"'At's where you makes a U-turn."

"Oh man you *so* dumb!"

Whatever its original attraction, the dictionary rivaled the success of the journal in the English program at Maxey and has been transplanted with equal vigor into the public schools participating in this program. The unavoidable conclusion is that children *like* dictionaries when dictionaries are part of a program designed to make language pleasurable as well as useful.

When a student first entered either the public or penal school, he was given, among other things, a paperbound dictionary. He was told that the dictionary was his, that it wouldn't be collected or replaced by the school, and that he could carry it with him or he could leave it at home or in his room or anywhere else he chose. If he chose to carry his dictionary with him, he would be able to use it in class—any class. If he did not have his own dictionary available, he found a set of paperbound dictionaries in every one of his classrooms. These sets ranged in number from class-size in English and social studies classes to smaller numbers in classrooms where the dictionary is less crucial to the subject. They were, according to the teachers, in constant *voluntary* use.

Our expectation at the training school had been that the dictionaries, if successful, would be transported constantly back and forth between the school and the boys' rooms. As a result, paperbound dictionaries were ordered for each student's personal use, but only one or two desk dictionaries were ordered for each classroom. Our mistake was quickly apparent: The boys wanted to use their dictionaries but they also wanted to keep them as part of their permanent possessions, safe in their own rooms. Experimentally and tentatively, we obtained paperbound dictionaries in class-size sets for each English teacher. Almost immediately we began to hear from teachers of other subjects. Why were they left out? The dictionary was as useful to them as it was to the English teacher. How about sets for their rooms? Happily, we purchased more books; soon, all over the school, dictionaries were in use. Teachers of all subjects discovered that an interest in words often becomes an interest in the ideas the words convey.

With the experience at Maxey as our pattern, we ordered individual books for every child and class-size sets for every classroom in the public school. The dictionaries were an immediate and resounding success. In one of her periodic progress reports, Mrs. Sylvia Jones, chairperson of the English Department, told the story of the boy who used the word "damn" in class. "That'll be enough of that swearing," said his teacher.

"Enough of *what?*" asked the boy.

Refusing to be baited, the teacher turned her attention elsewhere, but not before she caught a peculiar expression on the boy's face followed by activity at his seat. She had all but forgotten about him when his excited voice broke through the classroom conversation: "Swearing—that's cussing! The dictionary says so!" He hadn't understood the teacher, but he had possessed the means to arrive at understanding. No learning experience can be better than that.

Though the dictionary was equally successful at both schools, the pattern of its usage differs in one important respect—mobility. Where the protective sense of possession inhibited movement of the dictionary from bedroom to classroom at the Maxey School, the sense of pride in possession seems to have had the opposite effect in public school. Many of the children were proud of their very own dictionary; as a result, they carried and used it with a pleasure usually reserved for objects more familiar than word books.

"The English Classroom" is the title of this chapter in the book because one of the primary concerns of the program called *English in Every Classroom* is to place the teaching of

English in a context within which it can succeed. The reason for this preoccupation is the conviction that English is unique in its dependence upon other subjects for depth and reinforcement. An English class which does not draw some of its materials from other subjects, and which cannot make its influence felt in those subjects, might just as well be a class in Latin as in English. Given the proper surroundings— seeing a reflection of itself in all courses, even as it reflects them—the English class can be the meaningful focus of the student's education. Placed in a context where reading and writing are as necessary and inevitable as nourishment and sleep, the student, the course, and the instructor will thrive together.

Of first importance must be an appropriate definition of the general purpose of the English class. This purpose must not be defined in the usual impersonal and exalted professional terms; it must not be defined in the customary platitudes about improving the moral nature and verbal performance of the child through exposing him to the good and the great in literature. Instead, it must be expressed against the restrictive reality of the child's previous experience. Surely the *ultimate* goal of the English teacher must be to make humanists who are competent readers and writers; furthermore, this training must include competence in grammar and spelling. But, just as surely, the English classroom should be the place in which a learning experience of far greater importance than instruction in the mechanics of language takes place. To the means of effecting that end, the following recommendations are made for the philosophy and conduct of the English class:

(a) That the approach to literature be social rather than literary.

This recommendation is based upon a pedagogical philosophy which finds "He give me the Buk" a more desirable statement than "He gave me the book," if the former reflects a pleasure in its utterance which the latter does not. Best of all, of course, would be the coupling of the real accuracy of the one with the imagined enthusiasm of the other. But there can be little question as to precedence: pleasure and enthusiasm must be the first (and at times the only) goal of the English teacher. Literature chosen for the English class should be selected by the prime criteria of immediate interest and particular relevance to the students' situation. The important question to be asked is "What *will* they read?" and not "What *should* they read?" If teachers of English view themselves first as purveyors of pleasure rather than as instructors in skill, they may find that skill will flourish where pleasure has been cultivated.

One of the best examples of this attitude and its results is Gerald Weinstein's English lesson based upon a very small poem called "Motto" by Langston Hughes. Mr. Weinstein was Curriculum Coordinator for the Madison Area Project in Syracuse, N.Y. A teacher complained to him that her class "practically fell asleep" when she read "The Magic Carpet," a poem from a traditional school anthology. As an answer to the teacher's implied question—"How can you teach poetry to these kids?"—Weinstein reproduced copies of Hughes' poem and distributed them to the class. Here is the poem and a part of the class reaction, as it was quoted in the National Council of Teachers of English publication, *Language Programs for the Disadvantaged* (edited by Corbin and Crosby, 1965):

Motto

I play it cool and dig all jive.
That's the reason I stay alive.
My motto, as I live and learn,
Is: Dig and Be Dug in Return.

After the students read the poem, there was a long moment of silence. Then came the exclamations.

"Hey, this is tough."

"It's written in our talk."

But when asked the meaning of "playing it cool," the students had difficulty verbalizing the idea.

A boy volunteered to act it out.

Weinstein took the part of a teacher and the boy pretended he was walking down the hallway.

"Hey, you," said the teacher, "you're on the wrong side of the hall. Get over where you belong."

Without looking up, the boy very calmly and slowly walked to the other side and continued without any indication of what was going on in his mind.

That was "playing it cool."

When Weinstein asked a boy to show what he would do when not playing it cool, a verbal battle ensued.

The class began offering definitions for "playing it cool": calm and collected, no strain.

Weinstein suggested another: *nonchalant*. A new word. Next came a discussion of the phrase "dig all jive."

One student told how he once got into trouble because he didn't "dig the jive" of a group of street-corner toughs.

So the message of Hughes' poem, the class discovered, was that he "stayed alive" because he "dug all jive"— understood all kinds of talk.

Hughes' motto was to "dig and be dug in return"— understand and be understood.

The students were amazed at their own analysis.

Weinstein asked the students how many kinds of jive they understood.

Why all kinds, of course.

The Madison Area Project official launched into an abstract essay on the nature of truth, using all the big words he could find.

The students looked blank.

He then asked them to test his understanding of their jive.

They threw the colloquialisms at him and he got five out of six.

The class was impressed.

"According to Hughes, who has the better chance of staying alive," Weinstein asked, "you or I?"

"You," they said, "because you dig more than one kind of jive."

"The jive you have mastered is a beautiful one," Weinstein said. "But you have to dig the school jive, too, the jive that will occur in other situations. That's what school is for, to help you dig all jive and stay alive."

Which brings to mind the story told me by a young woman about her first year as an English teacher in a difficult inner-city high school. One afternoon a group of boys came to her with incontrovertible evidence that she had made it as a teacher. They had been looking at her car in the teachers' parking lot for months, and they were sorry for how she must feel because hers was the only hog in the pen that didn't have whitewalls. So they had copped four of them—one at a time, here and there—and now her car looked as tough as anybody's.

Because she understood all their language, she knew what they were telling her. Because she dug their jive, she knew what kind of compliment she had been paid. As for what she did about the tires, I leave that to the imagination of the reader.

One result of teaching English from a social rather than a literary point of view is that the English class will combine language training and social studies. This view of teaching literature makes the English–social studies "core" curriculum one of the most reasonable of modern educational structures. It is based upon the realization that all effective literature is related to life in the same way that a portrait is related to its subject. If the living model is caught and accurately interpreted at a vital moment, whether in painting or literature, it will be accepted because of its informing relationship to life. Such a reaction is the pleasurable first step that leads toward further study and understanding. Thus, reading materials selected for their actual and potential relevance to the student's own experience are likely to be doubly valuable: First for the absorbing interest in self which they exploit, an interest bound to promote a greater desire to read; and then for an understanding and acceptance of the social norm, an attitude which is any school's chief business to promote.

Speaking of portraits and their relationship to life, the same teacher who had her hog improved with whitewall tires tells another revealing story:

I remember trying to explain some insipid romantic intricacy in a sophomore text by drawing stick figures on the board to represent the characters. "This is Frank, this is Susan," I explained. Drawing a line to represent the barrier between them, I asked what problem or conflict kept Frank from his girl. "Well, ma'am," piped up an unchallenged wit in the back row, "that cat's biggest problem is he ain't got no arms."

She also reports that a similar incident confirmed her suspicion that our students often consider *us* "culturally deprived." "Talking one day of Robert Frost," she says, "I hoped to inspire my young writers with a striking photograph, in color, of the old poet's face. 'Does that look like your grandfather?' I hopefully asked one of the less inspired boys in the class. 'No, ma'am,' he replied, 'my grandpa's black.'"

A further implication of a combined English–social studies class is reliance upon a daily newspaper as one of the chief texts of the course. The newspaper is in many ways an ideal text for the English class; its format, style, and content all qualify it as an excellent vehicle for teaching reading and writing with special attention to the social point of view. The sense of informality and immediacy which the very presence of the newspaper conveys, a sense so useful yet so difficult to achieve in many other kinds of literature, is also communicated in many magazines and softbound, pocket-size books. Each of these three types of literature provides readily available materials designed to engage the interest of the most reluctant reader; each therefore commends itself for considerable and continuing use in the English class.

After a good deal of trial and considerable error, the English teachers at both the Maxey and Garnet-Patterson schools derived formulas for the use of newspapers and magazines which appeared to satisfy the needs of teachers and pupils at both institutions. With the customary hyperbole of the theoretician, for whom the problems of distribution and collection never existed, I asked myself why the newspaper could not be used every day in every English

110

classroom. Finding no answer that discouraged the idea, I stipulated such usage as part of the original Maxey plan. It worked. When that plan was adapted to the needs of the public school, the formula of daily usage for the newspaper remained unchanged. It didn't work, and the teachers soon told me why.

At the training school, no class had more than twelve boys in it. Although one B.T.S. boy may be a teaching burden equivalent to four public school children, he possesses only one pair of hands (however quick) and he sits at only one desk (however disarrayed). Getting a dozen newspapers out and back is not usually very much of a task even for the inefficient classroom manager. But when that number of hands and desks is multiplied by three, the job of distribution becomes formidable. This is especially true when the newspaper proves to be particularly attractive to the less able student, who gives it up as slowly as possible because he seldom has time to read as much of it as he would like.

A considerable number of teachers in the junior high school found that managing the newspaper in the classrooms was becoming unusually difficult. One result was the increase beyond reasonable proportions of the classroom time spent on newspaper study. Allowing the children to continue their reading was easier than battling them for the return of the newspaper, especially when so many of them were reading enthusiastically (or even just reading) for the first time. The answer to the problem was a change in the basic formula for use of both newspapers and magazines. Instead of employing the newspaper on a daily basis, and the magazine twice weekly, the two types of periodicals were alternated, so that newspapers were used three days a week and magazines two days. To decrease distribution problems still further, in most classes the two were seldom used on the same day.

(b) That the English teacher be encouraged to select and to create her own reading materials within the limits of type and format prescribed by this program.

One of the most common and most serious flaws in programs for poor readers is the relationship between the teacher and the material she uses to engage her students in the reading process. If the instructor does not take pleasure in the texts she uses, what then is the likelihood of pleasurable response from the pupil? The answer is not only obvious in the abstract, but all too obvious as well in schools I have visited, where texts were apparently chosen with neither the individual teacher nor the poor reader in mind. With these observations as a guide, I have refrained from prescribing specific classroom materials and have limited my suggestions to matters of type, format, and style. I do not believe that desirable results will be obtained unless English teachers are offered a freedom of selection which allows them to consider both the students' needs and their own inclinations.

This recommendation also speaks of "creation" by the English teacher of her own reading materials. Stories, plays, and essays written by the teacher who knows what her students' vocabularies really are, rather than what they should be; who knows particular facts rather than patent generalizations about their background, environment, and aspirations; who knows, in short, her students as individuals rather than types—such reading materials can be of unequaled value in involving students in the process of reading and writing. In response to the objection that few people, even teachers of writing, are effective creative writers, the answer must be made that anyone who can tell a child a bedtime story, or recount a narrative she has read in a newspaper, book, or magazine, can create stories, plays, and essays appropriate as teaching devices. Any teacher who has not written such materials before, is likely to be very pleasantly surprised at the ease with which she can create them and the readiness with which they are accepted by her students. In cases where teachers feel unequal to the demands of such a task, they may find their initial feelings of inadequacy dispelled by undertaking a writing project in cooperation with another instructor.

(c) That the teaching of language skills be accomplished through organic rather than mechanic or descriptive means.

This recommendation is meant to alter a great variety of common practices in the English classroom, ranging from spelling lists to workbooks of all kinds and schemes for analyzing sentence structures. What is wrong with one is wrong with all: they represent language *being* rather than *doing*. In that sense they are mechanic rather than organic, and they are self-defeating. They are always inefficient to some significant degree, but their inefficiency increases as the academic orientation of their student users decreases. This conclusion becomes inevitable when one considers the "practicality" of the mind either unaccustomed or unable to abstract and transfer information. For such a mind, real pleasure may be found in working up lists of properly spelled words. But unlike the pleasure of recognition in reading, which is likely to promote further reading and understanding, the pleasure which a student takes in a well-executed word list does not necessarily mean that he can spell those same words correctly in sentences or even use them comfortably in written discourse. The student who can spell words in lists, but who can neither use them nor spell them correctly in sentences, is a familiar phenomenon in all classrooms. If a list is used at all, it should be a list of sentences—a list of words *doing* rather than merely *being,* whose "carryover" is guaranteed if only in a single instance for each word. Such a list would be an example of the organic method of teaching language skills which this program advocates.

A consistent employment of this philosophy would bring the workbook under serious scrutiny. To begin with, there is the question of whether most workbooks are in fact cumulative. Do succeeding lessons really depend upon and build upon those which precede them? Or are the skills which the workbooks teach as fragmented as the workbooks themselves? These are unproved accusations, reflecting suspicion rather than hard evidence. What is *not* mere suspicion is the generic flaw of the workbook: it is viewed by teacher and pupil alike as a world unto itself, a repository of exercises which develop skills useful only for filling workbooks. Little evidence can be found to support the argument that the workbook participates in any meaningful relationship with the world in which language performs tasks more demanding than its own arrangement. Generations of students have exercised upon them and come away in the flabbiest sort of verbal condition. Therefore this program recommends that the English curriculum replace the workbook with exercises devised by the classroom teacher, exercises which are free of the book-grouping that suggests they have a life of their own.

Schemes for analyzing sentence structures are subject to many of the same criticisms which question the usefulness of the workbook. Most damaging perhaps is the simple question of their relevance. What do they tend to generate? Do they create understanding, or do they in fact merely re-create themselves? Does exercise of the schematic intelligence produce verbal understanding? We have all had students who take great pleasure in their ability to diagram a sentence, just as others enjoy making lists of spelling words. But even as a list of words in sentences breaks down one more mechanical barrier between learning and meaning, so does a sentence analyzed in sentences add organic dimension to a previously mechanical diagram. The making of a sentence diagram is evidence of little more than the student's ability to learn and the teacher's ability to teach the practice of diagraming sentences. The writing of even a one-sentence analysis is altogether more convincing evidence of the student's understanding of sentence structure.

A further illustration of the difference between organic and mechanic philosophies of teaching in the English classroom is the interesting example of the class-written story or play. In the usual curriculum, these exercises are remarkable by their absence. Stories and plays are of course employed with great frequency; but since they are the creations of others, they are far more likely to inspire the reluctant reader and writer to an interest in content rather than in form. That this interest in content is desirable, especially in an English class which emphasizes social studies, is undeniable; but that it need be at the expense of an interest in form is not so clear. If the student has a "practical" rather than an abstract mind, give him the first-hand experience he needs in order to learn. Occasionally let the words be his own. Let him witness words *doing* as he uses them to create a story or a play. Let him have the always pleasing experience of creating an art form, whether artful or not. Any reservations on the instructor's part as to the capacity of his students for such a performance are likely to disappear in the face of their enthusiasm. The group nature of the undertaking is usually effective in quieting individual fears, so much so that students who would ordinarily never consider creative expression on their own are sometimes influenced to try a piece of writing themselves. And, most important, many members of the group discover what a sentence *is* by making one, and thus discovering what it *does*.

Because most that is worth remembering in this book is a reflection of the experience and practice of good teachers in classrooms across the country, it seems appropriate to end this chapter on the English classroom with the words of such a teacher. Donna Schwab was a member of the Northwestern High School English faculty when she wrote the following paragraphs:

The classical school texts are a waste of time for a student who is crying out for information about his world, about himself as part of a race, part of a generation of men and women. The students who took part in the "freedom school" during a recent high school boycott in Detroit expressed a desire to know about laws affecting their rights as citizens, about their own history as a race in America, about their own minds' and bodies' workings. They wanted to talk about religion, Africa, and segregation in the South. It was obvious to all those who listened to them that public schools are doing very little to help the urban Negro youth answer his one burning question, "Who am I?"

Some classics can help him answer his question. I taught Shakespeare's *Othello* and Steinbeck's *Of Mice and Men* with encouraging results because we discussed the people as real and the social and moral questions in familiar terms. My greatest delight came when the argument over Othello's sanity reached such a pitch that one of my "juvenile delinquents" stood up and shouted—"You put your money where your mouth is, man. That cat's mind was messed up!"

That cat's mind was no more messed up on the Isle of Cyprus than the public schools are in the United States of America. Though Miss Schwab was writing about Black schoolchildren, she could as well have spoken of all the colors of the poor, the disadvantaged, and those other temporary and undesirable classroom residents who are not going on to college. Until school boards, administrators, and teachers can bring themselves to realize that they are elected, appointed and employed to serve *all* the people, and that serving *all* the people does not mean converting all colors to white and all values to middle-class, we will continue to damage and destroy those children, full of need, who want to value themselves even as they struggle to comprehend the values of a world they never made.

L. The Ludington Story

Some stories that should be repeated are left untold because they seem so implausible. For thirty years I never told anyone about the deer I saw bound across our Baltimore City front yard in the first light of Christmas morning, 1937. A deer in Baltimore on Christmas morning? Could a sleigh with a jolly old elf be far behind? Even at the age of seven I knew better than to tell anybody about that deer.

Or, twenty years later, when I was teaching in a California nursery school and neither the children nor the other two adults could net a handsome butterfly that flew persistently among us. Here, I said, give me the net and watch an expert at work. I was joking. I had never before netted a butterfly nor have I since. But I took the net, did a pirouette for the entertainment of the children, whipped the net behind my back, and joined everyone else in shock as that foolish, accommodating butterfly flew into the trap. When I told my wife about it that evening, she raised a single eyebrow, said "Certainly. Of course." and went back to her reading. Which was all I needed to place the butterfly beside the deer in my collection of stories not for telling.

Why do I tell them now?

Because the story you will read in this chapter is at least as implausible as the nursery school butterfly or the Christmas deer. But I will try to tell it anyway, believing that the story needs to be told for the hope that lies in it:

"Do he be Sandyclaws?"

"No. But he sure is like Sandyclaws, isn't he?"

"Sure is."

Christmas images associate themselves as naturally with Ivan Ludington as he associates with children. I have known kind and generous people who were painfully, obviously ill-at-ease with the recipients of their care. To see Ivan in one of the many Reading Rooms he has created or supported in public, private, parochial, and prison schools throughout southeastern Michigan—to see him among books and schoolchildren is to see a man in his natural habitat, no less at ease as he sits and speaks with a child than the child herself as she sprawls on the carpeted floor with a book. As he talks with her, another third-grader across the room peers at him intently before she shakes her head knowingly, in a perfect imitation of some older person in her life, and repeats her own emphatic words:

"*Sure* is. He be *just* like him."

He be. But unlike that other white-haired gentleman who works with his associates throughout the year to prepare for a single day, Ivan Ludington works with his associates throughout the year to prevent the arrival of that day when a majority of students, teachers, and parents acts upon its belief that reading is an anachronism in an oral/visual society. Neither he nor I think that day improbable of attainment, much less impossible. Because it is a daunting vision, we have worked together for more than a decade to prevent it from becoming reality.

On 26 July 1974, almost ten years to the day after Ivan Ludington and I had begun to search together for effective means to increase the value of literacy to schoolchildren, William H. Millikin, Governor of the State of Michigan, signed Act No. 230 of the Public Acts of 1974 into law. Section 33 of that Act is quoted here in full:

Sec. 33. The appropriation of $1,000,000.00 contained in section 1 for grants for paperback libraries shall be used for grants to school districts for the acquisition of high interest paperback libraries housed in reading rooms, reading centers in school libraries, or classroom collections to stimulate and sustain student interest in reading and to encourage children to use and expand reading skills. Paperback libraries shall be considered a service under section 622 of Act No. 269 of the Public Acts of 1955. For the purpose of this section a region of a first class school district shall be considered a school district. A grant made to an applicant school district shall be in the amount of $4.50 per membership pupil for each pupil in the first year of the program and $2.25 in each of the second and third years. In 1974-75, a first year grant for an applicant district shall be limited to ½ of the district's membership. A school district which received a first year grant for ½ of its pupils and applies for a grant in a subsequent year to start a high interest paperback library for the other half, shall receive an amount of $4.50 per membership pupil for that part of its program. A school operating a paperback library in 1973-74 may be funded for a second year grant.

At least 85% of each first year grant shall be used for

118

the purchase of paperback books and no more than 15% of each grant shall be used for display racks and devices. At least 95% and 100% of each grant shall be used for paperback book purchases in the second and third years, respectively. None of these funds shall be used for ordering, receiving and processing costs.

In applying for and accepting a grant under this section a school district shall agree to all the following:

(a) To provide physical space for the collection.

(b) To provide responsible parent volunteer, paraprofessional or professional supervision of the collection.

(c) To provide simplified circulation and book accounting procedures to encourage high utilization versus preservation. Cataloging is not intended.

(d) To provide direct student participation in the selection of the collection. Book selections shall be made by individual school committees composed of students, parents and faculty. Librarians and reading specialists related to the school shall be represented on the committees.

(e) To provide that the collection be open and available during school hours, and to permit operation of the high interest paperback libraries during preschool and postschool hours as feasible. The collection shall be available as an open library.

(f) To provide community use of the collection.

(g) To provide that the collection shall be made available at least 3 hours a week to every student in the program.

(h) To provide that student reading selections are free of assignments or other direction, reports, tests, or grades in direct connection with free reading opportunities provided by this program.

How easy now to cite this brief section, one of thirty-seven, of "An Act to make appropriations for the department of education and certain other purposes relating to education for the fiscal year ending June 30, 1975." In a

119

budget of 239 million for education, can 1/239 be very important? It can if you're attending a school where $4.50 per pupil is available to buy paperbound books *you* want to read; it can if you're teaching in a school where reading is made compelling to your students by hundreds or thousands of new paperback books; it can if you're two men, one from a Big University and the other from Big Business, who've worked for ten years to obtain such a bill.

One year after Governor Millikin signed Public Act No. 230 of 1974 into law, he signed Public Act No. 252 of 1975. Section 31 reads as follows:

Sec. 31. The appropriation of $400,000.00 contained in section 1 for grants for paperback libraries shall be used for pilot project grants to school districts for the acquisition of high interest paperback libraries housed in reading rooms or reading centers in school libraries to stimulate and sustain student interest in reading and to encourage children to use and expand reading skills. These pilot projects shall be considered a service under section 622 of Act No. 269 of the Public Acts of 1955. Each applicant school district that receives a grant under this section shall provide 25% funding from school district funds for each reading room or reading center that is funded under this section. The minimum grant for each reading room or reading center funded under this section shall be $1,500.00 together with an additional $500.00 in funds provided by the applicant school district.

At least 85% of each grant shall be used for the purchase of paperback books and no more than 15% of each grant shall be used for display racks and devices. None of these funds shall be used for ordering, receiving, and processing costs.

The determination of which applicant school districts will participate in these pilot projects shall be made by the state board of education. That determination shall be based upon which school districts are best able to meet the following requirements:

120

(a) To provide physical space for the collection.

(b) To provide responsible parent volunteer, para-professional or professional supervision of the collection.

(c) To provide simplified circulation and book accounting procedures to encourage high utilization versus preservation.

(d) To provide direct student participation in the selection of the collection. Book selections shall be made by individual school committees composed of students, parents, and faculty. Librarians and reading specialists related to the school shall be represented on the committees.

(e) To provide that the collection be open and available during school hours, and to permit operation of the high interest paperback libraries during pre-school and postschool hours as feasible. The collection shall be available as an open library.

(f) To provide that the collection shall be made available at least 3 hours a week to every student in the program.

With matching funds from applicant districts, that's over a million dollars in two years (even though the first appropriation was cut in half because of the severe recession in Michigan in 1974) intended for "high interest paperback libraries," where at least $17 out of every $20 appropriated had to be spent on the books themselves. That's a long way from 1964, no matter how the distance is measured:

One day in the late summer of 1965, a year after the Maxey experiment had begun, Ivan Ludington asked me how long it might take to spread the practices of *English in Every Classroom* throughout the schools of Detroit and Wayne County. "If you're speaking of curriculum change," I said, "it may take forever." "Suppose we forget curriculum change for the time being," he replied. "Suppose that we try to *give* magazines and paperback books to the schools free of charge. Would they accept our offer?"

121

I had to answer that I didn't know. What I did know, I said, was that public schools had been lacerated by criticism and burdened by do-gooders for so long that they'd certainly look any gift horse in the mouth to be sure it was toothless. "If you offer them something for nothing," I said, "they're going to examine it mighty carefully *and* they're still going to want to know what's in it for you."

"All right," he said, "I'll tell them. If I invite teachers, principals and other school administrators to lunch, will you talk about the Maxey experiment while I offer them whatever they want in the way of paperbound materials and tell them what's in it for me?" When I said yes, I had no idea that I was agreeing to address fifteen luncheons in five months. Even less, I think, did Ivan Ludington realize that within the year he would be supplying 92 public schools and 41 private schools with their free choice of magazines and paperbound books.

Measure the distance of a Ludington decade in terms of programs in effect instead of state funds appropriated for paperback books: Which is a better measure of progress (the argument is a pleasant one)—the space between zero dollars and one million plus, or the distance between fifteen luncheons that produced 92 public and 41 private school participants in 1965, and 523 distribution points throughout the Detroit Metropolitan Area that serviced 933 programs in 1975? In 1965, our luncheon guests were selected for their (reputed) openness to useful innovation and change. All too frequently, the openness was more reputed than real. In 1975, the Ludington Company received more than a thousand enquiries and applications for its magazine and paperback program, only about half of which it could accommodate and—by remarkable contrast to 1965—none of which it solicited.

When the latest numbers were all totalled and mapped, Ivan Ludington and his cooperating publishers found themselves supplying more than one hundred school regions, districts, cities, and counties in southeastern Michigan with free magazines (returns and overruns) and, in some instances, free paperbound books. Both types of materials, freely offered and freely taken, were seeds planted to bring about growth of the first legislation in North America that gives state financial support specifically and solely to the purchase of paperbacks for the schools.

Just as I write this chapter, saved for last so that it may be as timely as possible for its readers, the 78th Legislature of the State of Michigan has passed and the governor approved Section 25, Act No. 249 of the Public Acts of 1976, which for the third consecutive year provides more than half a million dollars in state ($400,000) and district (⅓ matching) funds solely for paperback books. I quote here two of the most important subsections:

(1) The appropriation of $400,000 in section 2, for grants for paperback libraries, shall be used for grants to school districts, for the acquisition of high-interest paperback libraries housed in *reading rooms* or reading centers in schools, to stimulate and sustain student interest in reading, and to encourage students to use and expand reading skills.

(4) Funds will be used to establish a *reading room* in a single school building within each district, except where this would result in the establishment of a *reading room* which would contain more than a maximum of 3 books per student in that building [In that case] a district may establish *reading rooms* in additional school buildings.

In both subsections the italics are mine, added because the Ludington Reading Room (LRR), the reality from which the legislative phrase is taken, has been the heart of our cooperative effort with the schools for the past decade. Its story begins in Detroit's Northwestern High School:

Northwestern opened its Ludington Reading Room on February 21, 1965. In the first ten days of its operation, over 1,500 of the school's 2,700 students visited the room and 1,850 books were put into circulation. All of us have seen the sudden upsurge of interest associated with a new program fall off to nothing when the newness wears off. But in this case we have comparable figures gathered seven months later. In nine September school days, 1,147 students visited the reading room and left with more than 1,000 books.

Some weeks after the Ludington Room was opened at Northwestern and its full impact was being felt throughout the student body, seventeen-year-old Joe approached a teacher outside the reading room. "Mrs. Gillis," he said, "I got to be in there! Can I be in charge of them books?"

Coming from another seventeen-year-old, the question might not have been so startling. But in Joe's case it was something special. Because Joe couldn't read. He had been the beneficiary (or victim) of the doctrine of the "social pass," a passive philosophy of school advancement which allowed him to reach the eleventh grade without being able to read. And now, still unable to read, having resisted learning the written language with all his strength—having resisted successfully and for so long—now Joe wanted to be a librarian. Why?

The answer is simple enough: Joe wanted to be where the action was. Over half the students in a large school is a lot of action, anyway you figure it. Joe figured that he couldn't keep his place on top unless he made the reading room scene. Improbably, impossibly, Joe became a librarian. He wanted to make it so bad that he memorized the covers of *all* the paperbounds and replaced them in their proper pockets in the wire racks solely on the basis of their identifying pictures.

Joe as librarian? Books as magnets? Librarians as heroes? Heroes as sandwiches? *Sandwiches* defined by the kids as three-book-borrowings, with one "heavy" book carried between two much-lighter ones? Listen to the teachers who experienced that first Ludington Reading Room:

Student response has been overwhelming. Never have I seen such interest shown in reading since my arrival here at Northwestern four years ago . . . . Students are seen reading everywhere—on hall duty, in lunchrooms, in study halls, and even in classrooms (undercover). *The* status symbol is the paperback.

At least half a dozen or more students have asked if they could serve as librarians. Boys seem to outnumber the girls in attendance. One teacher commented, "This is the best thing that's happened to Northwestern since I've been here."

Reading coordinator's report

I have watched students who have never before been coaxed into textbooks, pick up paperbacks and carry them around in their pockets for weeks, reading a few pages a day. What a breakthrough! I have watched supposedly slow students get through a paperback book every other day.... I am delighted to hear students recommending books to each other and having true literary discussions, even if about James Bond.

English teacher's letter

I think this program in our school may do for the teaching of reading what Sputnik did for the teaching of science.

English teacher's statement

We were not content, however, to take aim only at the schools with our program for providing thick concentrations of materials that children and young adults *would* read rather than thin diffusions of materials that they *should* read. Our target was broader than the classroom:

As every teacher knows, the full effectiveness of his work depends upon influencing the child's home environment as well as the child himself. He therefore values especially the Reading Room practice which makes paperbound books and magazines available to the community at large. One Ludington Reading Room, established early in the program in a Detroit grammar school, welcomed an average of more than 700 parents per week during the afternoon hours between three and seven. Watching a child progress of his own free will through comic books and Peanuts to *A Tale of Two Cities* is a rich experience for any teacher. Watching an adult, the parent of a "problem family," painstakingly read *Teen-Age Tyranny*, by Grace and Fred Hechinger, over a period of weeks, lips moving with the words, is as powerful and even more poignant. When one child writes, "Thang you for the magazines I like them because they has lots of thing we can do as a family," you know that she knows too much about things that fall apart, things that will not hold together without every kind of help—even that of magazines.

During the years between the 1965 opening of the LRR in Northwestern High School and the 1974 passage of the first paperback library legislation, perhaps the single most important advance of the Reading Room concept developed from the combination of Professor Kenneth S. Goodman's center for Reading Miscue Research (RMR) at Wayne State University with the Ludington News Company and the public school system of Garden City, a Detroit suburban community of some 50,000 people.

That combination led to the *Ludington Reading Room Study: A Report on Students' Perceptions* produced by and available from the RMR Center and directed by Dorothy J. Watson and Mervin F. Thornton. Nothing so well expresses and explains the purpose of the study as the directors' own words at the conclusion of their acknowledgments: "Finally, we want to express our appreciation to Mr. Ivan Ludington, Sr., who had the courage to put the concept of the Ludington Reading Rooms up for close examination and in-depth study." Courage, concept, and study together will sometimes produce results like these:

First, what did Watson and Thornton study? "Since 1965 Ludington has put his ideas into action by providing one-year pilot reading room programs in approximately two hundred schools .... In an attempt to determine the effect of the Ludington Reading Rooms on pupils, primarily as that effect was perceived by the pupils themselves, a study was designed by the Reading Miscue Research Center of Wayne

State University." The directors continue to explain that they used a sixteen item questionnaire in four Garden City schools—one k-3, another 4-6, a junior and a senior high school—plus a twenty-six item interview with 80 of the high school students. In assessing their conclusions, it is useful to remember that Watson and Thornton derived virtually all of their data from what students reported about themselves, and almost none from what teachers or other adults reported about students.

Who uses Reading Rooms? More than four-fifths of the Garden City students in grades three through twelve, with the percentages in the four schools ranging from 97% (elementary) to 70% (senior high). Do students read more when such Rooms are available? *Yes*, said a lot of them: 70% of the elementary pupils, 40% of the junior high, and 30% of the senior high students had read more since the paperback books arrived in their schools. Perhaps most interesting were the reasons they gave—wider variety, greater availability, and more attractive books—for their increased reading. Fully two-thirds of the respondents thought that the enormous variety of books was the single most important factor causing them to read more than they had before.

If they read more, do they read better? If the question is traditional, then asking it of students themselves is not. Watson and Thornton found that "nearly 60% of the total pupil population felt that their reading had substantially improved because of the presence of the paperback books provided by the Ludington Reading Rooms.... It is especially important to note that a majority of the Low readers perceived themselves as becoming better readers."

Careful examination of their data led the authors to conclude that the LRR's had "major successes" in the areas of pupils' attitudes and pupils' reading proficiency. The data demonstrate that "with the advent of the Ludington Reading Rooms, pupils' attitudes toward school, toward learning, and toward books and reading improved. The majority of students involved in this study felt that school had become more interesting since the LRR opened.... Students reported that they were encouraged by their reading successes, that they began to feel good about themselves, and

that the quality of their school experience had improved."
All of which are exceptionally good reasons for making the
Reading Room a state-wide, state-supported lever for
moving students and literacy closer to each other.

Chapter V

HOOKED ON RESEARCH

Elton McNeil

"I haven't got much time now," I said to the man standing in the doorway of my office. I didn't want to be rude to a colleague—even if he was from the English Department—but the fact was that I *didn't* have much time. After an hour and a half of the time I didn't have, I watched him leave my office and I realized I'd been had by an expert. I was hooked on *English in Every Classroom*.

Dan Fader is a former poolroom hustler who cares as much about kids as a child psychologist, which he isn't, and as much about language as a Renaissance scholar, which he is. He's also one of the great Idea-pushers of our time. Brushing aside my objections as though he hadn't heard them—and he probably hadn't—he pursued me from one excuse to another. What he wanted was nothing less than my unqualified commitment to spend part of the next three years testing his idea that kids could learn to *like* to read and write. What I wanted was to be left alone with my own writing, teaching, and responsibilities as director of graduate programs in psychology at the University of Michigan. By the time he left my office I had agreed to test his thesis. Without Fader, the idea is persuasive. With him, it's irresistible.

Irresistible though the idea seemed at the time, the more I thought about my commitment to test the premises and practices of *English in Every Classroom*, the more uneasy I became. I had spent many years laboring in clinical and educational settings with socially and culturally deprived children, and I found it difficult to believe that anything so simple as Fader's idea could make a significant difference in their behavior. I was reasonably certain that they could not read and write with pleasure unless some of their other problems were solved first. But the more I read what Fader wrote and listened to what he said, the less certain I became. Today I have quantitative proof of the quality my instincts responded to three years ago. The fact is that Fader's educational theory is as sound as his pool game.

During the six months following our initial meeting, I designed a program of research calculated to answer the most pressing questions raised by the theory of *English in Every Classroom*. From the beginning I realized that these answers were bound to be imperfect, for the techniques of psychology are not adequate to measure completely the changes in attitude aimed at by Fader's program. But this necessary imperfection bothered me less than the fact that this project had come alive just as I had abandoned hope for the classic and traditional forms of conducting psychological research.

I have no particular objection to the methods psychologists use, since they represent a massive improvement over the hit-and-miss subjective techniques of the past. What bothers me most about the stage to which psychological research has evolved is that we psychologists seem increasingly unable to answer simple questions. We have become very much like the man who was asked, "How's the weather?" and proceeded to answer with a statistically complex meteorological observation and prediction.

My feeling that research psychologists have become obsessively concerned with technique at the expense of purpose, is a personal issue that forced me to set conditions on the nature of the conduct and reporting of this research. My desire is to return research to something of its previous state, to have it become again, in part at least, a personal document that focuses its energies largely on the business of telling people, in an intelligible way, how the weather is.

As the form of this research report will indicate, neither

Professor Fader nor I was willing to settle for a traditional report directed to those who face the problem of adapting our findings to the challenges of school and classroom. Our sole objective was to make our answers to the questions we · raised useful to all those who must convert them into workable plans of action involving real human beings. The freshness, newness, and basic simplicity of the ideas of *English in Every Classroom* make demands of their own. I hope that I have been able to meet those demands in this report.

A. Who's Hooked and How Do You Tell?

We began with the assumption that *English in Every Classroom* had an unusually good chance of failure. Our research report, we calculated, might be devoted to intricate explanations of why it didn't work even though it had seemed like such a good idea. We had chosen an almost impossible terrain on which to do battle and we could hardly count on anything better than the bare survival of a few ideas. I know at least one hundred research settings less hostile to the basic premises of Fader's plan for literacy, but this was the battle site he had chosen and I was stuck with it.

The trouble is that "hooked" has a variety of meanings when applied to young people for whom reading, writing, teachers, books, and schools add up to nothing more than bitter failure. Response to such a program is certain to be uniquely individual and best recorded by collecting hundreds of highly personal case histories. These individual testimonials would contain the real heart of the experiment; unfortunately, anecdotes have never been an acceptable substitute for the more objective kinds of information that testing provides. We had to discover who got hooked, where the hook found its mark, and the depth to which it penetrated. We were aware that some young people learn the pleasures of the written word despite the crippling influence of the worst kinds of educational experience, and we were

131

also aware that some can resist all blandishments. Furthermore, we realized that we needed to compare changes issuing from the program of *English in Every Classroom* with the natural, self-induced, and accidental changes that time alone brings to a comparable group of human beings.

One inch away from the edge of a cliff may be a significant distance to a man walking in the dark, just as a linear mile may be an insufficient distance from the center of a bomb burst. Under the new program, microscopic gains in reading and writing by an educational loser might be greatly significant when contrasted to the regression of a similar child subjected to traditional methods. Thus a "control group" was necessary to the experiment. In another midwestern training school, we found a population of counterparts to the students at B.T.S.—boys similarly enmeshed in the toils of the law, burdened by similar social histories, and characterized by their rejection of everything that school is and represents. This training school became our control, while the program of *English in Every Classroom* was actually initiated in the W.J. Maxey Boys' Training School (B.T.S.) at Whitmore Lake, Michigan.

Selection of our control group (CG) marked the end of the beginning. We had matched populations available for study, we had measuring devices that looked good on paper, and we had all the confidence and enthusiasm that usually characterize a new venture. What follows here is a guided tour through the results of placing boys, books, newspapers, magazines, *and* teachers in continuous contact.

B. The Raw Material

What were the fundamental characteristics of the boys who made up our experimental and control samples? The boys at B.T.S. averaged fifteen years and seven months of age while their control counterparts were four months younger. From youngest to oldest, the boys ranged from twelve to seventeen.

Racially: The overall sample was divided between Black and White students with fewer White subjects in the control group than at Whitmore Lake. This possible bias in the sample is explored as a separate factor in our analysis. We have no reason to suspect that this differential representation by race is significant, since the sample is weighted heavily in both institutions in favor of membership in the lower socioeconomic classes. Our experience has led us to believe that social class, rather than race, is the prime determinant of the individual's attitude and behavior toward reading, writing, and speaking the language of the middle class. Comparisons of White and Black boys at the two training schools may clarify the relationship of race and social class to literacy. They will be cited where they seem to influence our research findings.

Racial Distribution by School

School	Black	White
Whitmore Lake	31	29
Control Group	21	10

Intellectually: A high-jumper with both legs amputated at the knees probably has no greater handicap than the prospective student entering school competition equipped with limited intelligence. Smart kids have always done disproportionately better than dumb kids in a formal educational setting, but we have also learned that it is awfully difficult to tell who's smart and who's dumb if our sole measure is the traditional intelligence test.

As every educator has learned the hard way, intelligence tests may measure the basic intellectual capacity of middle-class White children, but such tests are at best only very rough assessments of *probable* academic success for lower-class White and Black children. Intelligence tests are inadequate measures of the mental capacity of lower-class children because such tests are so heavily weighted with knowledge gained only by participation in the world of the middle class. Though no one knows the intelligence of lower-class White or Black children, our crude measures can tell us something of their probable response to a traditional education.

An intelligence test can be a threat and a promise of failure or it can be a showcase for the display of intellectual capacity. It can be a difficult task that is accomplished with verve, or it can be middle-class punishment visited on lower-class victims. For want of better devices, we used these inadequate indices as measure of the basic equipment our children brought to the fray. An average of five I.Q. points separated the boys in the CG from those at B.T.S. (approximately the number of Full Scale I.Q. points allowed for on the Wechsler to compensate for testing error). The Full Scale I.Q.'s of the B.T.S. sample average 95 and those in the CG average 90. Both scores are below the hypothetical statistical average of 100, and this fact sets an additional limit to our expectations regarding reading, writing, and literate attainment.

The relevance of skin color to intelligence that is measured by tests standardized on White middle-class youngsters is inescapable here. Being Black is, on the average, a condition that assures one of a lower score on any test of intelligence currently in use. Such is the case with the boys we studied. Whether the Full Scale Intelligence quotient or its Verbal or Performance subparts are used as measures, the Black child does less well throughout our sample. If we accept the Wechsler Intelligence Test as a representation of functional abstract and symbolic intelligence, then our Black children are less well equipped in this way than are the White. The Black child in the CG had a Full Scale I.Q. of 85.57 and the Black in B.T.S. scored 87.59. The White boys in the CG scored 98.91 for a Full Scale I.Q. and their counterparts at B.T.S. scored 104.60.

A rank-ordering of the boys in our sample from highest to lowest scores on individual intelligence tests is as follows:

1. White boys at B.T.S.
2. White boys in the CG
3. Black boys at B.T.S.
4. Black boys in the CG

Despite these differences in measured intellect, statistical comparison of the Whitmore Lake boys as a whole with the total CG sample of boys disclosed *no* over-all significant difference in intelligence.

In the analysis of our tests and measures and the interpretation of the research findings, we are primarily interested in determining how the boys at B.T.S. differed from the boys in the CG before and after the experiment. To reach scientifically reliable conclusions we must view each finding in terms of the qualifications imposed on it by age, intelligence, and race. This is an important research step to take since we need to know which children are most and least receptive to the program of *English in Every Classroom* and what characteristics identify each of them.

Age differences in the two samples must also be noted. Our typical subject at B.T.S. was 188.81 months old while the typical CG boy was 183.50 months old. It is reasonable to assume that some effect of this average age difference of five months between the samples is possible.

C. A Catalogue of Tests and Measures

There is no exciting way to describe the variety of measures we used to assess the progress of our pilgrims to literacy in the two training schools. Some of the tests and measures were modifications of research instruments proved effective in other settings with different children. We adapted, altered, and modified traditional instruments to meet the demands of a particularly difficult testing situation. Here we have grouped our research instruments in terms of the psychological and behavioral phenomena they were designed to tap. All catalogues are wearisome reading; the one that follows here merely hopes to convey the range and kind of devices employed in assessing this program for the teaching of reading and writing in the schools.

Intellectual Performance

Most of our children were administered individual intelligence tests at the time of their commitment to one or the other of the two correctional institutions. These tests served as a rough indicator of potential response to educational designs within the institutions and, indeed, we suspect that assignment to the CG school or B.T.S. was, in some part, a function of how bright the child was. B.T.S. has the deserved reputation of being a model correctional institution in the State of Michigan, and a bright child (if he is free of other grossly disqualifying characteristics) has a greater likelihood of being assigned to B.T.S. than to other correctional institutions within the state.

We used both individual intelligence tests (the Wechsler Intelligence Scale for Children) and scores on the Stanford Achievement Test as indicators of intellectual capacity. Scores on subparts of the Stanford having the greatest relevance to our study included those on language, word meaning, paragraph meaning, and spelling. Though we were unable to repeat the Wechsler for a significant number of children as they were released from incarceration, we do have Stanford Achievement Test scores for enough boys, both before and after the experiment, to warrant statistical analysis. On the average, eight months elapsed between intelligence tests or achievement tests.

In the Eye of the Beholder—the Teacher

We sought to measure certain values and beliefs which affect teachers' attitudes toward their pupils, since their view of the children they teach profoundly affects the pattern of educational and human interaction that takes place between them. On the *Teacher's Behavior Rating Sheet*, for example, we presented each teacher with pairs of words often used to describe pupils and asked for an estimate of the degree to which one or another of these words fit a particular student. A sample of the form used appears in Illustration 1, which follows.

Illustration 1

Teacher's Behavior Rating Sheet

Below you will find pairs of words or phrases which can be used to describe people. Each pair is separated by seven spaces. Please put an X in the space that best describes the student you are rating.

For example, if the student is really very much like either one of the words, you would put an X on the line to the extreme left or right as follows:

agile $\underset{\text{—}}{\overset{X}{}}$ — — — — — — awkward

or

agile — — — — — — $\underset{\text{awkward}}{\overset{X}{}}$

You would choose an intermediate position in accordance with how you feel about the particular student being described.

You will be rating a number of students, but do not try for balance. For example, it is possible that *all* the students in your particular class are agile or that all of them are awkward. You would rate them accordingly.

Be sure to check every item. Use only one check mark for each pair of words or phrases. Mark each item quickly. Your first impressions or immediate feelings are best.

dishonest — — — — — — — honest

bad — — — — — — — good

inattentive — — — — — — — attentive

unaggressive — — — — — — — aggressive

adjusted — — — — — — — disturbed

energetic — — — — — — — lazy

devious — — — — — — — forthright

137

From teacher ratings of these opposite word pairs, it was possible to construct the following broad stereotypes:

The Angel

The angelic student is one the teacher describes as honest, good, energetic, attentive, unaggressive, forthright, and well adjusted. Even in a population of delinquent boys in a training school, there are some who roughly approximate this model.

The Devil

The devil is everything the angel is not. The devilish student is dishonest, bad, lazy, inattentive, aggressive, devious, and disturbed. Few students are described completely in such terms, but our sample contains boys who have a startling resemblance to that portrait.

The Mixed Type

Only grade-B Western movies persist in dividing human beings into two classes—the good guys and the bad guys. In real life there are many shades of gray between those who wear white hats and those who swear black oaths. Where teachers reported mixed views of a child, we cast him into this category.

On a *Teacher's Evaluation Form* additional ratings were gathered to assess such dimensions as:

> The pupil's capacity to form interpersonal relationships
>
> The pupil's emotional adjustment
>
> The pupil's attitude toward school and motivation for school work.

Each of these broad categories was constructed by compiling a series of ratings of individual items, to form a total score. Thus, for example, "the pupil's emotional adjustment" is a composite based on teacher ratings of the pupil's frustration tolerance, his attitudes toward limits set in the classroom, his general emotional adjustment, his degree of self-control, and his ability to contemplate consequences before acting.

The *Teacher's Evaluation Form* also provided us with estimates of:

> The pupil's sense of self-worth and self-esteem
> The pupil's tendency to become withdrawn
> The pupil's relationship to the teacher
> The pupil's attention span in school
> The pupil's reaction to failure

All these aspects of the teacher's view of her pupils are important to the kind of educational and human interaction most likely to take place in the classroom. In any research project you have to make decisions and choices; these elements were our choices.

The *Teacher's Evaluation Form* provided for ratings on the same kind of seven-point scale used for the *Teacher's Behavior Rating Sheet* but the descriptive adjectives used differed somewhat. The *Teacher's Evaluation Form* is exemplified in the following illustration.

Illustration 2

Teacher's Evaluation Form

For each statement below, place an X in the space that best describes the person you are rating. Even though you may be unsure about some of the categories, do not leave any items blank.

1. Pupil's capacity to form interpersonal relationship with peers.

    High   __ __ __ __ __ __ __ Low

2. Pupil's capacity to form interpersonal relationships with adults.

    Low   __ __ __ __ __ __ __ High

3. Evidence of anxiety

Little
apparent — — — — — — — Overwhelming
and
debilitating

4. Frustration tolerance

Becomes upset easily
when things
happen — — — — — — — Rarely
becomes
upset

5. Sense of self-worth and self-esteem

Feels adequate
and
competent — — — — — — — Feels
inadequate and
worthless

6. Attitude toward classroom limits

Rebels — — — — — — — Accepts

7. General emotional adjustment

Good — — — — — — — Poor

8. Tendency to become withdrawn from people and things
   around him

High — — — — — — — Low

9. Relationship to teachers

Wants to be
accepted
and liked — — — — — — — Rejects all
overtures

10. Attention span in school

Needs constant
reminders and
direction — — — — — — — Capable of
sustained
work

11. Amount of self-control

Well
controlled — — — — — — — Frequent
breakdowns

12. Attitude toward school

    Negative — — — — — — — Positive

13. Motivation for school work and learning

    High — — — — — — — Low

14. Reaction to failure

    Gives up in anger or   Tends to
    gives up after denying   work harder
    concern — — — — — — —   for mastery

15. Acts without considering the consequences

    Usually — — — — — — — Rarely

In the Eye of the Beholder—The Pupil

Teachers' eyes and pupils' eyes do not always see the same events in the same light. It was therefore equally important for us to obtain before-and-after measures of pupils' views in both our experimental and control samples of young men.

We began by asking each pupil to tell us how much he liked (a lot or a little) "being in a school that has a library," "learning how to read and write well," "reading books and magazines" and "writing about things." The pupils' responses were converted into a single measure or score of *Attitude Toward Literacy*. This form includes eight items as follows:

Illustration 3

"How Much Do You Like" Form

Since all people are different, they like different things and they like them in different amounts. We would like to learn *How Much You Like* certain things about school. The way to mark this section is this: the more you like something, the more points you give it. The things you like very little, you mark 1. The things you like very much, you mark 7. You can choose any number from 1 to 7. Mark the number you choose by *drawing a circle* around it.

A. Playing games or sports at school

like a little   1   2   3   4   5   6   7   like a lot

B. Being in a school that has a library

like a little   1   2   3   4   5   6   7   like a lot

C. Learning how to read and write well

like a little   1   2   3   4   5   6   7   like a lot

D. Learning about people and places

like a little   1   2   3   4   5   6   7   like a lot

E. Learning about arithmetic or mathematics

like a little   1   2   3   4   5   6   7   like a lot

F. Being where there are many others my own age

like a little   1   2   3   4   5   6   7   like a lot

G. Reading books and magazines

like a little   1   2   3   4   5   6   7   like a lot·

H. Writing about things

like a little   1   2   3   4   5   6   7   like a lot

Seeking an alternative way to test feelings toward books and school, we gave a *Behavioral Rating Form* to each student and asked him to indicate which of fifty-one items were "like me" or "not like me." Illustration 4 depicts the experimental form we employed.

Illustration 4

Behavioral Rating Form

Please mark each statement in the following way:

If the statement describes how you usually feel, put a check in the column "LIKE ME." If the statement *does not* describe how you usually feel, put a check in the column "NOT LIKE ME."

There are no right or wrong answers.

	LIKE ME	NOT LIKE ME
EXAMPLE: I'm a hard worker.		

	LIKE ME	NOT LIKE ME
1. I spend a lot of time thinking and wondering.		
2. I'm pretty sure of myself.		
3. I often wish I was someone else.		
4. I'm easy to like.		
5. I find it very hard to talk in front of the class.		
6. I wish I was younger.		
7. I'd change a lot of things about myself if I could.		
8. I can make up my mind without too much trouble.		

9. I'm a lot of fun to be with. _____

10. I'm proud of my school work. _____

11. Someone always has to tell me
    what to do. _____

12. It takes me a long time to get used
    to anything new. _____

13. Lots of times I'm sorry for the
    things I do. _____

14. I'm popular with kids my own age. _____

15. I'm doing the best work I can. _____

16. I give in very easily. _____

17. I can usually take
    care of myself. _____

18. I'm pretty happy. _____

19. I would rather play with kids
    younger than me. _____

20. I like to be called on in class. _____

21. I understand myself. _____

22. It's pretty tough to be me. _____

23. Things are all mixed up in my life. _____

24. Kids usually follow my ideas. _____

25. I'm not doing as well in school
    as I'd like to. _____

26. I can make up my mind
    and stick to it. _____

144

27. It's better to be a girl than a boy. _____

28. I have a low opinion of myself. _____

29. I don't like to be with other people. _____

30. I often feel upset in school. _____

31. I often feel ashamed of myself. _____

32. I'm not as nice looking as most people. _____

33. If I have something to say, I usually say it. _____

34. Kids pick on me a lot. _____

35. My teacher makes me feel I'm not good enough. _____

36. I don't care what happens to me. _____

37. I don't do things very well. _____

38. I get upset easily when I'm scolded. _____

39. Most people are better liked than I am. _____

40. I often get discouraged in school. _____

41. Things usually don't bother me. _____

42. I can't be depended upon. _____

43. Books are things I like to have around. _____

145

44. I read a newspaper almost every day. _____

45. I like to write things down when I think about them. _____

46. I usually read something when I have some free time. _____

47. I get pretty nervous when I have to explain something. _____

48. I hate books. _____

49. There are lots of magazines I am interested in. _____

50. Writing is something I can do without. _____

51. It's better to be a grown-up than a kid. _____

By combining responses to items clearly related to one another, we devised a series of composite pupil views.

The Literacy Lover, for example, is a boy who indicates that he likes to have books around, likes to write things down when he thinks of them, usually reads something when he has free time, finds lots of magazines he is interested in, and does not consider writing unimportant. The *Literacy Hater* is a boy whose attitudes caused him to reverse all or most of these responses.

Literacy tends to be an abstract concept to most children despite attempts to translate it into everyday terms. Using other items in the *Behavioral Rating Form,* we established *School Lover* and *School Hater* categories. A *School Hater* tells us he "is not proud of his school work," "does not like to be called on in class," "feels upset in school," "thinks his teacher makes him feel he is not good enough" and "often gets discouraged in school." And of course the *School Lover,* by comparison, feels that in school he has found a home away from home.

It was obviously important for us to know something of the attitudes with which students in our experimental and control samples viewed the classroom both at the beginning and the end of their exposure to *English in Every Classroom*. But school is not all books and learning. School is the sum total of the work of the child and the forge on which he hammers out his self-image and self-esteem. Using several of the fifty-one items of the *Behavioral Rating Form,* we assembled a single score that would tell us something of the pupil's view of himself. A young man with a positive self-image and high self-esteem, for example, would report to us that he saw himself as a person who is "sure of himself, is easy to like, is a lot of fun to be with, is popular with kids his own age, can take care of himself, is happy, understands himself, has friends who follow him, and doesn't usually let things bother him." The reverse of this image is a loser who expects catastrophe in the academic world and has little hope for social or interpersonal success.

An additional measure of academic attitude was our form entitled *How Do You Feel About Things in Class?* This elaborate questionnaire includes thirty items, all of which addressed themselves to the issue of anxiety in the classroom. The students were asked to estimate the intensity of their feelings along four dimensions. The dimensions differed descriptively, *i.e.,* from "worry a lot" to "never worry," from "often" to "never," for various items, but the intention was to sum up anxiety in many of its forms in order to achieve a total index of its amount. Pupils then were asked to indicate intensity of concern for the following thirty items:

Illustration 5

How Do You Feel About Things in Class?

I am going to be asking you some questions—questions different from the usual school questions, for these are about how you feel and so these questions have no right or wrong answers.

147

No one but myself will see your answers to these questions—not your teacher, principal or your parents. Read each question with me as I read the question aloud. You can answer each question by circling just *one* of the letters right below the question.

These questions are about how you think and feel and therefore have no right or wrong answers. People think and feel differently. The person next to you might answer a question in one way. You might answer the same question in another way, but both would be right because you feel differently about the matter.

Remember, I shall read each question, including the kinds of answers you can give. Wait until I finish reading the question and then answer. Give only one answer for each question.

1. Do you worry when the teachers say that they are going to ask you questions to find out how much you know about a subject?

2. Do you worry about whether you will be promoted, that is, passing from one class to the next class at the end of a year?

3. When the teacher asks you to answer questions in front of the class, are you afraid that you are going to make some bad mistakes?

4. When teachers say that they are going to call on students to do some problems, do you hope they will call on someone else?

5. Do you dream at night that you are in school and cannot answer a teacher's question?

6. When you think you are going to be called on by a teacher, does your heart begin to beat fast?

7. When a teacher is explaining a hard subject, do you feel others in the class understand it better than you do?

8. Before you fall asleep do you worry about how well you are going to do in class the next day?

9. When a teacher asks you to write on the blackboard in front of the class, does your hand shake?

10. Do you worry more about school than other students?

11. When you are thinking about your school work for the next day, do you become afraid that you will get the answers wrong when a teacher calls on you?

12. If you are sick and miss class, are you afraid you will be way behind the other students when you return?

13. Do you dream at night that others in your class can do things better than you?

14. When you are thinking about your classwork for the next day, do you worry that you will do poorly?

15. When you think you are going to be called on by a teacher, do you get a funny feeling in your stomach?

16. If you do very poorly when a teacher calls on you, does it bother you and make you feel unhappy?

17. Do you ever dream that a teacher is angry because you don't know the material?

18. Are you afraid of school tests?

19. Do you worry before you take a test?

20. Do you worry while you are taking a test?

21. After you have taken a test, do you worry about how well you did on the test?

22. Do you dream at night that you did poorly on a test you had in school that day?

23. When you are taking a test does your hand shake?

24. When teachers say they are going to give the class a test, do you become afraid you'll do poorly?

25. When you are taking a difficult test, do you forget some things you knew well before you started taking the test?

26. Do you ever wish that you didn't worry so much about tests?

27. When teachers say they are going to give the class a test, do you get a nervous feeling?

28. While you are taking a test do you usually think you are doing poorly?

29. While you are on your way to school do you worry that you might have a test?

30. While you are taking a test do your hands ever feel sweaty?

From this test, a single measure was constructed based on the child's total anxiety score. Some children are made nervous by the classroom setting and others take it easily in their stride. We needed to distinguish between these two types and used this measure to accomplish our purpose. While the academically anxious child may worry about every aspect of the classroom encounter, there are those for whom the classroom is an arena designed to fit their personal specifications and they revel in it.

Finally, we adapted familiar test devices to form what has been given the rather pretentious title of a *Literary Attitude Scale* for children. This particular measurement is an adaptation of the semantic differential technique. On this scale, any object, feeling, attitude or behavior can be assessed along a variety of dimensions calculated to reveal the subject's fundamental feelings. Take *money* for example: Would you consider money very good or very bad, very weak or very strong, very interesting or very dull, very small or very big, very important or very unimportant? On such a set of rating scales we apprised ourselves of the value these children ascribed to literary efforts (reading and writing) and literary materials (newspapers, magazines, and books).

As an additional measure, we used the semantic differential style of questioning to allow the child to tell us about himself; *i.e.,* are you a person good or bad, weak or strong, interesting or dull, small or big, important or unimportant? Using this research technique we probed for reaction to sixteen different items. Illustration 6 demonstrates the descriptive adjectives attached to each concept and is followed by a list of the items we explored.

Illustration 6

Literary Attitude Scale

Example

Money

is

very good	good	sort of good	not good or bad	sort of bad	bad	very bad
very weak	weak	sort of weak	not weak or strong	sort of strong	strong	very strong
very interesting	interesting	sort of interesting	not interesting or dull	sort of dull	dull	very dull
very small	small	sort of small	not small or big	sort of big	big	very big
very important	important	sort of important	not important or unimportant	sort of unimportant	unimportant	very unimportant

Test Items (using above dimensions)

1. Cars are
2. Television is
3. Classes are
4. Newspapers are
5. I am
6. Sports are
7. Writing is
8. Food is
9. This place is
10. Reading is
11. Tests are
12. Teachers are
13. Home is
14. Magazines are
15. Work is
16. Books are

151

Few of the traditional measures of intelligence and achievement seemed to us useful in assessing progress in our students. We needed something more than these, something more directly concerned with literacy. We therefore modified existing techniques to construct a test of *Verbal Proficiency*. The *Verbal Proficiency Test* was nothing more than an attempt to provoke our anti-literate boys into producing words and ideas. The test included instructions such as the following:

1. Write all the uses you can think of for tin cans, bottles, or milk cartons.
2. Write all the things you think might happen if we could understand birds and animals, if people from Mars landed on the earth, or if we could reach each other's minds.
3. Write all the things you would say if you tried to tell someone what kind of person you are.
4. Write the improvements you could make in such items as bicycles, chairs, telephones, beds, cars, and shoes.
5. Write all the words you can invent by using the letters in CREATION, GENERATION, or MATURATION.

From these diverse assessments of literary production, we marked off measures of the number of words actually written and the number of separate ideas contained in these words. The scores on the various subtests were combined to achieve a total score reflecting the number of ideas and number of words produced by the student.

This, then, constitutes the catalogue of instruments, measures, and techniques we employed to find out what was happening to the boys exposed to *English in Every Classroom* as compared with what happened to their peers, who were given a more traditional education. Other methods, other devices, and other techniques might well have been used to assess what was happening, but the ones we selected seemed to us most likely to serve our purposes.

Our primary concern was to study our subjects, to assess the effects of the program, as contrasted with its absence, and to communicate the results in as direct and uncomplicated a fashion as possible. Thus, what follows here is our *interpretation* of our research results in a form relieved wherever possible of the burden of statistics and technical information. This has been recorded in full in the extended report furnished to the United States Office of Education and is available from that Office on request. To include true statistical analysis here would be irrelevant to the scope of this book and would require reproduction of more than 130 separate tables.

D. Two Years of Testing

The Self—Its Image and Its Esteem

When a child turns his eyes inward he gets an image of himself—of who and what he is—and he reacts intellectually and emotionally to his judgment of what he sees. With his inner eye he takes the measure of himself—his characteristics, his physique, his looks, his style of life—and compares this self-view, for better or for worse, with the way others see him. His view of himself is also constructed of reflected appraisals, i.e., the kind of person other people think he is. What do I think I am? What do others think I am? What do I want to be? Such are the questions asked of the self; in the answers to these questions we find a wellspring of motivation for human behavior.

The quest for a sense of identity continues throughout every person's life. Suppose, for a moment, that the seeker discovers an identity like this one:

I am a fifteen-year-old Black boy who has been in a lot of trouble with the police. Finally, one time they caught me, they took me away from my family and sent

153

me to this training school. All the boys here are tough and have got busted by the police, too. People think I am pure bad and don't trust me. My mother's ashamed of me, the neighbors don't like me, and kids at home are told to stay away from me because I'm "trouble." White folks don't treat me fair and they don't like me. Everybody thinks I am dumb and no-account and they think I am going to end up in Jackson Prison for the rest of my life. Maybe they're right.

Such a self-image makes its possessor unlikely to look to literacy as a means of changing his life. Hope and prospect are functions of how you value yourself and of the importance you attach to seeing youself as you think you are. Education and self-worth are necessary complements to one another.

We asked teachers to evaluate the sense of self-worth and self-esteem of each of their pupils. We asked the teacher to tell us whether a child feels adequate and competent, inadequate and worthless, or somewhere between these extremes.

There was no statistically significant difference between teacher estimates of self-esteem at B.T.S. and in the CG at the beginning of the experiment. The self-esteem of the boys in the CG was somewhat higher when we began, but it deteriorated during the year, while that of the boys at B.T.S. rose, until, according to their teachers, it matched the original starting position of those in the control group. In other words, self-esteem rose among the boys at B.T.S. while it was falling in the CG.

The details of this change are instructive. When the experiment began, high self-esteem characterized the youngest and the brightest of the Black boys in the CG. They valued themselves more highly than older boys of either race at either school. By the end of the school year this promising state of affairs ceased to exist. Superior self-esteem traded partners and became the possession of the older boys at both schools and, significantly, the particular pride of the brightest ones at B.T.S. At the end of the year, those with the highest self-esteem were the older, brighter, White boys at B.T.S.

One year in a penal training school must maim the psychological well-being of the young, bright Black, for he ends this period of intended rehabilitation with his view of himself greatly diminished. The significant early advantage posted by the young in the CG, compared with the young in B.T.S., disappears in the post-test evaluations. Pre- and post-test comparisons between schools by high and low I.Q. display a marked, significant shift.

The Self Through the Child's Eyes

We asked the boys to tell us how they viewed themselves. In the *Behavioral Rating Form* and in the *Literary Attitude Scale* they could tell us who and what they were. When we began to examine *English in Every Classroom*, the least bright in the CG possessed, on both measures, a superior view of themselves. The same finding appeared for the Blacks in both groups. In fact, being a Black in the CG was better than being a Black in B.T.S. if self-image is taken as the criterion. And a Black in the control school had a better self-concept than White boys at either institution.

When the smoke of a year in a training school had cleared, those with the highest self-esteem were found to be the boys in the B.T.S. population and a positive self-image was most apparent in the brightest among them. The Black boys in the CG maintain their superiority of self-view when compared with the general run of White boys at the same school, but both the Blacks and the Whites at B.T.S. do even better in maintaining self-esteem. It is clear that the two schools have a different effect on their charges' views of themselves; it is also clear that this view is not a function of the age of the boys tested. We believe this self-view is crucial to each child's ability to respond to the world of words. Something of a positive nature took place in B.T.S. that was missing in the CG. A part of this positive influence was *English in Every Classroom*.

155

One kind of truth about classroom and pupils can be seen through the eyes of the teacher. Her view of the classroom world is an essential one because it contains the key to educational success or failure. In time every student comes to understand that the teacher is the master of the class and is the dispenser of reward, punishment, success, and failure. Education is basically a process of child-teacher interaction and, given the form in which it is fashioned, any child at any given time has teachers who may or may not understand him, appreciate him, help him, encourage him, or teach him.

Teachers reach conclusions about children following very brief and superficial contacts with them and these conclusions are, unfortunately, emotional and cognitive stereotypes. Children extend similar treatment to teachers, but since teachers are vested with the ultimate educational authority, their stereotypes are the more dangerous. In common with all teachers, the teachers in both the CG and B.T.S. stereotyped their pupils and, perceiving surface rather than depth, reacted to them accordingly.

We asked the teachers about "devils" and "angels," for example, and discovered that the angelic student was White, bright, and older than the average at both institutions. What is most important is that this educational view of children was *invisible* when the semester *began* and only became apparent at the conclusion of our experiment. In this single academic year the stereotype for teacher discrimination of good versus bad students reared its ugly head to the detriment of Black, less bright, and young pupils. It is our conviction that the teachers' classroom responses to individual children followed closely the outlines of these stereotypes, but we cannot prove it scientifically. We also suspect that what we discovered in these detention homes is a reasonable facsimile of events in our national public school system, but we are again without adequate proof that this is true.

Inferential corroboration is available, however. We asked teachers at both schools to rate the general emotional adjustment of each child and to judge his response to the establishment of limits on his classroom behavior. The boys judged best adjusted by teachers when the experiment began were, at both schools, predictably White, and the ranks of the best adjusted were populated most significantly by boys at Whitmore Lake.

Being smarter than the average of the group made no difference in the initial ratings of teachers, but it came into its own after a year. Somehow, being smarter was confused with being better adjusted by teachers in both schools. This is an error of judgment that seems to be repeated over and over again in the history of education.

If you are seeking a good adjustment rating from your teacher, be White. To a significant extent, White was right for pupils in both schools. It may be that skin color will prove to be an insurmountable obstacle as long as our teacher population is as predominantly White as it is at present. It might also be that our teachers are responding to some inevitable facts of life and that they are responding honestly. In our schools as they are presently constituted, White pupils have an advantage denied to their Black peers. Though both explanations are defensible, our observations suggest that being Black carries with it the penalty of misunderstanding by White teachers.

What about teacher estimates of these children's interests, reactions, and attitudes more immediately and directly concerned with literacy? When we asked teachers to tell us about the child's attitude toward school, they consistently reported that older and brighter children have the best attitudes. What little influence race has on this issue favors the White rather than the Black child, but even this distinction disappeared by the end of the experiment. The clearly reliable finding is that teachers see bright students as better oriented to school. Perhaps this evaluation is both accurate and reasonable. After all, who else should respond best to confrontation with the mysteries of symbolism and abstraction? In this respect, geographical location makes less difference than measured intelligence. Teachers like smarter rather than dumber students and they view them as better disposed toward school.

Teachers' attitudes and beliefs about pupils may be most significant when things are going badly. What happens to the student who is experiencing failure? Does he give up in anger, does he insist that he "doesn't care, anyway," or does he work harder to master the problem that confronts him? The child's reaction to failure, as the teacher sees it at the beginning and end of our experiment, ought to be a reasonable indicator of the child's "learning how to learn" in the course of the year.

When *English in Every Classroom* was first installed, the boys at B.T.S. responded best to failure and buckled down to work harder and did better when academic catastrophe threatened. The age of the child at Whitmore Lake was not related to digging-in rather than quitting, but it was evident at the beginning of the experiment that a good response appeared most often in the bright and White boys at B.T.S. Being Black, being less bright, and being in the control school group combined to make "working harder" an alien reaction to failure.

At the conclusion of our experiment, the boys in the CG were reported to have improved slightly in their reaction to failure, while those at B.T.S. showed a slight loss in maturity of response to failure. Both sets of differences were slight and it was no longer possible to make a significant distinction between boys at the two schools. The advantages of intelligence and race disappeared by the end of our study. It was as if these protections were inadequate defenses against the continued onslaught of failure as symbolized by incarceration. Both young and old at B.T.S. scored better at the conclusion of the experiment than the young at the CG. Intelligence ceases to be a significant factor at the conclusion of the experiment, as does the advantage of being White. The reaction to failure becomes almost totally uniform during the year the boys spend in training schools.

Literacy and the Attitude of the Child

There are a number of perfectly respectable, more-or-less

scientific definitions of the word "attitude." But most of them are so stiff and stuffy that what we mean to convey by the term gets carried away in a flood of jargon. I once told a delinquent boy that I was worried about his "attitude" toward the crime he had committed (professors talk funny even when they try not to). He replied, "I don't know what a attitude is, but it's how I feel, baby. The hell with them." The "them" of course, was all the members of middle-class society who bugged him by their insistence that he should not do what he regularly did.

Perhaps we need no better definition of attitude than "it's how I feel, baby," for that's the level at which an attitude is experienced by its possessor and we must start where they are rather than where we wish them to be. How our subjects feel about reading, writing, the classroom, and things properly belonging to it is of vital interest to us. If literacy "feels bad," we must improve its feeling before we can accomplish any meaningful training at all. If we can influence the feelings people have, we can make fundamental changes in their view of the world.

It is conceivable that even if none of our subjects displays a change in literary habits and energy investment in the acts of reading and writing, we could yet proclaim ourselves victors in the battle. If how they *feel* about reading and writing can be nudged into a new posture, we may have achieved the stance needed to move their whole outlook on the world. Once a child stops fighting the system, he can divert his energy into making it work for him to get what he wants and needs.

Our scales were designed to reflect two aspects of attitude toward literacy: (1) the child's attitude toward literary effort on his part, i.e., reading or writing; and (2) the child's attitude toward literary material, i.e., books, newspapers, and magazines.

At the beginning of the experiment, the boys' attitudes toward their own literary efforts were statistically indistinguishable by age, I.Q., or race, although the boys at B.T.S. had slightly more positive feelings than the boys in the control group. In the brief period of exposure a number of differences did appear and all of them fitted our original hypotheses about the impact of *English in Every Classroom:* they all favored the Whitmore Lake setting. The attitude of the B.T.S. boys improved and they kept their edge over the boys in the CG. In particular, in both schools the older boys showed the greatest improvement in attitude. Literary effort had greater meaning for them than it did for the younger boys, particularly for those in the CG. Uniquely, being smarter or dumber and being Black or White made little difference on this measure when the experiment was finished.

When the children were asked to express their attitude toward books, magazines, and newspapers, intelligence played no part at all either before or after the initiation of *English in Every Classroom* at B.T.S. At the beginning, there was a clear-cut age difference in the schools. The younger boys at Whitmore Lake were happier about these instruments of literacy than were the older boys at the same school or the younger boys in the control group. Both the CG and B.T.S. had increased their interest in reading materials by the end of the experiment, but our findings favored the boys at B.T.S., whether young or old.

Initially, the White boys at Whitmore Lake felt better about the materials but this was not a significant difference. When the experiment was concluded, the significant finding was that the White boys at both institutions had more positive attitudes than their Black comrades, with those of the White boys in the CG significantly more favorable than those of Blacks at the same school.

Reviewing the data, we can only conclude once again that the White–Black differential response reflects the depth of our educational dilemma. In a variety of subtle ways the fact of skin color gets hopelessly entangled with notions about literacy. In the self-image of the child, in the teacher's view of him, and in his attitude toward education, the unbright, non-White child is so handicapped that massive educational reorganization may be necessary to help him. Getting him hooked on books may be a beginning, but it is only that. The educational climate within our schools and within ourselves as teachers must be modified to meet the needs of the Black student if we are to alter the way he feels about school and basic literacy.

In our next attempt to study attitude, we brought various items together to form the dimensions of "literacy lovers— literacy haters" and "school lovers-school haters." In the beginning, school lovers and school haters were distinguishable along only one dimension—race. Surprisingly, the Black students at both institutions brought with them the most positive attitude toward school and the tasks of education. Age and intelligence were not significant forces in shaping this attitude. The results at the conclusion of the experiment wiped out this initially significant difference in attitude. On an uneven pattern, the attitude to school of the White boys improved slightly while the attitude of the Black boys deteriorated. As a consequence of one year at these two training schools, no significant difference existed in the measurement of school lovers and school haters. All the boys in the sample occupied a position that could best be described as "alienated by the school experience." They didn't care much for school when they first arrived at the training center, and they didn't care much for it when they left.

Given a choice between books and schools, the children in our sample prefer books. Though our book lovers had only a modest passion for the written word, they clearly preferred it to school. As you might anticipate, the book lovers were, on the average, the older and brighter children at B.T.S. The older boys retained their interest in books at the end of the experiment, but intelligence ceased to contribute to this interest.

Thirty Things to Worry About

The questionnaire we titled "How Do You Feel About Things in Class?" actually addressed itself to the level of anxiety each child experienced as he thought about himself and education. We asked each child how much he worried about such things as tests, being promoted, reciting before the class, giving wrong answers, and being behind in his

161

homework. Summarizing the answers to thirty such questions allowed us to compare the academic "worry scores" of boys in the two schools.

These scores were almost identical at the beginning of the experiment for the boys in both institutions. By the end of the school year, the boys in the CG were more worried about the educational process than they had been at the beginning of the year. The reverse was true of the boys in B.T.S. The average boy there was significantly less anxious about school at the end of the experiment than he was at its inception.

Watching these changing levels of anxiety about education in the two schools was like witnessing a race in which the two runners left the starting line at the same time, but one ran backward while the other ran forward. By the end of the race, the boys in the CG were farther back than they had been at the start. Had no anxiety reduction taken place for the B.T.S. boys, they would still have won the race. As it was, they were clearly more comfortable with things educational as a result of their experience in the training school.

Who became more anxious and who less? At the beginning, age didn't matter at either school. On the average, all the boys at Whitmore Lake came to worry less, whether young or old, than those in the control group. Being in the brighter half of the student body and being at B.T.S. proved to be twice good for those seeking relief from school pressures. If you were sent to the CG, by the end of the experiment your chances of worrying less about school were in direct proportion to the strength of your intellect. At first, White boys in B.T.S. were less anxious than White boys in the CG; more surprisingly, Black boys in the control group were less nervous about school than were White boys at the same institution. By the time the experiment was completed, White children at B.T.S. felt better about school than their CG counterparts, both White and Black. Even more remarkably, the Black children at Whitmore Lake felt considerably less anxious about school than both White and Black boys in the other school.

Does *English in Every Classroom* really provide this relaxation of academic tension for the child exposed to its practices? We think it does. In part, we are convinced that providing the opportunity for children to get hooked on books is important and, in part, we know from observation that *English in Every Classroom* provides a new sense of excitement and enthusiasm for despairing teachers confronted with the hitherto hopeless task of forcing literacy upon unresponsive consumers. Teachers of reading and writing find new vigor and meaning in this English program because it returns teaching to where kids *are* and removes it from the esoteric realm of where they *ought to be*. *English in Every Classroom* offers an educational rationality that produces in children a measurable relaxation of distress about school and its problems. Perhaps this is enough to demand of any educational innovation.

Measurements of attitudes by paper and pencil tests given in a group setting are far from infallible indicators of the way children really feel. If actions do speak louder than words, then we may look to the following measures of performance to discover which offers the greater promise—what the boys actually do on tests of literacy or their own expressions of how they feel about it.

Verbal Proficiency

The Verbal Proficiency Test was really five tests rolled into one. Each test asked the students to perform with words and ideas in a variety of related intellectual tasks. Using separate scores based on the number of ideas and number of words students had at their command to meet each test, we compared the performances of the boys in the two groups.

Though the results are as we hoped they would be, they are nonetheless shocking for they are impersonal reflections of the fate of living human beings exposed to a crippling educational and social environment. In this measure of ease with words and ideas, B.T.S. boys were not significantly different from those in the CG when our experiment began. It was in the tests conducted after a year of work with and

163

without *English in Every Classroom* that meaninful differences came to be so painfully clear.

I reported earlier that the level of anxiety about school and literacy increased for the CG boys while it decreased for the inmates of Whitmore Lake. To look at these performance measures is to understand why. As in the race I described, a race with only two entries, our control group did worse than run second—it finished farther back than its own starting point. In their ability to generate ideas, boys at B.T.S. gained significantly by the time of post-testing; in the CG, boys not only failed to gain, but fell behind their initial levels of performance. When a count was made of the number of words used to meet testing situations, boys exposed to *English in Every Classroom* at Whitmore Lake took part in what can only be described as a runaway performance. While the B.T.S. boys performed so well, the boys in our control sample were unable even to maintain their unsatisfactory level of the year before.

This is a pathetic report but it is consistent with other reports in scientific literature which record intellectual regression following an absence of cognitive stimulation. We could, realistically, have expected little else. Given intellectual deprivation in an overworked and understaffed institution, we can hardly expect pupils to hold their own in the battle for verbal survival.

The facts speak for themselves. A calculated program of intellectual stimulation has a measurable impact on its consumers—the children. Verbal Proficiency, measured in our fashion, reflects the kind and quality of program an educational institution is willing to invest in. Though a great many events other than *English in Every Classroom* occurred simultaneously with our program, we are convinced that what we attempted must find its reflection in the results we have reported.

In both the CG and B.T.S., production of ideas and numbers of words were related to the students' measured intelligence. What is of particular interest is that the influence of basic intellectual ability was evident, not at the beginning of the experiment but at its conclusion. In the tests of number of ideas and number of words, a significant relationship with intelligence was revealed only at the end of the experiment. Using the Verbal Proficiency Test as our measure, it is clear that our best prospects for inducing changes in literate performance are to be found in the ranks of the brightest students. They are, of course, always our most promising prospects: in part, because measures of intelligence tap exactly those qualities best suited to deal with the symbols and abstractions of education, and, in part, because an intelligence test is in an odd way a measure of how far the child has already traveled in his journey toward literacy.

Much the same relationship exists between Verbal Proficiency and all the subsections of the Stanford Achievement Tests in the Whitmore Lake sample. The best achievers on the Stanford Achievement Test among the boys at Whitmore Lake turned out to be those who displayed the highest degree of verbal proficiency both before and after the research study. While these findings are hardly startling, they gain import when we note that measured achievement did not prove a saving grace for the boys in the control group. No significant relationship existed between high achievers and low achievers on the Stanford Achievement Test and the ability to produce ideas and words on the Verbal Proficiency Test. There is a reasonable basis for believing that the (typical) environment created in the control school suppresses the boys' verbal productivity to the point that their performances do not even reflect the differences in achievement they have already attained.

The only significant correlations with Verbal Proficiency for the CG boys were with their self-stated high valuation of literary efforts (writing and reading) and of literary materials (newspapers, magazines, and books). Those who displayed the greatest production of ideas and words on our tests were the same self-avowed lovers of reading, writing, and books whom we identified at the beginning of the project. At B.T.S., a boy did not have to be deeply committed to things literary to produce an abundance of ideas and words at final testing time.

An additional check was run to verify these observations. The section of the Verbal Proficiency Test asking each child to construct new words (using the letters available in a stimulus word) produced long and short words in unequal numbers. We decided to count the average number of letters in each word manufactured by each child in both schools. The outcome of this primitive means of assessment confirmed our previous conclusion about what had transpired between the beginning and end of our experiment. While the boys at B.T.S. showed a 20 percent increase in the length of words they could invent, the boys in the CG lost so much ground that they reduced by almost one-half the average length of words they could assemble from the stimulus word. There are many possible explanations of this turn of events, but it is evident that language production of even this simple variety is a sensitive response of children to their educational experience.

As the brightest among the children at both schools progressed most in the production of words and ideas during the course of the experiment, so too the White students achieved more idea production than did the Black population at Whitmore Lake. In the beginning of our program, White students at B.T.S. proved to be slightly superior to Black boys in their own school as well as to Blacks in the CG in the production of ideas and this trend became even more pronounced when the experiment ended. Interestingly, race played no part in determining proficiency with words either before or after the experiment. Our suspicion is that words are a more easily available currency than ideas, and that ideas are more subject to erosion when exposed to the abrasion of cultural disadvantage. The symbolic mental manipulation of words is a vital tool in the production of new and different ideas, but it is only one of a number of essential tools.

An additional technique designed to assess changes in language comprehension and proficiency was the Stanford Achievement Test. Our plan was to take advantage of the routine administration of this test at the time each child entered and left detention. This "routine" data collection, we discovered, was a hit-and-miss affair—more miss than hit. In particular, the boys in our CG sample often failed to take the post-test we needed to assess their progress in achievement in comparison with that of the boys at Whitmore Lake.

The part of the Stanford Achievement Test least subject to this erosion in numbers is the section assessing the pupils' capacity to comprehend paragraph meaning. The measure of paragraph meaning is, happily, a global measure of comprehension and understanding that relies on knowledge of the meaning of individual words that compose it. This is, in most respects, an ideal tool for our purposes, since it is unconcerned with such trivia of achievement as, for instance, spelling proficiency.

Analysis of before-and-after scores of boys in B.T.S. and boys in the CG restates an already familiar set of observations. The boys at B.T.S. are superior to those in the CG at the beginning of the experiment. Though both groups improve over the course of the academic year, the boys at B.T.S. make more than twice the progress of their control group counterparts. Their capacity to absorb a paragraph's meaning has clearly improved and the improvement is substantial.

A revealing subanalysis of this finding is worth reporting. We divided the Stanford Achievement Test scores of all the boys into upper and lower halves to see if the best achievers fared better than those who achieved less well when the test was that of ferreting out paragraph meaning. We discovered that having a high or low standing in achievement at the beginning of the experiment had little relevance for predicting a boy's progress during the ensuing year. Both the high and low achievers at B.T.S. made positive and substantial gains by the end of the study, while progress of the boys of the CG ranged between slight gains and equally slight losses. When we reduced our sample to those boys on whom we had pre- and post-achievement measures, it became apparent that the highest achievers at Whitmore Lake profited most from the year of schooling.

The results of the Verbal Proficiency Test and the Stanford Achievement Test were congruent with one another and confirmed our hopes when we designed the experiment initially: where it finally counts—in performance—*English in Every Classroom* was a vital part of the educational experience available to the boys at the

Maxey School. Furthermore, these changes in performance were directly attributable to a *change in feeling* generated by a change in methods and materials employed in the teaching of English.

E. "What I Done Last Summer"

Each September millions of kids face the impossible task of describing, in three hundred words or less, what they did during the summer. From the teacher's point of view, the gambit is foolproof: every child does *something* every summer, and he usually remembers it with pleasure, although children themselves aren't very demanding judges of a summer's quality—a summer is a summer is a summer. You don't have to go to school, so it's good. You come back to school, you've got to write, and that's bad. But you write because *they* want you to. Maybe you write like Reggie S., a twelve-year-old Black boy who lives at the St. Francis Home for Wayward Boys.

Reggie's police record began when he was eight. In four years he's been arrested nine times (the top of the iceberg) for a variety of crimes against society, including extortion, thefts, truancy, gang fighting, and breaking and entering. Reggie writes like this:

What I Done Last Summer

Last summer they say if I was a good boy and behave myself for a change I could git to go to camp. I done all what they say as good as I could and they let me go. A couple things I done I thought they wouldn't send me but they did on account I promised not to do them no more and some other guys started it anyway.

The camp has all kinds of free stuff. You don't pay

168

nothing to ride in the boats or jump on the tramp or go to the crap [craft] shop or drink all the milk you wants. Sometimes they has chocolate milk or Kool-ade. When you go to bed they has snacks. They don't hit kids even if you cuss them or fights them but they make you go into the session room and talk about what's making you act that way. The people ain't like regular Whiteys and when I called Mac a white soda cracker he said he didn't call me no race names so I can't call him none.

They say they don't whip us ever and they don't. I think they ought to beat on some of them kids who wreck stuff or smoke illegal when they ain't supposed to. I had a lot of fun and only trouble sometimes. The first day we was their they took us to the Ludington Liebarey and the liebareyan give us any two books we wanted to keep. They was tiny paper books we could stick in our pockets and trade at the liebarey for other books. We used to trade books and all them magazines with other guys and sometimes we could read to the guys in the cabin with a flashlight when we went to bed. I used to take my books to the waterfront and tell one of them sitting waterfront guys to put it under his butt so's nobody would swipe it.

They used to let us play with the typewriters in the liebarey and we could look at all the books and magazines we wanted. Even if books and things got a little wrecked they didn't mess on us. I want to go back to camp next year and be a counselor when I grow up. That's what I done last summer and I still got them books.

Reggie's "theme" is an accurate account of the view children at the Fresh Air Camp have of their month-long stay. The camp is an outdoor clinical center devoted to training budding professionals in the clinical management of emotionally disturbed and/or delinquent boys. The counselors are selected from the ranks of clinical psychologists, psychiatric nurses, psychiatric social workers, and teachers of special education for the emotionally disturbed. They don't holler at kids. They try to understand them.

In my years as director of this training center we had never made a meaningful attempt to incorporate literacy as a part of our basic program. We ignored the intellectual side of emotional and delinquent problems because I had no faith in the available programs of educational improvement for such youngsters. But I must report now that the *Hooked on Books* idea of a new approach to achieving literacy has changed our camp. The Fresh Air Camp is as corrosive an acid test for a literacy program as man or devil could invent. The odds against it were incredible. Who could imagine children who never read anything willingly, turning to books and magazines in an environment free of adult interference and full of fun and games?

The Odds Against Reading

The typical summer camp is populated by healthy, well-adjusted offspring of affluent American middle-class parents who view Mother Nature as a peerless developer of independence, maturity, and character in their children. If not quite all that, then at least fun for the child and freedom from children for the parents. Such campers generally have two sorts of reading material available to them—the backs of cereal boxes and clandestine comic books. The fact is that the typical American camper is carefully shielded from books while he is adventuring in the great outdoors. With very few exceptions (such as academic or scientific camps for the very bright or gifted child), the American camping movement is fundamentally anti-intellectual.

Camp directors and counselors are vaguely discomfited by the sight of a child absorbed with the stimulation to his inner life that the written word provides. A child lying quietly on his bunk bed, lost in a novel, smacks of the "introvert" and introvert means maladjusted in the outgoing, friendly, bustling, go-get-'em society of the summer camp. Why isn't he *doing something* instead of just lying there? The maxim is, "Campers who play together pay together." As any camp director knows, the kid who reads by himself is the one who doesn't come back.

The portrait is overdrawn, but it is an essentially accurate picture of the typical summer's hiatus from literacy of the middle-class child. Quadruple its intensity and you have a small idea of such a hiatus at the University of Michigan's Fresh Air Camp. The children whose patronage we solicit come from mental hospitals, detention homes, houses of correction, child guidance clinics, slum neighborhoods, and juvenile courts. These subjects of our experiment in reading are perhaps best characterized as children who hate. They are children from the worst sections of Michigan's large metropolitan areas. They are school kick-outs, smash-outs, and flunk-outs, and they are the debris of our educational and social system. They are nonreaders, almost nonreaders, pretend readers (picture lookers), and a host of slow, slow, slow readers whose lips move with every word their finger points to. There are some adequate readers, but very few.

Books are painfully alien to these children, who have read only when forced to by a teacher. Besides, camp is for fun, not for schooling; it's a place where all the cool guys go. At the top of the summer's agenda for most of these children is the attainment of power and leadership by force. The bespectacled, literate bookworm hardly fits the stereotype of a scabrous, irreverent, adult-defying leader whose credo is summarized in the Rule of the Golden Knuckle: "A punch in the mouth is worth a thousand words." From this improbable clay we were to mold a model of the reading nonreader. As one young man put it, succinctly and directly, "What you got that motha library for? My worker [psychiatric case worker] tole me I was coming here for a good time. He didn't say nothin about no mothering books. He said I could swim across the lake if I want to."

Given those crushing odds, it seemed only fair to demand a choice of weapons. We selected an armament consisting of the following pieces:

1. The Ludington Library (an unused camp cabin) was stocked with an assortment of paperback books and magazines selected to interest children ranging in age from

seven to fifteen.

2. On the first day of camp every child was taken to the library, allowed to browse, and to choose two books as a gift.

3. The camper was told that the books were his to keep and could be exchanged for any others in the library whenever the mood moved him.

4. Games, typewriters, crayons, paper, etc., were distributed on tables for the pleasure of the library's visitors. It was not a "quiet" library; it was an activity center.

5. The three librarians were instructed to participate actively with the children and to have fun with them even if it hurt.

6. The library was to be kept open at all hours when the children were not engaged in scheduled camp activities.

The library weapons were primed and ready to fire, but a target was needed. Traditional notions of what a camp should do for children and how it should plan for them had to be violated. These violations took the following form:

1. Every morning and all day Sunday were times for free activity. This meant that during approximately thirty-six waking hours of the seven-day week the children were free to visit the library, to read, to sit, or to stare vacantly into space.

2. Counselors were instructed not to annoy the reading child or to coerce him into physical activity. Reading was officially designated a worthwhile activity.

3. Teacher-trainees among the counselors were brainwashed in seminars to keep them from reverting instinctively to the classic role of the teacher-who-teaches-the-children-to-respect-books-and-to-take-care-of-them-properly.

Who's Hooked and Who's Not?

The battle was joined when the children arrived at camp and settled down to spend a summer month with us. The strategy was planned and we sat back to see what would happen. Our first observation post was set up in the library and we made notations of the length of time our restless charges spent in the Ludington Library and of what they did

172

while there. Our library was not only a place to check out books, it was a setting in which a boy could look at magazines and other books, read, type, play games or just mess around. Records had to be kept inconspicuously to keep the children from feeling watched. For these children, a scheduled activity is an adult plan to be destroyed and a grown-up purpose to be defiled. Once some of our boys found a tree-vine just right for playing Tarzan. When the fighting started ("Its *my* turn!" "The hell it is!" etc.), we installed a counselor at the site to arbitrate the mayhem. Within a day the children had lost interest in the whole affair. We feared the same fate might befall a library staffed by compulsive record-keepers.

On a typical library morning, between one and sixteen campers (out of the seventy children in camp) visited the Ludington facility. Averaged over a month's time, this works out to about six campers occupying the library at any one moment during the three hours of its availability in the morning. To put this number in proper perspective, it must be recalled that these free mornings could be spent swimming, boating, fishing, hiking, exploring, playing games or making "stuff" in the craft shop. Furthermore, no limitations were placed on out-of-library trading of books. Counselors reported a great deal of unrecorded book swapping—perhaps more than took place inside the library. Several counselors testified that a book became popular in proportion to the length of time a boy took to read it. If a boy and a book appeared to be going together, that book was likely to be coveted by the boy's friends who could obtain it only at the price of some personal service ("O.K., if you'll give me your dessert tonight") or if it gained the reader some immediate gratification ("Can I use your swimmin' fins?"). Finally, there was no discernible difference in library patronage between the first and last parts of the summer month, but a rainy day was as great a stimulus as the urge to read.

One boy checked out eleven books, after being given his initial two, while some (ten in all) checked out no more books once the original two were in their possession. On the average, the first two books were traded for two more during

173

the month's time (forty-three boys). In all, 224 books were obtained at the library by the sixty-two boys who frequented it on a semiregular basis. Consider for a moment how often you go to your local library and you have a rough basis for comparing the figures reported here. Given the nature of our camper population, I think this is an astounding record of voluntary traffic in books. Of course there was another kind of traffic, as our rate of book-crookery was predictably high. Nearly 100 books "disappeared" in one month. However, it could have been worse: for instance, *no* books might have been stolen!

Our observations made it apparent that something like a reading habit gets established for certain cabins and not for others. Our youngest cabin, in which the boys averaged eight years of age, traded a total of twenty-four books at the library during the month, with each cabin member exchanging at least two. The oldest boys traded only sixteen books during the same period. The younger boys consistently checked out more books than the older ones in all ten cabins in camp. It should be no surprise, then, to learn that *What's New, Charlie Brown?* and *Dennis the Menace* were the books most frequently issued. The books next in line are a wry commentary on our times—*The Man from U.N.C.L.E., Man in Flight, Voyage to the Bottom of the Sea,* and *Batman versus the Joker.* Witness the power of television! By contrast, *Mary Poppins* was, among these street-hardened young men, treated to the position of low eminence also accorded *Grimm's Fairy Tales.* One boy checked out a book entitled *Energy and Power* but returned it shortly with the cryptic comment that he "thought it was about something else."

A most fascinating and startling finding emerged from a careful study of casual comments the children made to the librarians. Since I was primarily interested in the campers' attitudes toward reading, I asked the librarians to record offhand observations the children might make about books and magazines. No comments were recorded for fifteen of the seventy children, but of the remaining fifty-five a grand total of twenty-seven reported at the beginning of the month they could not or would not read. These twenty-seven

174

checked out a total of sixty-eight books during the month of the experiment. Maybe they just liked to feel the weight of a book in the back pocket of their jeans or maybe they wanted to show the other guys they were "with it." But, for book haters, they certainly spent a lot of time with books. I prefer to take their words with a grain of salt and to believe their behavior.

And so our unlikely readers came to terms with paperback books and magazines. They visited the library on their own free time, and spent fifteen minutes there on the average. Some boys breezed in and out in five minutes while others stayed as long as an hour and a half. While they were in the library, their most frequent activity was the trading of one book for another, but typing ran an extremely close second in interest. Reading books and just messing around were the third and fourth runner-ups in popularity, followed by idle thumbing of and glancing at books and magazines. A library is still a library, however liberal an interpretation the word may be given, and playing games in the library was of the least interest to boys surrounded by 300 acres of games-playing possibilities.

There was a marked increase in idle time spent in the library during the last two weeks of the month-long camp session. It became apparent that the mere inert availability of reading material was not enough for children unaccustomed intellectually to self-direction. A positive, active program of reading and writing is necessary for children unused to surmounting obstacles simply because they are there. "To the stars through bolts and bars" is a middle-class slogan ranking with the homily "A job worth doing is worth doing well." When told of these strange philosophies, our campers only smile tolerantly and say, "Sure, baby. *You* believe it."

To Library Is One Thing; to Read Is Another

A place for books that avoids resembling a traditional library can attract customers who don't usually shop in that part of town. Business may be brisk and children wise in the ways of the adult world may learn to say those library-kinds-of-things that so endear them to library-type adults. But do they read, or do they smile gracefully and later rip the covers from the books in some secret setting? We can report convincingly about book-cover ripping. Though paperbacks seem particularly susceptible to destruction, the event rarely took place. Books were husbanded and nurtured as prize possessions. Placed carefully in locked footlockers, slipped under pillows or guarded on request by adults in camp, the books survived as few other material objects did. Windows were broken by irate fists, chairs hurled in anger, doors kicked akimbo in rage, and staff bodies bruised in focused resentment. But books and magazines seldom were torn or damaged. We had hoped to gauge the average life span of these reading materials with such children as ours, only to discover that with proper care even these insubstantial items can probably live forever.

But what of reading as distinct from library behavior? The most popular time for immersion in literature proved to be the half-hour allotted to getting ready for bed. Sometimes, and much to our chagrin, reading was used as a means of provoking adults who were tired from the day's labors and more intent on sleep than developing interests in literacy. Our boys used whatever tool was available to get the job done; when they discovered the simple trick of reading only at the wrong time and the wrong place, they mastered it superbly. Shouts of "Don't turn out the damn lights, I'm reading!" rang through the camp and every literacy-loving adult found himself disemboweled by ambivalence. The lights always went out (after some reasonable compromise) but flipping the light switch began to seem like an act destined to be recorded in history on the same pages as book-burning.

The second most appealing time to read was mealtime. We did not demand that the children devote their attention exclusively to mastication and digestion. Consequently, they read books before, during and after eating. Next in frequency of patronage were our planned Free Activity Periods each morning. Those who read, read longer in the free morning time but more children were reading at meals

176

and bedtime than at any other time of the day. The accuracy of these counselor recordings of reading is attested to by the fact that for an entire month no child was listed as reading during the free swim time each afternoon. The greatest frequency of reading as well as the greatest length of time spent at this activity was recorded for one child who was confined to the infirmary with a severe case of poison ivy. As he said, "I been scratchin' and readin' all day."

There were, of course, avid readers in the group who turned to their books at any moment that activities slackened or became uninteresting. I heard one boy in a boat tow (five rowboats strung together and towed by a power boat) shout to slow down and stop rocking the boat so he could read. The portability and availability of books and magazines were invitations to such reading. Probably the last word in portability was expressed by two boys on a three-mile hike to the village of Hell (that's really its name), Michigan. A Black boy was reading *Black Like Me* while being led by the hand by a White cabin mate as they hiked down the road. Their bargain was completed on the return trip when they switched positions.

Any figure reflecting the average time our typical camper devoted to reading during the average camp day would be meaningless, and would obscure the important observation that reading is a highly idiosyncratic and personal event that is not susceptible to mass motivation. Some times of day and social settings are more conducive to the act of reading than others, and this is clearly reflected in counselor observations of the children. Still, there are nonreaders to whom words are totally alien and there are avid readers to whom the time for reading is anytime and anyplace.

In the cabin of our very youngest children (aged seven and retarded three years, on the average, in reading skills), the eight members of the cabin devoted a total of two hours to reading during a two-week period of observation. All but twenty minutes of this reading time took place just before going to bed. By comparison, the reading rate of boys in the adjoining cabin (populated by eight-year-olds) doubled that of their younger friends. In a sample of the older boys in camp (three cabins in the Senior division), a total of twelve hours beyond library time was spent in reading by each cabin during the same two-week period. The sight of a teenager immersed in a book was a familiar one despite heavy involvement of older boys in activities of great variety and number. Most remarkably, I have seen older boys reading books even when the evening's activity was television viewing in the cabin.

In the middle age range (ten to twelve), we discovered a steady progression, on the average, in the frequency of reading in the camp setting. Reading appears to be an age-related phenomenon whose joys are learned by practice and whose pleasures increase with the growth of greater skill. Even these primitive children violate our expectations when the proper setting and supplies are provided for them. They don't read much, from the point of view of the literate middle-class child; they read an astounding amount compared with our usual stereotype of their literary interests.

The Odds for Tomorrow

It is highly unlikely that the cerebral pleasures of reading will ever replace the unique sensations of gross bodily movement or the sensory experience of water, wind, and just being alive. Yet, in this hopeless experiment, I think we managed to demonstrate a fundamental and meaningful fact about the relationship of children of action to the world of words.

If ever a deck was stacked against us, this was it:

1. Our subjects were selected from the youthful intellectual dregs of modern society; they were academic retards in every sense of the word. In the most congenial of circumstances and settings, little could be expected of them in the way of reading involvement.

2. We constructed a three-ring circus of outdoor activities to lure these deprived children away from the solitary pursuit of reading.

3. We asked harried counselors to make objective recordings of when, where, and how much time each child spent reading.

4. We found no means to control or properly assess the exchange of reading materials between children. Even camp bathrooms were sometimes converted into temporary markets for bartering books.

The entire experiment was only a crude and approximate match to the traditional models of pure science and perfectly hygienic methodology. It was impressionistic in the extreme despite the sanctification of numbers, percentages, and levels of significance, all duly recorded day after day. And I am certain it contains no more than a rough sampling of the total interaction with books that took place in our camp population. However, the absence of methodological perfection troubles me very little, for the quarry being tracked was an unusual species seldom captured in nature.

One of our original assumptions was that if delinquent and emotionally disturbed boys could be induced to read at all, we would feel we had succeeded in our assigned task. If they were to substitute reading for the call of the outdoors, we could have achieved goals we barely dared hope for. So strenuous a test as this was necessary for a number of reasons, not the least because a massive superstructure of doubt about the capability of such social rejects looms ominously over our society. We had to prove that books and magazines could be made compatible with a variety of ways of life other than that of the middle class in our social structure. We wanted an acid test: we got more acidity than we had bargained for.

In the words packaged between the covers of paperbound books and magazines I think we have finally found a common and exciting ground for conversation and contact between the dominant and dominated socioeconomic groups in our society. Books and magazines are a drug that anyone can become addicted to. You are hooked on books, I'm hooked on books, and **THEY** can become hooked on books too. The clearest testimonial I know of is contained in the reaction of a teacher from a detention home in Detroit.

While we were discussing the case of one child he had sent to camp, I mentioned some of the books the boy was reading. The teacher interrupted to point out. "But he can't read a word!" He should have added, "Except when he wants to."

Chapter VI

THE ELEMENTARY SELF-CONTAINED CLASSROOM

James Duggins

Grouping

The twin principles of SATURATION and DIFFUSION are natural to elementary school classrooms. The heart of the program for these classes lies in the ways in which classrooms are organized and the ways in which children are grouped. In the past decade, attention to "accountability" has frequently come to mean partite skills, fractionated bits of reading and writing. In attending to these skills, we have often forgotten to attend to human nature.

Even though the elementary classroom is divided into "Centers of Interest"—social studies, the sciences, the library table, music and art centers—we tend to forget that those same interests define the growing child. Instead of *interests*, we emphasize phonic *skills*, writing *skills*, comprehension *skills*, study *skills*. Because a cadre of reading and writing specialists has told us more about the *skills* of reading and writing than about the development of readers and writers, we have come to equate those skills with both learning and wanting to read and write. That same cadre of specialists has interpreted failing test scores to be a failure at skills processes. But I am convinced that the failure is primarily attributable neither to skills, teaching, nor learning; instead,

I believe it has been caused by our failure to give children reading materials that touch their lives.

Children who have scored poorly on standardized tests, supposed composites of reading skills, are not necessarily poor readers. Instead, what may be true is that we have taught them to place little or no value on reading in school. Persistently they have denied our ditto worksheets which emphasize word attack as well as cognitive and affective *skills* development. Denying their denial, we spend twelve years of their lives teaching them *how* to read; during those years, almost no time at all is devoted to persuading them *why* they should read.

We have so much evidence to suggest that if most people know *why* to read they can easily learn *how* to read. Many of us learn to read at age four from an older sibling (age 6). That six-year-old did not need a baccalaureate degree plus two years of graduate preparation to teach us to read. We wanted to read. We had an interest in learning to read. We had interests which reading satisfied. The self-contained classroom must be organized about those interests—they must be true "interest centers." In order to encourage the growing child to recognize his need to read, they will incorporate such materials as Grosset and Dunlap's *Wonder Starters* and the Young Reader's Press' *"World of..."* series along with the many episodes of Rey's inventive *Curious George* and the escapades of *Encyclopedia Brown*. Such baldly factual and transitional, fictionalized accounts begin to meet the youngster's need for information. The more those interest areas are satisfied, the more likely he or she is to develop an interest in reading.

Grouping in this classroom will be based upon the interests of the children—what they want to read about rather than the skills they are supposed to need. The curriculum in the elementary classroom is composed of the stuff of the child's world—his city, her home, his friends, her world of fantasy and imagination. The interest centers of the classroom should mirror that world with physical properties such as hats, paints, ant farms, and books, books, books. Children should be able to choose from such books as *Sing Down the Moon, Old McDonald Had an Apartment House,*

A Dog's Book of Bugs, A Tree Is a Plant, Helen Keller, and *The Courage of Sarah Noble.* Today, on every reader's level, materials are available to meet a myriad of interests.

Book Acquisition Resources

A major dimension of this program is the process of acquiring books. Wherever possible, they should be chosen locally. Books should be seen and plucked from the shelves and taken away—all on the same day, rather than ordered from catalogs and then long awaited. A kind of magical aura surrounds the book that attracts itself to you at the moment it is found on the shelves. Children and adults are motivated by the new treasure both found and taken home on the same day. This program depends upon that moment of selection, the testing of that sudden desire to possess a book, to peel it and devour it almost on the spot. The youngster who sees *The Snowy Day* or *Titch, Blueberries for Sal* or *Crow Boy,* should be able to touch them and decide among them and take the chosen one home that same day. Paperback publishers know that the cover alone can influence the sale of any new title they issue. If that is so for the bookbuying adult, how can we, in schools, deny that attraction for children, especially those who do not read much or well? The teacher who would bring the free-ranging use of paperbacks to the classroom must use local sources so that books can be seen and handled, for the books themselves can invite the would-be reader to literacy.

Jobbers and wholesalers usually offer the greatest range and quantity of children's books. Unless you live in one of those cities fortunate enough to have a good children's bookstore, your local wholesaler will be the only single source able to provide the variety your classes need and want. The general bookstore or book department of a larger store cannot supply that variety since they must handle hardbound as well as paperback editions. Appendix D provides a list of major wholesalers committed to working with you and your students.

Once having located a place to obtain paperback books, you must then involve the children themselves in the selection process. If the wholesaler or children's bookstore is nearby, don't hesitate to ask their help in making arrangements for bringing children to the book display or warehouse. Nothing is more important than the participation of these ultimate consumers in the choices that determine what they will read. Several key principles justify this aspect of the program. First, we want children to make choices which cause them to consider the suitability of printed materials to their needs. In that process they begin to form attitudes and values about books and reading that will be appropriate for them as adults. Second, we want children, particularly those who have become disenchanted with reading, to begin to see themselves as readers, as discriminating users of printed materials. And, third, in the process of choosing what they will read from thousands of available titles, children make a commitment to reading itself as a satisfaction of their personal needs.

One teacher, in taking children on book-buying field trips, has fourth grade children choose books for absent members of the class. They may choose Wolfe's *Jokes and Riddles* for Sammy whom they know personally to be a prankster, or one of the *Madeline* books for Sally Ann. For still another classmate they might take *Colonial Life in America,* or *This Is Washington, D. C.* Almost more important than the books the children choose, is this excellent teaching practice that causes them to consider carefully the mesh of personal need, personality, and books available. Another teacher on such a field trip has each child choose three books, then decide which one she wants most. Having taken *The Pushcart War, About the B'nai Bagels,* and *Are You There, God? It's Me, Margaret* down from the shelves, they must decide which they want most. These acts of conscious choice-making can often bring even diffident children to care about books and printed materials.

Still another compelling reason for involving children in selection of reading materials is that non-children do not know enough. As adults we cannot depend upon ourselves to anticipate what children will like. We can make some generalized guesses about types and fields of interest, but the final decision must lie with the reader's peculiar interests and circumstances at the moment she chooses something to read.

Book Display

The Centers of Interest in your classroom are an excellent chance to sample books that students have chosen. At each of these centers you can have spinner racks displaying books related to that subject. These subject area books can also be used to teach reading. If you want to teach figurative language, what better way than through *The King Who Rained* or *Amelia Bedelia*. You can teach both science and alphabet recognition with *ABC Science Experiments*. *The Enchantress from the Stars* can be used to teach the social studies and reading comprehension skills of "ordering events" as well as "the use of details to make conclusions" at the same time that students are having a great science fiction read.

In the primary classroom where books are often outsized, ordinary spinner racks can be used if the alternate metal rods are removed and the central core is cut down to the eye level of primary grade youngsters. We know a teacher who found a stationery-card store going out of business. Display cases for greeting cards are ideal for displaying outsized books. One can imagine almost limitless possibilities made from cardboard. Another teacher has constructed cardboard castles whose battlements hold books. A third has created a magical Alice in Wonderland rabbit hole, providing an intimate inner space for book selection. In yet another classroom, a mysterious grotto contains mystery stories. In these special places, book selection itself becomes an enchantment.

Young readers should be enticed with the contents of books. Objects in the classroom such as bits of fur, feathers from a variety of birds, and collections of rocks that provide children with direct experiences should be supplemented with books that provide further information. The collections of feathers and rocks might be near *What Is A Bird, Birds,* and *Rocks and Minerals.* Such arrangements provide resources of information at the moment that childrens' curiosity may be highest.

All classrooms should include the daily experience for children of being read to. The continuing story in the classroom becomes a special time whose pleasantness can carry over into the students' independent reading. Once having heard the story, large numbers of elementary school children will want to read the book for themselves. They will look forward each day to the new chapter or episodes of *The Borrowers*, adventures stemming from *The Little House on the Prairie*, and, more recently, the saga of *Watership Down.* It does not matter that the teacher does not have a professionally trained voice. The power of the literature itself affects children as they listen. And there is also a special "affect" for the teacher whose class demands that the *teacher* read (for the third time) that exciting moment as the scorpion climbs down the cord to wound Coyotito in Steinbeck's *The Pearl.* Just this year we saw again the power of that experience: It was a few minutes before the final bell. Both class and teacher unsuccessfully fought back tears as the teacher read the last pages of *Julie and the Wolves.* Thirty-eight slum children filed slowly out of the room, unashamedly red-eyed as they shuffled down the hall to the waiting school buses. One lone Chicano stopped by the desk to ask, *"Por favor,* Mr. Martin. Can we read that book again? Tomorrow?" Few pleasures in a teacher's professional life can surpass this.

To entice young people to read independently, the teacher must read. Teachers and students together must make exciting discoveries in the classroom collection. It counts for much when a teacher, walking about the room, has good things to say about the selections that children have made. One child praises and defends his book (*Goldilocks and the Three Bears*) simply because he likes bears: "And the most horrible thing in the WHOLE world was when she ate *all* the porridge and *broke* the chair." As the teacher circulates among the young readers, a cunning bit of salesmanship can be introduced. As important as the supportive comments about books the children have chosen, is the prepared but informal booktalk offered each day in the classroom. The reluctant, the timid, the child who never reads—all can thus be introduced to exciting reading. Voracious readers who read narrowly, glutting themselves on a single kind of fare, can be led to widen and deepen their tastes.

Though the daily booktalk requires only a minimum of planning, it does not just happen. A few principles carefully applied can assure successful salesmanship in presenting a new book. First, announce the book as a new discovery and show a shiny, new copy of it if possible. Established readers and book-people will seek a book unseen or enjoy a battered, well-worn copy, but children universally want to see the book and prefer clean, new editions. Then, tell some of the story, but not all of it. Tell some of the mystery or danger, show a good illustration, but withhold some, too, for the sake of those who would find out which of the three princes is able to slay the dragon to win the princess. Choose a few paragraphs or passages to read aloud for flavor or to lead into the plot, but read only enough to entice your audience.

Booktalks can do double duty, too. On one hand, books can be presented for sheer delight. On the other, books can also be chosen to introduce or reinforce specific reading objectives. (This technique will be demonstrated in Appendix A.) The following examples of booktalks are chosen from books young readers find delightful, but which can also be used to develop specific reading skills.

Primary Grades

Books:
and/or

Beady Bear, Don Freeman
Corduroy, Don Freeman

Reading Objective: Sequence of Events

Precis: Fantasy adventures of a young man and his mechanical Teddy Bear. Using these warm stories, a teacher could illustrate figurative language or differentiation between fact and fiction. Or these books can be used to elicit discussion of love and what it means to be wanted. For a wide range of readers, both books could be supplemented by the teacher's reading of *Velveteen Rabbit*.

1. Show the book and ask, "Who likes stories about bears?"; "Who remembers Goldilocks?"; "Has anyone read *Corduroy*?"; "Does anyone know about mechanical toys?"

Beady Bear is the story of a fuzzy toy bear who belonged to a boy named Thayer (show picture). They play together (show pictures) until Thayer goes away. Left alone, what happens to Beady? Of course he becomes curious, then finds out that he is a bear and that bears live in caves. Beady sets out to find a cave where he can live as other bears do. In the cave, he can not sleep. Why do you think he can not sleep?

(reading) "And yet it's awfully dark and stilly here inside! And a wee bit chilly, really!"

Now who would like to read more about Beady and Thayer?

Intermediate Grades

Books: *Season of Ponies*, Zilpha Keatley Snyder
and   *Black and Blue Magic*, Zilpha Keatley Snyder

Reading Objective: Figurative Language

Precis: These are fantasy adventures of intermediate age children who discover a special kind of magic that enables them to escape the ordinary in their lives. Two books are chosen since *Season of Ponies* has greater appeal for girls because of its heroine; *Black and Blue Magic* is more likely to appeal to boys.

With these adventures one might teach recognition of the absurd, memory for details, or affective responses to imagination and the need for adventure and special events in life.

1. Show the book and ask, "Who believes that magic *is* possible?"; "Can we always explain everything that happens to us?"; "Do some of us ever have special powers?"

Season of Ponies is the story of a girl left alone for the summer with two maiden aunts. She has no friends or companions until a mysterious young man and a herd of magical ponies come to her in the night. We are never entirely sure that the young man, the ponies, or the adventures they share are real. One of the fine things about this book is the descriptive language it uses. Listen to these paragraphs: (It is easy to choose examples which promote interest in the story and demonstrate the use of figurative language.)

Now, who would like to read more about Pamela and Pony boy and their adventures during that mysterious summer?

The salesmanship of enticing young people to books extends beyond the pleasure of booktalks and being read to. Classroom displays created by teachers must be frequently changed. And just as one does not tell all the story in a booktalk, one should withhold enough new books so that unfamiliar titles can appear in the collection throughout the semester. We have had success with using the formula of three books for each child, but we begin with only half that many and then allow five or ten new titles to appear each month. Children look forward to this new stock. On the mornings when the teacher appears carrying a box from the trunk of her car, children come from all parts of the playground to follow her so that they may be the first to know about the new books. The promise of new books to appear on the rack will be a constant enticement, a treat that will send them back to the book racks again and again for another look in order to select just the right one to read.

In this country, where reading improvement is most often said to be the number one goal of the schools, the great poverty of books in classrooms is a special sadness. Children who would read are deprived of reading substance. In a field potentially so fertile, many patterns of cultivation are popular. In Hooked on Books classrooms, some teachers never let books leave the room, while others practice one-day or weekend lending. In our schools, where a single teacher may be the only one using the Hooked on Books approach, we invariably find children from other classrooms standing at the doors, greedily eyeing the collection their classroom does not afford. Even though the book collection is large enough for only one class, few of our teachers can resist occasionally sharing with youngsters from other classrooms.

Another problem almost universally faced is the slow return of a book that is making the rounds of an entire family. In order to assure that the classroom library will be large enough to serve their students, many teachers have regularized brief circulation-return patterns.

Who, after all, can insist upon a weekend interruption of the final chapters of *(George)*? Or who would delay the suspense between Commander Feric and Elana in *The Far Side of Evil*? And who can be adamant to the student who cannot return a book because "My mother's reading it now and after her my sister wants it." When we learn that the parents of recently migrated Maria Ching are slowly, laboriously, carefully, profitably making their way through the *Story About Ping*, we can only wonder at this rich country which is so poor that it does not afford the school-wide saturation of inexpensive paperback books.

Chapter VII

SECONDARY SCHOOLS

Tom Finn

Two Departments

Only a very few fortunate secondary schools have adopted the Hooked on Books program on a school-wide basis. For the great majority of schools, use of the program is as varied as the needs of students. Different subject areas and departments combine to follow the program with all of their students or with selected classes. Some English departments modify the program for one or more grade levels or limit it to their general students. Although DIFFUSION of responsibility for teaching literacy is a basic principle of *English in Every Classroom,* the program and its advocates also recognize that students can be reached without commitment of the entire teaching faculty.

The Naked Children, the book which tells the story of the program in Washington's Garnett-Patterson Junior High School, vividly describes how difficult it is, even under fairly good conditions, to move an entire faculty to one course of action. In a junior high school I regularly visit, English and Social Studies teachers, aware of this difficulty and knowing their own students' need for immediate action, decided four years ago to join forces in an attempt to fight the battle for literacy. Multi-cultural and often bilingual students in this school shared as their most common bond a defiance of attempts to make them literate. The majority had been in the school district since kindergarten; their reading test scores were low when they entered junior high school and would be low when they left. Though the faculty knew that their students had been taught the elements—the pieces—of reading for seven years before they came to the junior high, they also knew (from test scores as well as from their own direct experience) that these students couldn't or wouldn't read. Maybe it was time for their kids to experience the *why* of reading. Hooked on Books was the approach that the teachers wanted to try.

From a faculty of 70, eight teachers and two department heads chose to try *together* to change the predictably anti-literate future of two hundred entering seventh grade students. Ten faculty members plotted to capture the initial enthusiasm of two hundred youngsters on the first day they entered junior high school and to keep that enthusiasm high for three years. Late in the preceding spring, after intense planning sessions, the group took its ideas to the principal. They knew what little hope of success they had without his administrative support. As weary of low reading scores as his faculty, he was willing to listen to almost any proposal. What he heard sounded possible, and he agreed to support it for a year's trial. During the summer, principal and faculty *together* spent six weeks developing their ideas and finding funds to provide for paperbacks, magazines, newspapers, and field trips. Squeezing his small budget heroically, the principal put everything he could into the experiment.

The eight teachers, four from English and four from Social Studies, paired by choice into four teams of two. Each teacher would teach four periods of seventh graders. In order to give added strength to the experiment, the principal squeezed his class schedules as hard as he had his budget, and found enough teaching time to allow the eight teachers two preparation periods instead of one—the second to be devoted to team planning. In fact, teachers used this time primarily to evaluate the progress of each of their students. Two teams exchanged students first and second periods and fourth and fifth periods, while the other teams shared the same students during the school day but not in so immediate a fashion.

When school opened in September, seventh graders entered English and Social Studies classrooms that were different. Walls were covered with posters calling for young readers to choose this book or that. Newspapers were piled in the front of the room, a spinner rack of paperbacks was nearby, and magazines, face up, lay on open shelves under the windows. According to the students, even the teachers in their English and Social Studies classes seemed different. How? Well, for instance, they seemed happy as they encouraged students to explore the room and its contents. And they had rearranged desks and chairs out of rows and into U-shaped groups or semicircles or around large tables.

In each English class students were given a spiral-bound notebook to write in. They were told that this journal was theirs, that it was to be written in daily, and that they could write in it anything they wanted to write. In the Social Studies class, they were asked to write about human events taking place within the school or without. As a first assignment in English, they each made a collage of clippings from old magazines and newspapers that reflected their interests and identified them as individuals. The results were images of larger-than-life athletes, pop singers, bike riders, pet lovers, movie goers, TV watchers, jokers, and even readers. After much discussion and comparison, students hung their collages from the ceiling and pinned them on the walls, letting everyone know who occupied those rooms.

Social Studies classes began by using the newspaper as a point of departure for studies in American history. In each class a great deal of time was given to individual reading of magazines and newspapers. By observing and conferring with each student, teachers determined their approximate reading level and their specific interests. Different teams decided on different plans. Two teams decided to have group activities three days a week and individual instruction for the remaining two days. Another plan allowed students to pursue individual interests for two or three weeks and then to join in a group activity for an equal length of time, always allowing at least one day a week for student-selected reading.

No, it wasn't the easiest of teaching semesters for those eight teachers. Each teacher took a great deal of time to assess student strengths and weaknesses; none found it invariably easy to work so closely with one colleague as well as to attend in-service sessions with six others. Fellow faculty criticized the "Hooked on Books group" for their togetherness and their separateness, parents asked about the absence of traditional textbooks, and some students wanted to know when they were going to have spelling and grammar tests or have a quiz on names and dates in history? Team members supported each other through this difficult time, while weekly meetings of the entire group with department heads helped to bolster the teachers' feeling that what they were doing was taken seriously and supported fully by the school's administration. Best of all, attendance remained high as students continued to be curious about their new teachers and new surroundings. Books, magazines, and newspapers were being read at an extraordinary pace, provoking the librarian's joyful complaint about all those seventh graders using up the library.

Other teachers began to comment on how this seventh grade class was different—they wrote and they used books. It was hard to believe, but they actually seemed almost *comfortable* with literacy. As their apparent comfort grew, their teachers were being asked by colleagues to explain what was going on in the Hooked on Books classes. Parents commented on how much time their children were *willingly* giving to reading. By Christmas, the teachers were convinced that things really were different. During the autumn, field trips had been taken to public libraries, book stores, and wholesale book outlets so that students could select books for their classroom libraries. Together with teaching strategies and materials, teachers shared popular titles with other teachers. Kids told teachers that they liked reading, they really did. And perhaps most gratifying of all, journal entries became longer and much more interesting to read.

At the end of the term, Hooked on Books teachers evaluated their efforts by selection of writing samples from students, observation of reading habits, and collection of attitude surveys indicating how students felt about themselves as readers, writers, and students. So positive were these final evaluations that everyone involved was convinced the program should be continued. It was clear to all that the outgoing seventh graders were better equipped than ever before to handle the regular school program in the eighth and ninth grades. Because of the quality of the evaluation, some teachers at the upper grade levels looked more closely at their own teaching methods and decided to try some of that "Hooked on Books stuff."

The original seventh grade group has graduated from junior high and gone on to high school, and the fourth group of seventh graders is now following a program similar to the original one. Though book titles and reading interests are somewhat changed, teachers have come and gone, and the administration has changed, those involved are convinced that the seventh grade experience is a turning point for their non-readers and non-writers. The cost of the program is far less than many others the city supports. And it is composed solely of teachers who *volunteer* to work in it, an understanding administration which *financially supports* it, and continuing *in-service education* (in the form of team meetings and entire group seminars) which refreshes and renews its participants.

Going It Alone

Those eight teachers had a lot going for them, but what happens when one teacher in a building has no support from the administration, the department, or even other teachers? Can that teacher embark alone on a book-oriented program? Yes, and there are perils, but all good teaching has risks worth taking.

Consider this example: Byron, a recent graduate from a local teacher training program, was hired in a suburban intermediate school because he had an interest in teaching reading and had taken some course work in reading while completing his English major and teaching credential. The reading test scores of the children from this middle-class white suburb had fallen far enough for the school district to decide that it needed a "reading person." While student teaching, Byron had given considerable attention to the non-readers, turned-off readers, and "general" students who would be his primary clientele in his new job. In June he knew his school assignment, visited the site, met the principal, and was shown his classroom. He checked out the textbook supply and school library, and found he would have five English classes of eighth graders. He attended summer school and participated in a two-day reading workshop exploring a Hooked on Books approach. As summer vacation came to an end and teacher planning days took place, Byron decided on appropriate sets of anthologies and awaited his first classes.

After the third week of school, a depressed Byron came back to the campus to talk about his teaching. Only a month before he had been excited about the prospect of having his own students in his own classroom. Now, though he liked his students and found them to be good people, he could find nothing that interested them. There was no life in his classes. He had tried all the best selections in the anthologies; nothing happened. His best lesson plans from student teaching days didn't work. Suggestions from other department members were of little help. Worse yet, most of them confided that, "These kids are just like that—nothing will turn them on to English."

Seeking a way to help him, I asked about his students' interests. His dejected reply was that he really didn't know because he couldn't find out. Maybe, he said, they didn't have any. Nothing I said or asked seemed to help. Though he said, at the end, that our conversation had been useful to him, I doubted it, for I had been able to offer nothing immediate or concrete. As he was leaving, we walked together past a box of examination copies of young adult novels in paperback that I had recently read. Unwilling to have him leave with nothing, I said, "Here. Take these. Give them a try." He took the box.

Several weeks later Byron phoned me to ask if I could

come to observe his teaching. It was a simple request with no mention of what was happening. We found an agreeable date, and on that day I drove to a new school which had clusters of buildings containing two or three classrooms and one small administration/library building. Byron's classroom, in the building furthest from the principal's office, was a pleasant room with movable chairs, attention-getting bulletin boards; and about twenty-five kids sitting in groups while reading paperbacks and magazines. Not a head turned as I entered the room. Byron left a student he had been talking to and came to greet me. His smile kept getting wider and wider as he gestured around the classroom at his preoccupied students. His happiness was contagious. I couldn't stop smiling either.

Three girls were in a group reading *The Pigman*; four boys on pillows were in a corner, and each had a copy of *On Two Wheels*. Another boy was reading a magazine, *Road and Track*, while a girl was lost in *Gone with the Wind*. Byron left me to discuss *The Chocolate War* with two students who had a question. *Every student in the room was immersed in a book or magazine*. The period ended but the students were slow to depart, reluctant to leave their reading. Before the room was empty of one class, the next was already entering. Chairs were moved, new clusters formed, and each student took a folder from a file; inside the folders were loose papers, each dated. Students quickly settled in their chosen seats and most had begun to write even before the second bell rang. "I couldn't get any bound writing journals," Byron explained. "So they write on loose paper that's dated and placed in their individual folders."

After five or ten minutes, students began putting away folders and producing paperbacks from pockets, purses, and book bags. A few went to make new selections from a table in the rear of the room covered with paperbacks and magazines. There was a low buzz of conversation that seemed to disturb no one. Byron was available to everyone, chatting easily with groups and individuals. At times students would come to him with comments or questions. One boy asked for a pass to go to the library; he wanted a book that the room collection didn't have.

Byron's free period came quickly. I was amazed at the discrepancy between what he'd described and what I'd seen, and I told him so. "It was that box of books you gave me," he said. "You told me to give them a try and I did. Then my whole Hooked on Books summer workshop came together for me, and you can see what's happened. I can't get them out of books and magazines."

With Byron's help I kept myself informed about his first year of teaching. He taught all of his classes by using journals, paperbacks, magazines, and newspapers. At times, for a week or longer, he would engage the entire group in a single title or theme that they had all decided upon. They read plays together, and wrote and read poetry as a group, but Byron thought the greatest successes were with the individual books that students had selected.

Except for class sets of books and the school library's titles, no financial support came from the school. The box of books Byron carried from my office was his original library. He added to it initially by selecting a large number of individual titles from the school library and textbook room. Then he scoured his personal library for appropriate paperbacks and brought them into the classroom. Used-book shops, thrift shops, and garage sales were other rewarding and inexpensive sources. Where else could he buy ten books for a dollar? He also located an excellent paperback distributor who liked what he heard about Byron's classroom and gave generous discounts, even on very small purchases. Students began bringing in favorite paperbacks; others asked to visit the paperback distributor to make their own purchases, or they placed orders with their teacher for specific titles or types of books. And the book collection grew.

The nearest metropolitan area's largest newspaper had the policy of providing class sets of day-old newspapers to schools that asked for them. Byron took advantage of this service because he knew that few of his students read the paper at home. Even a day-old edition was fresh to them. Magazines originally came from Byron's basement and the basement of friends. Like the newspapers, their age did not discourage his students. In fact, age was often the reason for their popularity. One particularly popular stack of magazines had many copies of *Life* dating from the late fifties. Students could hardly believe that their parents came from a world as bizarre in costume and custom as the pictures revealed. Other teachers, friends, and students themselves replenished the magazine collection.

Byron kept up a fresh and endless conversation with his classes—as a whole, in small groups, as individuals—about what was in the books, magazines, and newspapers that they were reading. When new books entered the class library, he would briefly describe each one, give some information about the author, read a short selection, and point out where possible its connection with a currently popular movie or TV program. Articles in newspapers were brought to the attention of students with special interests in those topics. On Tuesdays, the Monday newspaper sports page that summarized the weekend's events was always a favorite among both boys and girls. Most important, with the great variety of available materials, every day there was always something for everybody. Nobody ever had to feel left out.

Other students began to visit Byron's classroom before school, on the way to their classes, at lunch time, and after school. They had heard so much talk about his classroom collection that they wanted to check it out for themselves. Before school began, at lunch, and after school, clusters of students sat reading and browsing in Byron's room. When the sunny California skies turned to showers, students from many classes came to ask if they could eat their lunches and read in his room which had come to be known throughout the school as "the reading place." By the time parents' night came around, Byron was not surprised when many students brought their parents to see his room. He was even ready for their repeated statement and question: "My child has never read so much in his life. How do you do it?" His only reply was to point to the magazines, newspapers, and paperback books that filled his classroom.

The principal and many teachers in the school had been initially skeptical of Byron's program, but their skepticism diminished as they saw eager learners who wrote and read with increasing ease. Parents gave their support to the teacher who was bringing pleasure in literacy to their children. Most important, students were full of praise for the program even as their lives were full of reading. They and Byron had made the same discovery—one teacher *can* make a difference.

Epilogue: Crossing the Line

In the spring of 1975, the San Francisco Unified School District had a teachers' strike. This was about a year after many teachers had experienced "Hooked on Books" in-service courses and had built-up extensive classroom libraries. A teachers' strike can be a traumatic experience for all involved, especially for young, non-tenured teachers. Two young, untenured high school teachers had decided that they must honor the picket line in spite of the very real threat of losing their jobs. But on the first day of picketing, a rainy and miserable day, the two women approached the picket captain at their high school that normally housed over two thousand students and asked permission to cross the line. After much discussion they were allowed to enter the building and to remain for no more than half an hour.

The line that was honored by hundreds of students and most teachers was opened only enough for the two raincoated, wet-haired women to slip quickly through. About twenty-five minutes later they reappeared followed by eight students, each laden with two large boxes. The picket lines opened again and the ten walked together to the two teachers' cars where back doors and trunks were opened and the bulging boxes loaded inside the vehicles. Though they were being handled with exceptional care, one large box dropped to the sidewalk and paperback books spilled onto the wet concrete.

The picket line actually stopped for a long moment as teachers and students alike realized that these two teachers, in the midst of professional and personal turmoil, had refused to risk their Hooked-on-Books library. As they said later, they didn't know who would be using their classrooms and what care would be given to the books their students had so carefully selected and meant to read. They knew those books were worth crossing the line for, and so did the picket captain.

Chapter VIII

ADMINISTERING THE PROGRAM

James Duggins

This story begins at the annual convention of the International Reading Association. We had pulled away from fiery Board of Education budget sessions. The city's program of reading instruction seems always under attack. As in so many other areas, our district faced overwhelming reading problems. Reading achievement scores continued to plummet despite supplementary funds and immense investments of energy. Nothing seemed to give positive results. At the IRA convention we told our troubles to friendly members of the Children's Book Council. Even after adjourning to the bar, the more we talked about reading problems in our schools, the less possible of solution they seemed. In desperation, moved perhaps by the conjunction of our problems with members of the Book Council, we made the radical decision to try something different, something innovative, something seldom attempted in reading programs: We decided to try BOOKS.

Outlined here is what we did and what happened when we made books the basic medium for reading instruction in those first 140 classes. We hope that what we learned from 140 classrooms will help others to profit from our successes, to avoid our errors, and to help themselves. If we learned nothing else, at least we learned this: That attractive books can be a remedy for unwilling literacy. Their power to illuminate the lives of children and adults is a miracle for a disbelieving world.

"My students' first reaction was one of disbelief. They couldn't accept the fact that the Board of Education was going to provide them with the kind of book that they would buy for themselves! They found it even more difficult to believe that they could actually select the books for this library. This was unheard of!"

"When I found out I could get paperback books for school, I asked my class to help select the books. I cannot express the change in my classroom after I received the first order of paperbacks. Most of the children seem to enjoy reading for pleasure, but new interest really seemed to grow."

"Many of the books selected were in the school library and were books the children liked. They really were overwhelmed with the idea that the books they like would be in the classroom all the time, and they could read them when they wanted."

"After I received the second group of books, I assigned a student who cannot read to act as the class librarian. It was amazing to see how he arranged the books and could tell when books were not there."

A Checklist of Considerations

Our 140 miracles did not rise unaided in the eastern sky. We had read about others who had tried similar programs and we wanted to avoid their disappointments. In our design for success we tried to guard against the failure that grows out of administrative unreadiness. Therefore, though beginning with children and books, we proceeded to give careful consideration to five more elements in our design:

1. The Teachers
2. The Budget
3. The Suppliers
4. The In-Service Program
5. Evaluation

1. The Teachers

Today, as never before, teachers are aware that the success of their teaching often depends upon their involvement in selecting programs and materials they use in their classrooms. This is as true of the selection of the most attractive books as it is of the rejection of the dreariest workbook materials. As an administrator beginning such a program, you should begin only with teachers who want to be involved. Before you begin, call for teacher-volunteers to help plan the structure of the program and the in-service learning. When you have profited from their preparation, ask for volunteers among teachers who want to use paperback books in their classrooms. Nothing will so effectively doom the idea at its birth as teachers who are arbitrarily enlisted in the project.

Before our project began, we decided how many classrooms we could coordinate and then accepted volunteer teachers on a first-come, first-served basis. We felt we could reasonably begin with 140 classrooms, 70 in elementary schools and 70 in junior-senior high schools. Such a group of teachers, we knew, would be widely scattered in their expectations and experience about reading and books, as well as in their information about how to order and obtain materials. To bridge the distances between them, we required that all teachers in the program attend after-school, in-service meetings once a week.

We printed the first notice of our plans in the Superintendent's Bulletin; the response was enormous. Teachers poured into the program like ants into a honey jar.

'Hooked on Books' In-Service Stresses Reading

All District teachers, librarians, and administrators, regardless of grade level or subject field, who are interested in learning more about individualizing reading with motivational materials, are invited to attend a new in-service program, "Hooked on Books."

Sponsored by the District's Reading Office, the program strives to develop approaches which make reading instruction more exciting for the reluctant reader.

Because of the different management requirement of an individualized program utilizing a broad range of materials and the added competence teachers must have with reading diagnosis, prescription, and evaluation, this in-service opportunity has been created. It is designed to help participants learn the principles and practices of such individualization.

In addition to classroom methods, major Bay Area resources for such programs will be reviewed. The course staff, Roy Minkler, Mrs. Fannie Preston, and Dr. James Duggins, will be supplemented by Bay Area librarians, publishers, children's authors, and resource personnel.

Those who are interested will begin "to tool up" in January so classroom programs can be started in the spring.

The course will offer one unit of in-service credit for developing skills in diagnosis, prescription, book selection, and evaluation of individualized reading programs.

Meeting times and places will be established when it is known how many teachers would like to take part in the program.

All interested individuals are asked to call the Reading Office, 863-4680, Ext. 408, and leave their names and schools.

Our teachers came from every kind of school and every academic discipline. It was humbling to see them come, for their numbers and speed of response made clear to us that teachers know best how badly they suffer from the eroding malnutrition caused by lack of books. They came hungrily from schools on the rich side of town as well as from schools on the poor side. They came from schools (with lavish federal programs) which did not buy books as well as from schools (with no special support) which cannot buy books. They came from special service schools for delinquent youths, drop outs, and pregnant girls. One was from a hospital school with acute surgery cases: "Paperbacks are easy to hold while reading in bed." We accepted them from PE and IA, from English and Social Studies, from primary and intermediate grades. Five librarians came, agreeing to the stipulation that they must work closely with a teacher for this project. We had math and music teachers, shop teachers, and even ROTC. After all, we were told, reading must be taught in *every* class.

Who was it who said that no administrators are really effective, that they invariably stumble up some Peter-principle ladder? That person was wrong. In our program one could know the administrator by the responses of his or her teachers. Some schools had many teachers represented; others produced only one, or none. Soon we knew the philosophy, the children, the operation of the school, and even the building by the teachers represented in our program. We soon *knew* the outstanding principals of buildings we had never entered.

Those were our 140. A heterogeneous group to be sure. Seventy of them met on Wednesday (35 elementary; 35 secondary) at a northtown school from four to six p.m. The other 70 met on Thursday at a southtown school. Our program could accommodate them for location, north or south, as well as for their free evening. Our job was to teach them how, to demonstrate, to encourage, but always to accommodate.

Accommodate them we did, though we failed in some of our best efforts. For instance, we could never seem to help in ROTC. The failure was ours, resulting neither from want of books nor want of possibilities. Nothing worked. On the other hand, some of our accommodations were (modestly speaking) brilliant. In several schools we established spinner racks of paperbacks in the locker rooms of boys' and girls' gymnasiums. After all, every student takes PE every day; what better chance to assure that they see books all about them?

2. The Budget

We want everyone to know that the Individualized Reading Program of Hooked on Books is the cheapest game in town. During these days of financial gloom and doom, we want everyone to know that this program can be done for less per pupil-cost than anything now in the schools. Our program *cost less than a hundred dollars per classroom* while another district reading program, very popular with a trim-and-squeeze board member, cost as much as $4,000 per classroom. Before *Hooked on Books*, we were presented a program of packaged materials that would cost $7,500 to set up a laboratory for 150 students in a senior high school with nearly 1,500 illiterate young people in need of special help. We could hardly bear to think of what we might do for those students with $7,500 worth of paperbacks. Again and again our economic advantage took on a stark clarity when compared with other programs.

Paperback books in the classroom are probably the least expensive teaching material you can buy. Most classrooms can be stocked for less than $3 per student. If your school now has few or no classroom libraries, you should plan for three to five books multiplied by the number of children in the classroom. With school discounts, books will average 90¢. Later, when you have a classroom library established, you can manage with a budgeted dollar and a half per student to buy replenishment stock and the new books children are eager to read. Although books for primary grade children are less expensive, they require more frequent replenishment because they are more perishable.

As the program progresses, other book sources free to the schools begin to replace classroom dependence. One of the miracles of the program is the large number of children who have never read but who now go voluntarily either to the public library to select more good books or to a local bookstore to buy them.

The voices of these young people clearly demonstrate that transition and change:

> "I think this program benefits me because I usually do not have enough time to go to the library to borrow a book, while I could borrow one right from English without wasting any of my lunchtime, and usually I see more books that I like from the ones in English rather than the ones in the library."

> "The book program benefits me because it gives me a wider range of books to choose from. I can get books free from my father's store but those books are mostly love stories and movies. I read a lot in my spare time, but I choose books very carefully."

> "What I like the most are mysteries. Because I really like to figure out myself (plot). Well anyway it makes me feel confident and I can talk better without being nervous or anything like that. I guess I talk better by getting things from books or ideas I don't know but I feel like I'm a little ahead of everyone else when I'm reading 'cuz I get new information. I guess I do feel a little smarter too. And now I go to the library for more books like I started reading here."

> "Even my boyfriend who didn't even want to talk about reading after he saw me so interested in books and I told him how interesting they were; he started to read and now he reads more than I do; he buys books which he never done before; its really a miracle if I think about how he used to hate books."

3. The Suppliers

You will probably want to use more than a single source for purchasing books, for one supplier will seldom have all the titles you want. Therefore, when you introduce the resolution for your project to the Board of Education, you must be sure to specify "multiple vendors" so that you have the flexibility to buy from several sources. It is important, too, that you meet with these companies to plan together before you begin the program. The variety of book supply houses we found helpful were: a) jobbers and wholesalers, b) publishers, c) bookstores. Each of these distinct operations offers a resource you can rely on.

a. Jobbers and Wholesalers

Jobbers and wholesalers keep in stock thousands of paperback books, but they may not carry large quantities of children's books if your community has not asked for them before. When you meet with representatives of jobbers and wholesalers, discuss your plans, the magnitude of the project, and the age levels of the students. If you can, give them an idea of the publishers whose books you believe you will want. This forewarning allows them time to negotiate contracts and acquire stock from publishers whose books they do not now handle.

Another purpose of this meeting will be to investigate the possibility of a showroom or exhibit area where teachers may bring students to select books. The jobber or wholesaler often operates from a working warehouse employing trucks and pallets of encased books moved about by forklifts. Without preparation, such an environment is simply too dangerous for school children. We discovered the wholesalers who were eager to help, who were willing to open after school and on Saturdays so that our teachers could bring their classes to select books when warehousemen were not working.

The amount of discount you receive will vary, but most jobbers will grant the greatest discount for books that teachers and children choose directly from the shelves and take with them as they leave. Our teachers and children wheeled grocery market baskets among the aisles of the jobber's stock. When their selections were complete, the books were packaged and the packing slip/invoices signed at the door. A great deal of valuable time is saved in this way. You and your teachers are not forced to do the endless listing of titles you want and the jobber can afford a generous discount for the time saved picking single-title orders. Our evidence is that such an arrangement can be good for everybody!

"My class had our complete set of books almost immediately. Not because I was smart; simply because I was lucky. I had by chance chosen to take my students directly to the jobber to select our books and bring them home. My students had a great time pulling the books from the shelves and exploring the maze of paperbacks. . . . (Six kids accompanied me to the jobber. They had received suggested book titles from their fellow students and were responsible to them for their selections.)"

You must also be sure that the school district accounting office is prepared to accept abbreviated invoices for quantities of books (e.g. 15 paperbacks @ 45¢; 12 paperback books @ 70¢) rather than asking for listings of individual titles. This needs to be negotiated within your district before you begin submitting invoices.

Seen from the single perspective of efficiency, trips to book resource centers will be another of the miracles of your program. Teachers and students will be elevated into a state of ecstasy by the act of choosing from so many books, especially from books that they can take home that very day! No one has to wait while books they're anxious to read are listed, requisitioned, ordered, received, processed, stamped, and delivered to individual schools. That new book is in your classroom the next day.

b. Publishers

Some materials may not be in stock locally, but must be ordered directly from the publisher by using a catalog. Public and school librarians can be of great help in choosing books and advising you about processing your orders. They may be able to help you find a publisher's nearest warehouse or a wholesaler who carries a complete line. Publishers' representatives will be helpful in advising you about time of delivery. A general rule of thumb is that a minimum of 30 days must be allowed for receipt of such orders. The best advice that we can give from our experience is to depend most heavily upon books your teachers and students can see and handle, books that they can get NOW.

In case of orders that you must place directly with publishers, indicate on each order that you will not accept back orders. Back orders may take months to receive. The delay is usually too long for the original motivation that inspired the book's choice to survive in a child's mind. In addition, keeping track of your budget becomes a nightmare when you have dozens or hundreds of single copy backorders waiting with publishers. Publishers' representatives will be helpful in announcing new titles and trends, tracing orders, and determining reliable shipping dates. They will be helpful, also, in securing quantities of the extraordinary teaching materials produced by publishers—such as lesson plans, wall charts, posters, bibliographies of special interest collections, reviews of new books for young readers, and many other materials to make the teaching of tradebooks more attractive. And you can take advantage of them in your in-service course as well.

c. Bookstores

You will also want to use local children's bookstores, if you are fortunate enough to have one, or the rare general bookstore that has a good children's section. Since one of the major tasks in getting started will be to get books into the classroom as quickly as possible, these stores can offer an excellent opportunity for you to stock up and give your classes the experience of seeing books well displayed. Your school discount may not be as large, but stores with the books you want in stock offer a fine "fail-safe" system to insure that you can get books into the classroom while teacher and student enthusiasm is high.

4. *The In-Service Program*

The literature of school reading programs is packed with case histories of good programs that have floundered for lack of continuing direction. The book-oriented reading program is a radical change for many teachers. Even teachers who are themselves avid readers and devoted to books in the classroom, may feel insecure when they find themselves alone in a room with 30 children and 90 different books. Necessary to almost every teacher is a staff development program designed to alleviate anxieties about "What do I do now that I have all these books?"; "How do I group them?"; "How do I organize for instruction?"; "I know the kids are reading, but are they improving?" Answers to all of these questions must be offered and demonstrated, taught and exchanged during in-service meetings.

Still more positive benefits from in-service meetings come when they provide the opportunity for teachers to share their experiences, to exchange new or favored titles, and to brag a little about the miracles in their classrooms.

a. Book Selection

Teachers are not trained in book selection and will need help from the very beginning. Using multiple titles in every class involves decisions of readability, format, and legibility as well as investigations of student motivation and interest. Generally teachers will not know the vast number of publishers producing juvenile books. They will not know the resources available to aid them in choosing books to fit the special needs of each child and each classroom. Often they have had no opportunity to host local authors, illustrators, or storytellers in their classrooms. Publishers' representatives, school and public librarians, specialists in children's literature, knowledgeable book suppliers—all are happy to assist with demonstrations and presentations. They will themselves introduce new books, present films to accompany books and arrange for authors and illustrators to visit your classrooms. You can hold your in-service meetings in the stores and offices of these book people so that teachers can become familiar with their employees and procedures as well as their stock and services.

b. Introduction of Skills and Activities

After the first books are in classrooms and students are reading, teachers naturally want to know how to encourage the growth of reading skills. In this, you will find at least two distinct groups of teachers in your program. One group will know much about reading instruction, will have taken formal courses in reading, and can immediately begin considering the added dimensions introduced by the new variety of materials. Still another group will need some basic instruction in the processes of reading.

Our experience suggests, too, the need for separate staff development programs for elementary and secondary teachers. This seems largely dictated by the differing concerns of self-contained and subject-oriented classrooms, though the books they use are far more overlapping than many school people suspect. Grouping within the in-service program should include special attention to grade levels taught and previous preparation of teachers for teaching reading. Your own staff or outside consultants can be used to guide teachers in diagnosis, prescription, and the introduction of skills to students using many different books.

5. *Evaluation*

As we look back to the past year in planning for the next, we realize how broad a spectrum of success and failure we have known. It's clear to us that our greatest need in this program is for better techniques of staff development. Though our project accommodates 140 classes, it includes less than two percent of the total number of classrooms in our district. When six or eight teachers from a single junior high school volunteer (three such schools), we have seen them produce almost revolutionary excitement about books and reading in their schools. By contrast, the lone teacher from a school seems so isolated and vulnerable that we spend much of our time searching for ways to support him or her.

The most observable changes among both students and teachers were attitudinal. Students became and remained enormously enthusiastic about having paperback books in their classrooms. Our greatest pleasure, however, was in seeing the same enthusiasm among teachers. Teachers who had become cynical after years of attempting to control and teach children whose values were in conflict with their own, children who could not or would not read, now were teachers who came to school anticipating the pleasure of settled classes that were manageable because they looked forward to reading. These are the same teachers who report that the ripoff rate is lowering and damage to books lessening. Now, they say, their students care about books as once they never did. They offer the example of ungraded classes (Grades 10–12) in which juniors and seniors lead new sophomores through Hooked on Books classroom protocol. That is very heavy evidence indeed.

Our in-service program needs improvement. There is so much to be learned about book selection and suppliers that we have not yet had time enough fully to incorporate the teaching of skills into the paperback program. Next year we will offer an advanced in-service class for teachers who have mastered the selection/supply process, but who want more help with teaching the skills of reading.

Chapter IX

SCHOOL AND PUBLIC LIBRARIES

Tom Finn

The School Library—Ten Years Later

Many school libraries now have a look that invites those of us who worked reluctantly in them in 1966 to enter them with joy in 1976. Yes, there are spinner racks of brightly covered paperbacks; and even hardcover books are no longer spines staring at us, for their attractive jackets have been put under plastic and placed flat on the shelf to beckon readers. Posters like those that announce rock concerts or popular movies hang from the walls, extolling paperbacks. Spinners, visible jackets, posters—all provide evidence that school librarians are concerned about kids who don't come to the library and are attempting to lure them into discovering the pleasures of books.

Now that federal and local school library funds have diminished or disappeared, some librarians who were previously buckram-bound are finding paperbacks attractive because of their great advantages of cost. Even for those to whom permanency is irresistible, the midway point of the Perma Bound book, a reinforced paperback, is always available. No matter what the inclinations or budget of the librarian, no school library need ever be unattractive again.

Eight-thirty in the morning. Enter the inner-city junior high school library and see the large red and white sign above the male librarian which reads NO SILENCE. The room is full of all sorts of seventh, eighth, and ninth graders, and very few are not reading—the morning paper's sports page, a wide variety of magazines, paperbacks, hardbacks, and a few textbooks. The sign's surprise is greater than its impact. What little conversation there is does not seem to bother those readers intently involved in *The Pigman, Ebony, TV Guide, The Friends, Muhammad Ali,* or *Mad Magazine.* A small cluster stands by the librarian, inquiring about books in their areas of special interest. Spend fifteen minutes in this warm room and recall other less friendly libraries and less happy library experiences. The change from 1966 to 1976 has been very great indeed.

Students check out books and leave for classes at 8:45. The librarian finishes last-minute check outs, assigns two student assistants their morning duties, then turns to greet me as a familiar visitor. We talk about books currently popular among his students and I am amazed at the breadth of their interests—fiction and nonfiction relating to movies or TV, bodybuilding, hobbies, sports, biography, and a host of other topics. He works as we talk because he's got so much to do. "At nine o'clock I'm giving book talks in a ninth grade social studies class. See the shopping basket over there? It's full of paperbacks dealing with the idea of survival. The teacher wants her students to examine some of man's basic needs and she thinks the best way to do it is to have each student read a book on the subject. I've included *The Diary of Anne Frank, Alive, Manchild in the Promised Land, Earth Abides,* and many more. I'll try to talk just enough about each book to arouse their interests. If I do my job right, I should return here with an empty shopping basket."

As he added more books to his basket, he told me that a seventh grade English class was going to come to the library during second period for its weekly visit. "There're some really poor readers in that group," he said, "but we recently bought a large number of paperbacks especially for them. The books are behind the counter, and I'll put them on spinner racks before they come in. No matter how often I see it happen, I'm still a little surprised at the power of a good book cover to attract our poor readers."

This librarian and the English teachers in his school have arranged their schedules so that every English class visits at least once a week for "free reading." That's when they browse through newspapers, magazines, paperbound books, the general collection—the only requirement upon them being that they *don't* do homework and *don't* bring in a textbook. According to the librarian, lots of kids go systematically through big picture books like *The Best of Life, Pumping Iron*, and illustrated art books, as well as animal and nature books. More interesting, I thought, were his observations about the use his clientele makes of the library's extensive collection of stories recorded on tape:

"I often see our best readers listening to a tape while reading along, and it's amazing how many poor readers will check out a book after they've listened to it on tape. They all just like to be read to. Several teachers make a habit of taking a small group of kids to the rear tables and reading whatever they've requested. The funny thing about that is, it's often an article from a magazine or from the newspaper and they can easily read it for themselves, but they like to listen to the teacher. In fact, they like it so much that we've begun a tape collection of all kinds of readings by teachers and even some by students. They're every bit as popular as the commercial tapes, and a lot less expensive."

"What about teachers in other subject areas—do they use the library?"

"Sure do. It's like a contagious disease once you've got carriers like our English teachers and their classes. For instance, the physical education teachers have been a big help in telling us what sports the students are most interested in so that we can order heavily in those areas. One book that's always in somebody's hands is *Rules of the Game*. Fantastic! It's got rules for every sport there is. Before that, the *Guinness Book of World Records* was so popular that we finally had to place one in each English class library."

He told me that Social Studies classes visit his library about twice a month, and not only to use reference materials. "We've got so many good paperbacks," he said, "that teachers have students reading as many individual titles as possible. It's a two-way relationship, because Social Studies teachers know and recommend a lot of good supplementary titles for our collection. And homemaking students give our magazines on fashion, cooking, and home decoration a real workout because the teachers use them and refer to them so often in class. We also get a big play from industrial arts students who want to read magazines dealing with mechanics, architecture, and home repair. Some of them are pretty expensive for one person to buy, but they can go through a lot of hands in our library."

Our conversation took place in pieces throughout the morning as my librarian friend divided his time and attention between classroom book talks, visiting classes in his library, the normal survival duties of a librarian, and speaking to me. After two teachers on their break together had borrowed four books and left, he told me that one of the changes brought by the Hooked on Books program was in the number of teachers who now used the library for their own recreational reading. "It's great to see one of the coaches in here during his conference period browsing or reading. Their presence can really do something for a kid who thinks books are nowhere. I've had students ask me what book a particular teacher is reading and then check it out themselves."

At the end of the morning I asked him what accounted for such strong student patronage in the school library when every English classroom had its own collection?

"In this school, books seem to beget books. What I mean is, the more books they have, the more books our kids want. It's books that teach them to like to read, and then they can't get enough. For instance, I've got a situation I never had to deal with before. Some of the ninth graders are coming in and asking for 'real books.' They say that paperbacks are OK, but they want to carry around some 'real books' so that everybody will know they're reading. If I don't have the book here, they go to the public library for it. I have to remind myself that those are the same kids who came here three years ago and didn't want anything to do with reading, books, or the library."

A few mornings later, in a different school in San Francisco, I entered the library and sat close to the check-out desk, where a bulletin board displayed some student-written book recommendations I wanted to read. Being an eavesdropper by nature, I listened to the librarian's conversations with the various students who approached her for help and information. Fifteen minutes after I began to read and listen, I realized I had heard six different girls ask for the same book. In this school, *different* was *very different* because the kids came from such a broad spectrum of White, Black, Asian, and Chicano families. Not only were their differences racial and ethnic, but they ranged between a pre-pubescent seventh grader and a remarkably mature ninth grader. What in this world, or in any other, could have caused all six to ask for *Jane Eyre*?

Knowing all the English teachers in the school, I knew that none had assigned that title. Why then were the last three of the six girls so obviously disappointed when they discovered that the library's three copies had already been checked out? No, they told the librarian, they didn't want to go to the public library to get a copy, but they sure did want to see that book. Could they put their names on a list or something? This librarian did, responding with a pleased but perplexed smile as one declared that she was going to come back "two times every day" until she got that book!

Being not only an eavesdropper but a questioner of strangers, I waited until the three disappointed girls had left and then went to sit beside one of the two girls who was reading her copy of *Jane Eyre* in the library. When I asked her why she'd chosen that particular book, she detached herself from it just long enough to ask in an irritated tone, "Didn't *you* watch television last night?"

Indeed I had, but not *Jane Eyre*. I retreated, feeling culturally impoverished, and sought the preceding day's paper. Between four and six p.m., the magnificent Orson Welles and Joan Fontaine version of *Jane Eyre* had been offered by one of our educational stations and I had missed it, but *not* six girls from this ghetto school.

How had they known that the movie was based on a novel? A friend who had seen it reminded me that the opening scenes of the movie reproduce the first pages of the novel as they are read aloud. What he did not have to tell me or the school librarian was that the visual images of television and movie screens can be a first rate come-on for the pleasures of the printed page.

Libraries, students, and experiences like these become the rule rather than the exception as more and more school librarians open up their libraries to make them accessible for pleasure and profit to all students in the school. Recently a large high school was built in the southern part of San Francisco; principal and teachers were extensively consulted by the architect on its layout, which became basically a large open space with "learning areas" along the walls that took the place of classrooms. Much debate took place about where the library should be located—some wanted it housed in a separate building, for it didn't seem to fit into the spacious feeling that the open design created. Instead of opting for isolation, however, the faculty made the brilliant decision to have their library and media center at the focus of the interior. Consequently, it was built in the middle of the building, opening on all sides to the learning centers. In so doing, it provided a perfect embodiment of the Hooked on Books philosophy: The school library should be the central focus of every school.

The Public Library—Hang Around the Library Forever and They Don't Notice You

Schools open in the morning, close near sundown, and are locked Saturdays, Sundays, holidays, and summers. When schools are closed, what happens to students who have been turned on to reading? If they are lucky enough to be of elementary school age and attainment, then they will be welcomed and their habit supplied in one of our oldest public institutions, the public library. Traditionally, public library services for children (from preschoolers to twelve years old) have been excellent. Libraries large and small have children's sections and personnel trained to work in them. Story hours, movies, dial-a-story, puppet shows, and other activities are regularly scheduled. A vital part of any good school reading program is teaching children how to make use of public libraries. Visits to the school by librarians and field trips to libraries by students are an essential interchange in the process of creating lifelong readers who know how to utilize community resources.

Good children's librarians are aware of the vast number of excellent books which appeal to their clients. As librarians, they have been trained in book selection, and their acquisition budgets provide for children's programs. Unfortunately, teenagers and young adults often do not fare as well. At the age of twelve or thirteen they have outgrown children's chairs and tables and often children's books. Though there is a growing concern among librarians for the young adult, the holdings of many libraries still reflect a minimal understanding of adolescents' interests and tastes. Faced with a collection that leaps from children's to adult literature, the competent thirteen-year-old reader may actually profit from the initial difficulty of choice. But for the poorer reader, less certain of self and therefore much less adventurous in literature, the sheer numbers of volumes and the complicated cataloging may turn him away from his only free, out-of-school resource.

Fortunately there is a vigorous movement among young adult librarians to serve their clients better. Carol Starr, a leader in this movement, publishes the *Young Adult Alternative Newsletter*, an underground librarian's journal, and reports promising practices across the country. Working relationships between secondary schools and public libraries are being cultivated. For example, in Westchester County, New York, under the influence and guidance of an energetic Young Adult Coordinator, Mary Kay Chelton, the county public librarians are in secondary classrooms. At White Plains, Pat Thorsen says, "Well, I did it! After all the excuses... I've talked to nine classes and all were great. Their response was marvelous. It's great to see the kids in the library that afternoon looking for the books I talked about."

Yonkers has a minimobile librarian who spends two days a week giving booktalks in the schools.

Librarian Nancy Rolnick of Croton reports that she has "launched on the booktalk circuit at our junior high, having talked to two eighth grades and with invitations to do more. The kids took all but three of the books and I needed multiple copies for some of them. But the best response was from kids coming into the library—boys, in fact. One told me that it was a nice speech I made in his English class and asked for a mystery. Another lit up and said, 'You were in our school yesterday.' It seems as though you can hang around the library forever and they don't notice you, but once you go to visit them, you're a friend." Once the barriers between school and public libraries are broken, new library use develops in both directions. According to Joan Grott of Tarrytown, "If you want kids in your library—give booktalks."

Public librarians are also encouraging students to become published book critics. One- or two-paragraph reviews by students carry much more weight with their peers than reviews written by adults. In a similar practice, summer reading lists solicited by librarians from students, printed by the library and distributed to all students in the public schools, keep kids reading during summer vacation.

In Philadelphia, the Free Library cooperates with schools by giving special lecture tours and programs at the Central Library, and some of the alternative schools conduct classes there. Branch libraries also provide tours for students and present film programs for young adults. The Free Library cooperates with the Youth Study Center, a detention facility, and each youngster is given a paperback book. Teenagers on probation are counseled in film and book-oriented sessions cooperatively organized by the librarians with probation officers. Such out-reach programs are made possible through a Young Adult Specialist/Community Service Librarian.

Other bridges between schools and public libraries can be built. Jon Ballard of the Orlando Public Library, Florida, and the library's young adult staff host a breakfast each year for the local school librarians. At this informal affair Ballard hopes to "dispel the myth that there is an air of friction between public school librarians." The Orlando staff gave booktalks in schools to over 5,400 young adults in 1975. This type of service and cooperation should be at the heart of every public school library program.

The Prince Georges County Memorial Library, Maryland, makes an all-out effort to serve its school population. An incomplete listing of their program topics indicates the varied interests of today's young readers: Babysitting Workshops, Grooming, Make-up, Macramé, Sandpainting, Terrariums, String Art, Job Exploration Fair, Job Trends, Sex Roles, Rock Concerts, Folk Jams, Occult/Parapsychology, Photo Contests, Poetry, Sports, Sharks, Socio-dramas, Motorcycles, Book Discussions, and a film series. Programs are book-related by printing reading lists on the back of colorful flyers announcing the events.

The Los Angeles Public Library System made a survey to determine who its clients were in four neighborhoods—one Black, one Mexican-American, and two White middle class. The survey revealed that the dominant users in all four cases were juveniles and teenage students. From 65% to 75% of all L.A. library patrons are the youth of the communities. The Young Adult Coordinator has emphasized a collection of high interest/easy reading books, and has carefully cultivated good relations with elementary and secondary schools. Branch open houses for teachers are held, and the school system conducts in-service credit courses taught by public and school librarians on how teachers can effectively use the libraries.

Another example of city departments coordinating their efforts to promote youthful literacy is cooperation between the School Superintendent, the District Attorney, and the City Librarian in San Francisco. Under the mayor's guidance, the library and school system joined forces to help students develop basic reading skills by emphasizing better utilization of school and public libraries. Realizing that many consumer frauds are brought about by illiteracy, the District Attorney has added his support. Plans include literacy centers, located in public libraries and in schools, where both youths and adults can be tutored in reading as consumer complaint. With public funds in short supply throughout the country, this model of cooperation by several public agencies under one roof may prove to be as beneficial to municipalities as it is to their individual citizens.

Chapter X

BOOKS THAT ARE WORTH IT

James Duggins and Tom Finn

Pleasure and Self-Discovery

A revolution has taken place during the past ten years among authors as well as publishers of books for children and young adults. Nat Hentoff's *Jazz Country* appeared in paperback in 1966; along with it and following it came a stream of *different* young adult and children's novels—novels by serious authors attempting honestly to describe the world in which young people live. In their books for young readers, this new group of authors and their publishers defied the previous taboos of no four-letter words, no drugs, no sex, and no unhappy endings. Their primary concern was with the often turbulent, confusing, awesome, and always real world of their readers:

John Donovan, in *I'll Get There. It Better Be Worth the Trip*, writes with powerful realism of a boy named David who faces the death of his grandmother and his own subsequent adjustment to a new life style with his alcoholic, divorced mother in Manhattan. David's encounters in a new school and apartment life, his experience of parental conflicts and emerging sexuality are all shared in a believable way with the reader. *The Soul Brothers and Sister Lou*, by Kristin Hunter, looks at the hopes, fears, and successes of urban Black youth. *The One Dollar Man* and

Mom, the Wolfman, and Me share the concerns of youth being raised by single parents. For even younger readers, *Velveteen Rabbit* and *Whose Mouse Are You?* express in quite different ways the need to love and be loved. *The One Hundred Dresses* and *What Mary Jo Shared* show the sadness of poverty in the search for peer approval. As the list of titles and authors concerned with youth increases with the printing of each new publisher's catalogue, so does both the breadth and quality of the offerings.

Many books from this new wave of publishing have met with problems of acceptance by teachers, librarians, and parents. *Go Ask Alice*, a book about a young girl's destruction through drugs, had especially stormy times in many American communities. The "community," a force often invoked by book-burners but seldom defined, decided this book should be removed from many schools and libraries. In a town in the Northern San Francisco Bay Area, the Furies of Purification vented themselves at school board meetings while junior high students, including those possessing every degree of literacy, checked out all copies at local public libraries. Student demand was so high that local vendors couldn't keep the book in stock. Meanwhile, adults wrangled for weeks, then decided students who had written permission from their parents could borrow the book from their school library. As is so often the case with censorship, the community had waited too long to speak. Every child who was interested in the book had already read it, and no note-carrying borrowers were to be found.

We who witnessed the event could not help but wonder what a considerable list of banned books might do for the literacy of our school community. But banning books is an act that places schools in the untenable position of occupying a "school world" not only different from but opposed to the "real world." *Helter Skelter* becomes the most viewed weekly TV program, but the book can't be placed in the schools. Students can't avoid the graphically described "X"-rated movies in local newspapers, but discussion of this portion of the real world is inappropriate for purified classrooms. Even magazines, newspapers, and paperback books that are readily available throughout the

226

community, that attract readers at supermarkets, drugstores, and public libraries, are not allowed to enter the classroom. Almost as if by design, many schools still make the act of reading so unrelated to life that students who can find little profit in the classroom are also those who can find little reason to read.

Reading is, after all, a very personal act that requires very personal motivation. A reader's choice may be influenced by what friends are reading, by television and movie viewing, or by happenstance. But always that choice, where successful, is based upon a sense of self-value and self-definition that is heightened by each reading experience. One seventh grader writes:

> It's been a long time since I've had a favorite kind of book, but I used to read a lot of science fiction. I think it's sort of neat to read a book about an almost completely different civilization. *RUMBLE FISH* isn't science fiction, it's almost the opposite, but its characters act differently and think differently than people I know. The story is told by a boy named Rusty-James—he's about 14 and in a gang called the Packers. The book centers around a war between him and Biff, the leader of another gang. Rusty-James' older brother, Motorcycle Boy, is another important character—he's almost like a god to the other boys.... I was sort of surprised to find out S.E. Hinton is a woman. All the characters are boys—they act like boys, and girls don't take much part.

However, another student in the same class closed the same book after the third page, saying, "I don't like fish stories!" Both responses are easily admissible in a school or classroom full of alternate choices that encourage and attract students to find their own level of understanding. *Watership Down* is a rabbit story for some readers, a social commentary for others.

As adults and teachers we too often presume to know what is and should be of interest to our students. Perhaps the most useful thing we can know is the fact of change itself.

The realistic books of the past decade may fall out of favor with many readers of the next ten years. Phyllis Anderson Wood, a remedial reading teacher and author of successful young adult novels, has an interesting view of her audience's tastes:

> For the past five years I've been watching enormous changes come over the young, and it seems to me that many writers have been mis-reading the cues. While young adult novels have been becoming what adults call increasingly "realistic"—embodying more and more cynicism, disenchantment, sexual permissiveness, and antagonism toward adults—the young have been moving in the opposite direction.
>
> This demands of the author a kind of new old-fashioned book, or an old-fashioned new book. Anyone writing this kind of book to please these new readers, however, must face one predictable problem. Reviewers who are not really close to the young and haven't sensed this new trend will write these books off as "naive, overly sentimental, and wholesome." This is a moment of truth when the author has to decide if he's writing for the reviewers or the young readers.
>
> Personally, I'll choose the youngsters and take my chances with the reviewers. It's well worth the risk when some student closes one of my books with a satisfied air and announces, "That's the first book I ever read all the way through . . . have you got any more like it?"

Just as some of the books on adult best-seller lists are of poor quality, so are some of these books of new realism for young people. But the quality of even the poorest is less important than the remarkable change these books as a group have accomplished. Students who were reading nothing from the schoolroom and the school library are now asking for everything written by their favorite authors or for books about their current interests. This new audience has been neither numbered nor especially noted, but it is increasing and demands attention. These books speak loudly and persuasively to their audience, often creating a desire to read where little or none existed before. Until the reading appetite has been aroused, teachers and librarians are always at the near edge of defeat. Once that remarkable event has occurred, we must be thoroughly familiar with what the marketplace offers in order to provide further nourishment.

Many of the books that lure our reluctant readers come from authors writing for adults. Here again much has happened since the mid-60's. Then, for example, such books as Maya Angelou's *I Know Why the Caged Bird Sings* and *Gather Together in My Name* had yet to hit the paperback racks. Neither had the Houstons' *A Farewell to Manzanar*, nor Ernest J. Gaines' *The Autobiography of Miss Jane Pittman* nor Richard Vasquez's *Chicano*. And still limited to hardcover publication or no publication at all were vast numbers of titles in fiction and non-fiction dealing with Native American, Asian American, Chicano, Latino, and other ethnic groups full of youngsters anxious to read about themselves. Now, where there is a lack of titles for particular ethnic groups in schools, the fault more often lies in the work of the selector than in the availability of authors and titles.

Prominent, too, among the events of the past ten years is the steady movement of the paperback press toward serving elementary school children. Often imitative of the paperback revolution for older folk, producers of these works for young readers made some of the same mistakes and happy discoveries. Even now far from firm conclusions, the experiment continues as publishers learn to use book covers, size, and format to appeal to young readers.

Imitative of events in the adult world, the nature of content in the children's press also continues to change. The symbolic fantasy and fairyland of old favorites like *Hansel and Gretel, The Three Bears,* and *Three Billy Goats Gruff,* are supplemented with the more direct messages of *In the Night Kitchen, A Doll for William,* and *Charlie and the Chocolate Factory.* Older readers may still find adventure and excitement in *A Date for Diana, Hot Rod,* and *Deputy from Furnace Creek,* but often these titles gather dust on the shelves as students read *Your Bird Is Here, Tom Thompson, On Two Wheels,* and *Millie's Boy.*

As in an earlier era for adults and young adults,

paperbacks for young readers now most often must first prove themselves in clothbound editions. Paperback books still sit at the back of the bus, in the rear of publishers' catalogues. Sales of hardback editions to libraries and to adults as birthday presents continue to dictate what is available for children of elementary school age. Publishers, booksellers, and schools are just beginning to realize the massive potential of the young people's market for paperbacks. We see the foreshadowing of a new decade of experimentation in the publication of paperback supplements to standard school fare and in the materials for teachers produced by mass market publishers. As we learn to use the medium, we can expect more and more paperback originals, best seller sensations for young people, and the deliberate, commercial preparation of young appetites for new paperback releases.

If students are to have the largest possible selection, teachers and librarians must keep up with publications in hardback for adults, young adults, and children. At the same time, they must bring pressure upon publishers for simultaneous printings of cloth and paperback editions. S.E. Hinton's newest book, *Rumble Fish*, was released in hardback with a 1976 copyright; given normal publishing procedures, the paperback will be released approximately one year later. Rather than merely await the paperback, wise teachers and librarians will share a hardbound copy with as many students as possible in order to whet their appetites and to estimate probable demand for the paperback.

Many avid readers and perhaps even more reluctant readers find it very comfortable to stay with one author until all of that author's titles are consumed. Once readers have had success with one book by M.E. Kerr, Paul Zindel, Virginia Hamilton, or Richard Peck, they frequently decide to read all the author has written in spite of wide varience in topic and treatment. The reader who was enthralled by Alice Walker's short stories or novel is easily led into poetry upon finding the author's name on her collections of verse. Young readers who are hooked on Isaac Asimov as a science fiction writer pursue him through his many books of science nonfiction and thus become aware of reality that is as fantastic and fascinating as fiction.

Ten years ago one-eighth of the *Hooked on Books* booklist was devoted to science fiction. At that time Dan Fader reported that:

Of 125 titles describable as science fiction, approximately 100 are divided into two almost equal parts. One part is the work of eleven highly regarded practitioners of the craft, while the other part (approximately fifty titles) is produced by two indefatigable writers. The group of eleven ranges through such modern masters as Asimov, Bradbury, Heinlein, Sturgeon and Leinster to Pohl, Simak, Knight and Leiber, back to nineteenth-century romantics like Jules Verne and H.G. Wells. The two most prolific S.F. authors, whose output nearly equals that of the other eleven, are Edgar Rice Burroughs and André Norton.

Who that knew them will ever forget *Tarzan of the Apes* or *Beasts of Tarzan*? But who remembers that Tarzan's creator was as comfortable on Mars and Venus as he was in the jungles of Africa? It comes as something of a surprise to discover that Burroughs devoted as many of his fifty-odd books to other worlds as he did to this one. Together, he and Miss Norton provide almost half a hundred titles for readers of science fiction in the rough. Their books are no less read in 1967 than they were in 1965. Rather, the change has come in the increasing number of readers attracted to the more polished S.F. novels, such as Asimov's *Currents of Space*, Bradbury's *Martian Chronicles* and *Illustrated Man*, and Heinlein's *Green Hills of Earth*. Are the boys (and girls) learning the *pas de deux?* Not exactly. But they are learning to appreciate its performance.

Today we have the *Star Trek* freaks, the *2001: Space Odyssey* fans, and science fiction devotees of every description. We could easily build our entire booklist on S. F., but we will include only a few remarkable titles because

231

science fiction reading lists are so readily available. If this field is not familiar to you, ask student S.F. fans for their favorite authors and titles. Their responses are a guarantee of books your students will read. And you may be surprised at the number of your female students who are steady re-run watchers of Captain James Kirk, Lieutenant Uhura, and the Star Ship *Enterprise*.

Tarzan of the Apes is alive and well under exotic, new paperback covers, and Edgar Rice Burroughs has his following in that camp as well as among S. F. fans. Tarzan's popularity is being shared by more apely creatures from Boullé's *Planet of the Apes*. If these creatures have captured your non-readers, many titles stemming from the TV series offer them a broad choice. Alfred Hitchcock, too, flourishes on TV screens, with a variety of offerings in paperback to satisfy all tastes. TV repeats keep James Bond a sure winner for adventure lovers, just as each repeat showing of *Born Free* brings a stream of students to the library for the book and its sequels.

Charles Schulz has celebrated twenty-five years with *Peanuts*, and Hank Ketcham's *Dennis the Menace* must be in middle age, but they are both fresh and attractive to some of the same students who today enjoy Trudeau's *Doonesbury* and Morrie Turner's *Wee Pals* in a variety of paperback forms and titles.

As well as limiting its science fiction titles, this list deliberately does not attempt to encompass the very popular how-to-do-it books. We believe that the teacher in direct contact with students' interests is better able to choose a macramé, skate board, funk clothing, or scuba diving book for the class library. Books of poetry and popular song lyrics are sure winners with reluctant readers, and publishers have provided a wealth of paperbacks in these areas. Again, in our view, students and teachers together are the ones to judge these individual titles. Few plays appear on the list for similar reasons, but teachers are strongly encouraged to include stage, movie, and TV drama.

In response to questions about the *one* book they would like to have in a class of reluctant readers, teachers mentioned the *Guinness Book of World Records* most frequently. A great variety of record, almanac, and trivia books invariably arouses student interest. From spelling through grooming to speaking—all types of self-improvement books are popular, and multitudes exist from which to choose. Word, mathematics, and science game books may also become favorites. Since 1966, many excellent books on sexuality and drug abuse have been written for children and young adults; we believe that teachers and students together can best determine which of these books are most appropriate. Finally, no one should find this list entirely acceptable, for no general list can apply in its entirety to particular individuals. To use this list as an order blank for students would be to mistreat its best intentions.

For those unable to experience hands-on book choice, here's how one teacher and her students became expert book selectors:

Publishers' catalogues usually make their way too quickly into the teacher's trash basket. Usually, but not always. In one eighth grade classroom I recently visited, students were avidly paging through catalogues during a Friday "book selection" period. The room held twenty different catalogues in quantities of five to ten each. Toni, the teacher, told me that she had recently been on a book selection committee for new library books, and she chose titles by paging through catalogues while sitting at her desk before class. One day she entered her room to find several students reading through the stack of paperback catalogues. "What are these?" they asked, and were surprised to learn that such things existed when she explained that she was using them to select paperbacks for the school library. "What books are you going to order?" they wanted to know. To the gathering class Toni pointed out the check marks and number of copies beside selected titles. As more students came in, more questions were asked and answered. By the time the class bell had rung, her students had made their wishes clear: They wanted to help her choose those books.

And help they did. Though she had only single copies of the catalogues, two, three, and four students chose one and made lists of the books they liked. Toni told the class how

233

much they could spend and explained discount facts. Students rank-ordered their choices, and each group presented its choices to the entire class, explaining why they chose this book or that book. Students were forced to defend a title or explain a choice. The entire process took several class periods, but in the end it was the students' selections that made their way to the library.

This experience has caused Toni to involve all of her classes in selecting books for her new classroom library. The enthusiasm of the students is great and rarely do they choose a title that goes unread. Knowing her book budget at the beginning of the semester, Toni fixes three buying periods so that fresh student-selected books can be added to the collection as the semester progresses.

At the end of last semester, one of her classes decided to write its own paperback catalogue. Each student chose favorite books and wrote captions which were meant to sell that book to a fellow student. These efforts were put on ditto with student art work and distributed to other eighth graders. Now all of Toni's classes want to get into the publishing game. And her students would no more throw away a good catalogue unread than they would a good book.

Readability

Many formulas claim to identify the reading difficulty or grade level of a book. Though most of these were originally intended for non-fiction, they have been adapted to fiction as well. There are also formulas to determine the interest levels of books. Many of the major publishers supply a code indication of readability and interest level for their children's and young adult books. Teachers and librarians not only need to be aware of these codes and use them where helpful, *but* they need also to beware of them. The ultimate turn-off for many reluctant readers occurs at the moment when they bring themselves to inquire about a title and the teacher or librarian responds, "I'm afraid that book may be too hard for you. Let me find you something at *your* reading level."

"Thank you, sir; thank you, ma'am; but how about letting me reach that decision for myself?" The resolution is clear: Let the reader determine whether the book is too difficult.

Jim, an adult volunteer tutor, prepares a library visit for Willie, his street-wise, inner-city, poor-reading, junior high student, by carefully assessing the paperbacks in the school library. He makes certain that the meaty, realistic, easy-reading titles are there. Jim and Willie visit the library, and Jim extolls the "relevant" books about life in the city. Willie browses through these with little interest; the well-meaning and eager tutor is at a loss as his tutee wanders away from the carefully pre-selected books. In a short while tough Willie returns with a book he has decided to read: *The Adventures of Robin Hood*, not a book on sex, drugs, or ghetto life, all of which he may feel he knows too much about. Jim now asks Willie what *he* wants to read.

Reading tests will tell us that Mary, thirteen, is a third grade reader, that Joe, sixteen, is a second-grade-three-months reader, and Bill, eleven, is a seventh grade reader. But has anyone ever really met a thirteen-year-old *second grade reader?* Should the teen-aged student who reads at that level be given second grade materials with second grade vocabulary, interest, and approaches? The question is as foolish as the teachers and librarians who persist in making that mistake.

We all know that peers have the greatest influence on the reading choices of students, but are we all aware that this influence is customarily more powerful upon less rather than more able readers? Whether motorcycles, exorcism, or sharks—competent and incompetent readers alike want to know and to read about the topics that currently preoccupy their friends. When considering what group or individual reading tests tell us about students, we must consider equally the individual and group interests of these students if we wish to spark their desire to read.

Bill, one of those thirteen-year-old second grade readers, deep into bikes, sports, TV, movies, and a dozen other teenage interests, enrolled in a special summer program for remedial readers working on second grade vocabulary. His parents were worried about his progress in school and at considerable expense and some sacrifice were sending him to a private clinic to improve his reading skills.

I spent a morning visiting the clinic and found much of what was going on very valuable for the kids involved. Bill caught my eye early in the visit because he was large for his age, was dressed in a makeshift baseball uniform, and wherever he went he carried an athletic bag with a bat thrusting out. I noticed the variety of skill-building exercises he engaged in—some programmed materials, word games, individual oral reading with an instructor, and a group exercise in language experience. All of these activities appeared worthwhile for Bill and were individually geared to improve his skills.

Half an hour before the end of the two-hour session, all organized activities were concluded. Materials were put away and the students moved into a separate area with a rug and large pillows on the floor, casual chairs, and bookcases full of books and magazines. Various students headed for different materials and locations. Bill sat in an easy chair, unzipped his athletic bag, and pulled out a worn paperback. Opening the book near the middle, he began to read. I watched him as the pages moved slowly and regularly. Despite surrounding motion and some noise, his eyes never left the pages. When the half-hour was done and it was time to leave, some readers departed hurriedly while others left more reluctantly. Still absorbed in his reading, Bill completed the page or paragraph, turned down the corner, closed the book, glanced at the cover, placed the book in his bag, and started for the door. Intrigued by this thirteen-year-old *second grade reader*, I crossed his path at the door and walked with him as I asked, "What are you reading?" *"Jaws,"* he replied. "Is it good?" "Yeah!" "But isn't it hard?" "Sure it's hard, but its worth it!" With that, I moved back into the classroom and he moved out into the world of thirteen year olds.

"Sure it's hard—but it's worth it!" Is that what makes the difference between school-selected reading materials and student-selected materials? *Jaws* was not easy for Bill, but it was *worth* the effort because he wanted to read it. To know

his reading test scores and grade placement may be information important to helping him gain skills. But to know that he can and will struggle successfully through a book he wants to read is information of far greater importance.

The following book list, product of "A Thousand Authors," ranges from primary through secondary grades and is grouped beneath these headings: Careers, Challenges, Differences, Family, Fantasy, Nature, Peers, and Sports. Just as the interests of students overlap in their lives, so do some of the titles extend beyond a single group. For example, *Julie of the Wolves* is significant to its readers for a variety of reasons— either as a story of survival, courage, and determination, or as a tale of different cultural customs set in a faraway place, or as an informative account of the ways of wolves, or all of these. We place the book under the heading "Challenges," knowing that students and teachers will relate it to other of our themes as well.

The books we have chosen are popular today. The interests of young readers have been our *major* criteria for book selection, *not* the books' suitability to teachers, administrators, or parents. Titles in each segment of the list are rank ordered from least to most difficult. The first listings are geared for kindergarten children, the middle for fifth and sixth graders, while the last listings in every section are meant for eleventh and twelfth grades. When a very prolific writer is cited, an asterisk has been placed after the name to indicate that many more books by that author are available.

Chapter XI

The Reading List: A Thousand Authors

James Duggins and Tom Finn

A. CAREERS

TITLE	AUTHOR	PUB.
Mommies at Work	Merriam, E.*	SBS
Busy Wheels	Lippman, P.	Rand
Changes, Changes	Hutchins, P.*	Cllr
Big Joe's Trailer Truck	Mathieu, J.	Rand
Busy Day Busy People	Gergely, T.	Rand
The Tool Box	Rockwell, A.	Cllr
The Day Daddy Stayed Home	Kessler, E. and L.	Dday
Friends Within the Gates	Grey, E.	Dell
The Plant Sitter	Graham, M. B.	SBS
Cap for Mary Ellis	Newell, H.	Berk
Second Year Nurse	McCulloch, M.	SBS
Wren	Killilea, M.	Dell
Three Strong Women	Stamm	Puff
Girls Can Be Anything	Klein, N.*	Dutt
Maria Tallchief	Tobias, T.	Crow
Dorothy Thompson: A Legend in Her Time	Sanders, M. K.	Avon
Captain of the Planter: The Story of Robert Smalls	Sterling, D.	Arch
Maria Tallchief: American Ballerina	DeLeeuw, A.	Dell
Cesar Chavez, Man of Courage	White, F. M.	Dell

238

Malcolm X	Adoff, A.*	Crow
Fannie Lou Hammer	Jordan, J.*	Crow
Gordon Parks	Danska, H.	Crow
The Day of the Cowboy	Ulyatl, K.*	Puff
The Mayo Brothers	Goodsell, J.	Crow
The Story of Thomas Alva Edison: Inventor	Conpere, M.	SBS
Digging into the Past	Kay, S.	Puff
Six Black Masters of American Art	Bearden, R. and Henderson, H.	Dday
Shirley Chisholm	Brownmiller, S.	Arch
America's First Trained Nurse: Linda Richards	Baker, R.	Arch
Sidney Poitier: The Long Journey	Ewers, C. H.	Sig
Margaret Sanger: Pioneer of Birth Control	Lader, L. and Meltzer, M.	Dell
My Shadow Ran Fast	Sands, B.	Sig
Bound for Glory	Guthrie, W.*	Sig
I'm Done Crying	Ferris, L.	Sig
To Be Young, Gifted and Black	Hansberry, L.*	Sig
Lives of Girls and Women	Munro, A.	Sig
The Making of Star Trek	Whitfield, S. D. and Roddenberry, G.	Bal
Probing the Unknown—The Life of Dr. Florence Sabin	Pehland, M. K.	Dell
The Senator from Maine — Margaret Chase Smith	Fleming, A.	Dell
Woman in the Year 2000	Tripp, M.	Dell
The Last Laugh	Berger, P.	Bal
Report from Engine Co. 82	Smith, D.	Pkt
Some are Born Great	St. John, A. R.*	Sig
Lady Sings the Blues	Holiday, B.	Avon
Make a Joyful Noise Unto the Lord	Jackson, M.	Dell
Carrying the Fire	Collins, M.	Bal
W. C. Handy, Father of the Blues	Handy, W. C.,* ed. Bontemps	Dell
Sea and Earth: The Life of Rachel Carson	Sterling, P.*	Dell
The Basic Book of Photography	Grimm, T.	Plume
The World of Mary Cassatt	McKown, R.	Dell
The Police	Leinwand, G.*	Pkt
Ida Tarbell: First of the Muckrakers	Fleming, A.	Dell

Max's Wonderful Delicatessen	Madison, W.	Dell
Bob Dylan	Scaduto, A.*	Sig
Rising Voices	Martinez, A.	Sig
The Gentle Tamers: Women of The Old West	Brown, D.*	Ban
Serpico	Maas, P.*	Ban
Choice of Weapons	Parks, G.*	Dell
All Creatures Great and Small	Herriot, J.	Ban
Ossie	Ledner, C.	Ban
Nothing By Chance	Bach, R.	Avon
Golda, The Life of Israel's Prime Minister	Mann, P.*	Pkt
Getting Yours, How to Make the System Work for the Working Woman	Pogrebin, L. C.	Avon
A Matter of Conviction	Hunter, E.	Avon
P.S. You're Not Listening	Craig, E.	Sig
Ladies and Gentlemen Lenny Bruce!	Goldman, A.	Bal
Clive, Inside the Record Business	Davis, C.	Bal
The Civil Service Examination Handbook	Krulik, S.*	Sig
Seven Long Times	Thomas, P.*	Ment
Getting Even	Allen, W.	Warn
Working: People Talk About What They Do All Day and How They Feel About What They Do	Terkel, S.	Avon
Jimmy the Greek, By Himself	Snyder, J.	PP
Gemini	Giovanni, N.	Peng

B. CHALLENGES

A Mouse to be Free	Warren, J.	Avon
Bedtime for Frances	Hoban, R.*	Harp
The Green Hornet Lunch Box	Gordon, S.	Sand
Look Out Mrs. Doodlepunk	Dodsworth, D*	SBS
Magic Michael	Slobodkin, L.	Cllr
The Three Robbers	Ungerer, T.*	Athen
Mostly Mary	Rae, G.	Avon
Henry the Explorer	Taylor, M.*	Athen
Pancakes, Pancakes	Carle, E.	Knopf

Barney's Adventure	Austin, M.	SBS
Obadiah the Bold	Turkle, B.	Puff
Song of the Swallows	Politi, L.*	Scrib
In the Forest	Ets, M. H.*	Puff
House on East 88th Street	Waber, B.*	Sand
Amelia Bedelia	Parish, P.	SBS
Curious George	Rey, H. A.*	Sand
Harry by the Sea	Zion, G.	Harp
Blueberries for Sal	McCloskey, R.*	Puff
Higher Than the Arrow	Van Der Veer, J.	Avon
Petunia	Duvoisin, R.*	Knopf
The Mysterious Prowler	Nixon, J. L.*	HBJ
The Courage of Sarah Noble	Dagliesh, A.*	Scrib
Who's Got the Apple	Loof, J.	Rand
Someone is Eating the Sun	Sonneburn, R. H.	Rand
Cockleburr Quarters	Baker, C.	Avon
What Do We Have for the Witnesses	Trudeau, J.	Holt
Giants Come in Different Sizes	Bradfield, J. R.*	RM
Rocket in my Pocket	Wiesnert and Withers*	SBS
Encyclopedia Brown Finds the Clues	Sobol, D.*	SBS
Madeline and the Gypsies	Bimelmans, L.*	Puff
The Cat's Stand Accused	Townsend, J. D.	Sand
Clifford Gets a Job	Bridwell, N.	SBS
Tony and Me	Slote, A.*	Avon
The Grizzley	Johnson, A. and E.*	Harp
Marta and the Nazis	Cavanah, F.	SBS
Zoe's Zodiac	Stephens, M. J.	Sand
Henry Huggins	Cleary, B.*	WM
Maggie Marmelstein for President	Shurmat, M. W.*	Harp
Five Caught in a Treacherous Plot	Blyton, E.*	Athen
River at Green Knowe	Boston, L. M.*	HBJ
Swiss Family Robinson	Wyss, J.	Dell
The Gammage Cup	Kindall, C.*	HBJ
The Marvelous Misadventures of Sebastian	Alexander, L.	Dutt
Harriet the Spy	Fitshugh, L.*	Dell
Mystery of the Angry Idol	Whitney, P. A.	Sig
A Room Made of Windows	Cameron, E.	Dell
Ghost in the Noonday Sun	Fleischam, S.	Dell
When Hitler Stole Pink Rabbit	Herr, J.	Dell
Deathman, Do Not Follow Me	Bennet, J.	SBS

When Lightning Strikes	Ellis, M.	SBS
The Great Brain	Fitzgerald, J. D.*	Dell
Two-Wheeled Thunder	Gault, W. C.	SBS
Grover	Cleaver, V. and B.	Sig
Sasha, My Friend	Corcoran, B.*	Athen
West from Home	McBride, R. L.	Harp
Julie of the Wolves	George, J. C.*	Harp
Freaky Friday	Rodgers, M.*	Harp
Mrs. Frisby and the Rats of Nimh	O'Brien, R.*	Athen
Nilda	Mohr, N.	Ban
Dominic	Steig, W.	Dell
Story of my Life	Keller, H.	Dell
Island of the Blue Dolphins	O'Dell, S.*	Dell
One to Grow On	Little, J.	Arch
The Call of the Wild/White Fang and Selected Stories	London, J.	Dell
Watership Down	Adams, R.	Avon
Mavericks	Schaefer, J.*	Dell
Admission to the Feast	Beckman, G.	Dell
Sink the Bismarck	Forester, C. S.*	Ban
UFO's Past, Present, and Future	Emenegger, R.	Bal
The Fool Killer	Eustis, H.	Dell
Flight from Riversedge	Simmons, M. K.	Dell
Death is a Noun	Langene, J.	Dell
Golden Girl	Francis, D. G.	SBS
The Frogmen	White, R.	Dell
Fair Day, and Another Step Begun	Lyle, K. L.	Dell
Forever Island	Smith, P. D.	Dell
The Long Black Coat	Bennett, J.	Dell
Dreamland Lake	Peck, R.*	Avon
The Slave Dancer	Fox, P.*	Dell
Survive the Savage Sea	Robertson, D.	Ban
The Cross and the Switchblade	Wilkenson, D. and Sherrill, J. and E.	Pyr
Me and Jim Luke	Branscum, R.	Avon
Jed McLane and the Stranger	Honig, D.	Dell
Fanny Kemble's America	Scott, J. A.	Dell
Queen of Populists—The Story of Mary Elizabeth Lease	Stiller, R.	Dell
Somebody's Angel Child: The Story of Bessie Smith	Moore, C.	Dell
Friedrich	Richter, H. P.*	Dell
True Grit	Portis, C.	Sig

Millie's Boy	Peck, R. N.*	Dell
Freedom Road	Fast, H.*	Ban
Johnny Tremain	Forbes, E.	Dell
Against a Crooked Sky	Lamb, E. and Stewart, D.	Ban
Hey, Big Spender	Bonham, F.*	Dell
Shark Attack	Baldridge, H. D.	Berk
The House of Dies Drear	Hamilton, V.*	Cllr
Not the Usual Kind of Girl	Tate, J.	SBS
Nightmare	Chilton, I. M.	SBS
Operation Neptune	Nicole, C.	Dell
The Barefoot Mailman	Pratt, T.	Sig
The Other Side of the Mountain	Valens, E. G.*	Warn
A Wild Thing	Renvoize, J.	Ban
Why Me: The Story of Jenny	Dizenzo, P.*	Avon
The Iceberg Hermit	Roth, A.	SBS
Transport 7-41-R	Degens, T.	Dell
A Horse Came Running	DeJong, M.	Cllr
Runaway's Diary	Harris, M.	Arch
Macho	Villasenor, E.	Ban
Fireweed	Walsh, J. P.	Avon
If You Could See What I Hear	Sullivan, T.	Sig
Christy	Marshall, C.	Avon
Guests in the Promised Land	Hunter, K.*	Avon
A Sound of Chariots	Hunter, M.	Avon
Dove	Graham, R. L.	Ban
The Ra Expeditions	Heyerdahl, T.*	Sig
Soul Catcher	Herbert, F.	Ban
Bonnie Jo, Go Home	Eyerly, J.*	Ban
Johnny Got His Gun	Trumbo, D.	Ban
Nobody Else Will Listen	Holmes, M.	Ban
In This Sign	Greenberg, J.	Avon
Dollmaker	Arnow, H.	Avon
Alive: The Story of the Andes Survivors	Read, P. P.	Avon
Sasquatch	Hunter, D. and Dahinden	Sig
The Little Girl Who Lives Down the Lane	Koenig, L.	Ban
Rites of Passage	Greenberg, J.	Avon
Fig Tree John	Corle, E.	Pkt
Ordeal by Hunger	Stewart, G. R.	Pkt
Can You Wait Till Friday? The Psychology of Hope	Olson, K.	Fawc
Staying Alive	Bailey, M and M.	Bal

The Andromeda Strain	Crichton, M.*	Dell
When all the Laughter Died in Sorrow	Rentzel, L.	Ban
The Poseidon Adventure	Gallico, P.*	Dell
The Mound Builders	Silverberg, R.	Bal
Sunshine	Klein, N.*	Avon
I Heard the Owl Call My Name	Craven, M.	Dell
I See by My Outfit	Beagle, P. S.*	Bal
Centennial	Michener, J. A.*	Fawc
I Never Promised You a Rose Garden	Green, H.	Sig
The Black Swan	Sabatini, R.*	Bal
Scarlet Plume	Manfred, F.	Sig
Black Sunday	Harris, T.	Ban
Jubilee	Walker, M.	Ban
Alexander Dolgun's Story: An American in the Gulag	Dolgun, with Watson	Bal
The Massacre at Fall Creek	West, J.*	Fawc
The Jacaranda Tree	Bates, H.	Peng
Hunters Point	Simms, G.	Peng

C. DIFFERENCES

Eagle Feather	Bulla, C. R.*	SBS
Jambo Means Hello	Feelings, T.*	Dial
Black is Beautiful	McGovern, A.*	SBS
The Color of Man	Cohen, R.*	Bant
Taro and the Bamboo Shoot	Matsuno, M.*	Pant
Jeanne-Marie Counts Her Sheep	Françoise*	Scrib
Angelo, The Naughty One	Garrett, H.	Puff
Amigo	Schweitzer, B. B.	Cllr
Mei Li	Handforth, T.	Dday
Crow Boy	Yashima, T.*	Puff
Moki	Penny, G. J.	Avon
Once Under the Cherry Blossom Tree	Say, A.	Dell
Little Pear	Lattimore, E. F.	HBJ
J.D.	Evans, M.	Avon
In My Mother's House	Clark, A. N.*	Puff
Arrow to the Sun	McDermott, G.	Puff

Nilda	Mohr, N.	Ban
Notes of a Processed Brother	Reeves, D.	Avon
Harold and Maude	Higgins, C.	Avon
Uncle Tom's Cabin	Stowe, H. B.	WSP
Tongue of Flame: The Life of Lydia Maria Child	Melitzer, M.	Dell
Talking to Myself	Bailey, P.*	Pkt
The Man Without a Face	Holland, I.*	Ban
Narrative of the Life of Frederic Douglass, Slave	Douglass, F.	Dday
Chicano Cruz	Cox, W. R.	Ban
All God's Danger: The Life of Nate Shaw	Rosengarten, T.	Avon
Go Ask Alice	Anonymous	Avon
Sarah T: Portrait of a Teen-Age Alcoholic	Wagner, R. S.	Bal
No Place for Love	Lingard, J.	SBS
Mighty Hard Road: Story of Cesar Chavez	Terzian, J. and Cramer, K.	Arch
Black Elk Speaks	Neihardt, J.	Pkt
Only Earth and Sky Last Forever	Benchley, N.*	Harp
Coming of Age in Mississippi	Moody, A.	Dell
Black Boy: A Record of Childhood and Youth	Wright, R.*	Harp
Long Journey Home: Stories From Black History	Lester, J.*	Dell
In the Trail of the Wind: American Indian Poems and Ritual Orations	Bierhorst, J.	Dell
Felisa Rincon deGautier: The Mayor of San Juan	Gruber, R.	Dell
Bury My Heart at Wounded Knee	Brown, D.*	Ban
Nigger	Gregory, D.*	Pkt
The American Poor	Liston, R. A.*	Dell
Liberation Now! Writings from The Women's Liberation Movement	————	Dell
The White Dawn: An Eskimo Saga	Houston, J.*	Sig
The Fourth World	Hamalian, L. and K.*	Dell
Harriet Tubman: Conductor on The Underground Railroad	Petry, A.*	Arch
Miriam	Sommerfelt, A.	SBS
The Man Who Killed Deer	Waters, F.*	Pkt
Ramona	Jackson, H. H.*	Avon

Dave's Song	McKay, R.*	Ban
The Learning Tree	Parks, G.*	Fawc
Farewell to Manzanar	Houston, J. W. and J. D.	Ban
Flowers for Algernon	Keyes, D.	Ban
A Hero Ain't Nothin' But a Sandwich.	Childress, A.*	Avon
The Autobiography of Miss Jane Pittman	Gaines, E. J.*	Ban
The Cool World	Miller, W.*	Fawc
Ethnic American Short Stories	Newman, K.	WSP
Black Like Me	Griffin, J.	Sig
Circle of Children	"McCracken," M.	Sig
Sticks and Stones	Hall, L.*	Dell
West Side Story	Shulman, I.	Pkt
Hot Land, Cold Season	Soto, P. J.*	Dell
Winter in the Blood	Welch, J.*	Ban
A Woman Named Solitude	Schwarz-Bart, A.	Ban
The Chicano, From Charicature To Self-Portrait	Simmen, E.*	Ment
Why Have the Birds Stopped Singing?	Sherbourne, Z.*	Dell
Book of the Hopi	Waters, F.*	Bal
Who Wants to Be Alone	Craig, J.*	SBS
Long and Happy Life	Price, R.*	Avon
Laughing Boy	LaFarge, O.*	Sig
Down These Mean Streets	Piri, T.	Sig
Ali and Nino	Said, K.	Pkt
Manchild in the Promised Land	Brown, C.	Sig
Are We There Yet	Breuls, D.	Avon
His Own Where	Jordon, J.	Dell
Trout Fishing in America	Brautigan, R.*	Dell
The Outnumbered	Brooks, C.*	Dell
Lisa, Bright and Dark	Neufeld, J.*	Sig
Rabbit Boss	Sanchez, T.	Bal
Thieves Like Us	Anderson, E.	Avon
Apprenticeship of Duddy Kravitz	Richler, M.	Bal
Hatter Fox	Harris, M.*	Ban
Mary Dove	Rushing, J. G.	Avon
The Car Thief	Weesner, T.	Dell
Sula	Morrison, T.	Ban
The Bell Jar	Plath, S.*	Ban
Nunago, Ten Years of Eskimo Life	Pryde, D.	Ban
The Female Imagination	Spacks, P. M.	Knopf

I Will Fight No More Forever: Chief Joseph and the Nez Perce War	Beal, M. D.	Bal
Charbonneau, Man of Two Dreams	Blevins, W.	Avon
Zen and the Art of Motorcycle Maintenance: An Inquiry into Values	Pirsig, R. M.	Ban
Anya	Schaeffer, S. F.	Avon
The Chosen Place, The Timeless People	Marshall, P.	Avon
Things Fall Apart	Achebe, C.*	Fawc
Man Alone: Alienation in Modern Society	Josephson, E. and M.	Dell
Loneliness of the Long Distance Runner	Sillitoe, A.*	Sig
The Chosen	Potok, C.*	Fawc
Helter Skelter	Bugliosi, V. and Gentry, C.	Ban
Hell's Angels	Thompson, H.	Bal
Flying	Millet, K.	Bal
One Flew Over the Cuckoo's Nest	Kesey, K.*	Sig
Listen to the Silence	Elliott, D. W.	Sig
Autobiography of a Schizophrenic Girl	Sechehaye, M.	Sig
My Sweet Charlie	Westheimer, D.*	Sig
King of the Gypsies	Maas, P.	Ban

D. FAMILY

Ask Mr. Bear	Flack, M.*	Cllr
Titch	Hutchins, P.*	Cllr
Whose Mouse Are You?	Kraus, R.*	Cllr
Cinderella	Perrault, N.	Scrib
A Bear Called Paddington	Bond, M.	Dell
Lazy Jack	Werth, K.	Puff
Sad Day, Glad Day	Thompson, V.	SBS
Top Cat	Shura, M.	SBS
The Turnip	Domanska, J.	Cllr
Grand Papa and Ellen Aroon	Monjo, F.	Dell
The Little Brute Family	Hoban, R.*	Cllr
Always Room For One More	Nicleodhas	Holt
Spectacles	Raskin, E.*	Athen

Dennis the Menace (series)	Ketcham, H.	Fawc
A Year in the Life of Rosie Bernard	Brenner, B.	Avon
Picture for Harold's Room	Johnson, C.	SBS
All of a Kind Family	Taylor, S.	Dell
Adopted Jane	Darringer, H.	HBJ
Pippi Longstocking (series)	Lindgren, A.	Puff
The Lone Hunt	Steele, W. O.	HBJ
. . . And Now Miguel	Krumgold, J.	Apol.
Charlotte's Web	White, E.	Harp
Little House on the Prairie	Wilder, L.*	Harp
Girl Named Sooner	Clauser	Avon
Changeling	Snyder, Z.*	Athen
By the Highway Home	Stolz, M.	Harp
The House Without a Christmas Tree	Rock, G.	Ban
Grandma Didn't Wave Back	Blue, R.	Dell
The Borrowers	Norton, M.	HBJ
J.T.	Wagner, J.	Dell
From the Mixed-Up Files of Mrs. Basil E. Frankswiler	Konigsburg,* E. L.	Dell
Canary Red	McKay, R.	SBS
Nobody's Family is Going to Change	Fitzhugh, L.	Dell
The Secret Life of T.K. Dearing	Robinson, J.	Dell
Mary Poppins	Travers, P. L.	HBJ
Sounder	Armstrong, W.	Harp
A Long Day in November	Gaines, E.*	Dell
Requiem for a Princess	Arthur, R.*	Athen
Where the Lilies Bloom	Cleaver, B. and V.	Sig
Family Failing	Arundel, H.	SBS
Nothing Ever Happens Here	York, C.	Sig
Sing Down the Moon	O'Dell, S.*	Dell
Mom, the Wolf Man and Me	Klein, N.*	Avon
Of Love and Death and Other Journeys	Holland, E.*	Dell
Walking Away	Winthrop, E.	Dell
The Night Daddy	Gripe, M.	Dell
Twin Spell	Lunn, J.	Dell
My Dad Lives in a Downtown Hotel	Mann, P.*	Avon
Dinky Hocker Shoots Smack!	Kerr, M.*	Dell
Dollar Man	Mazer, H.	Dell
The Pearl and The Red Pony	Steinbeck, J.	Peng

The Boy Who Could Make Himself Disappear	Platt, K.*	Dell
A Figure of Speech	Mazer, N.*	Dell
Tiger Kittens	Zuckerman, A.	Dell
The Year of the Three Legged Deer	Clifford, E.	Dell
Getting It All Together	Dickenson, C.	SBS
In a Blue Bird's Eye	Kornfeld, A.	Avon
The Human Comedy	Saroyan, W.*	Dell
Red Sky At Morning	Bradford, R.	Pkt
None of the Above	Wells, R.*	Avon
Day No Pigs Would Die	Peck, R.*	Dell
Jesus Song	Knudson, R.	Dell
Nobody Waved Goodbye	Haggard, E.	Ban
Pistol	Richard, A.	Dell
Remove Protective Coating a Little at a Time	Donovan, J.	Dell
Mr. and Mrs. Bo Jo Jones	Head, A.	Sig
Phoebe	Dizenzo, P.	Ban
Richie	Thompson, T.	Ban
Ellen	Levit, R.	Ban
Summer of my German Soldier	Greene, B.	Ban
Run, Shelley, Run	Samuels, G.	Sig
Pudd'nhead Wilson	Twain, M.*	Ban
Lovechild	Hanes, M.	Sig
The Friends	Guy, R.*	Ban
Eric	Lund, D.	Dell
Daddy was a Numbers Runner	Meriwether, L.	Pyr
Songs My Mother Taught Me	Thomas, A.	Bal
If Beale Street Could Talk	Baldwin, J.*	Sig
Listen for the Fig Tree	Mathis, S.*	Avon
A Cry of Angels	Fields, J.	Bal
Chicano	Vasquez, R.	Avon
A Husband's Notes About Her	Merriam, E.*	Cllr
Twice Born	Lifton, J.	Peng
Stop-time	Conroy, F.	Peng

E. FANTASY

Three Little Kittens	Obligado, L.	Rand
The World Is Round	Stein, G.	Avon
Three Billy Goats Gruff	Asbjornsen and Moe, J. E.	HBJ

Little Red Riding Hood	Grimm, Brothers	SBS, HBJ
Three Little Pigs	Du Bois, W. P.	Puff
The Three Bears	Galdone, P.	SBS
The Ugly Duckling	Andersen, H. C.	Scrib
One Is No Fun, But 20 Is Plenty	Vogel, I.*	Athen
The Island of Skogg	Kellogg, S.*	Dial
Elephant Who Liked to Smash Small Cars	Merrill, J.	Pant
There's a Nightmare in My Closet	Mayer, M.*	Dial
Alexander and the Terrible, Horrible, No Good, Very Bad Day	Viorst, J.*	Athen
Stone Soup	Brown, M.*	Scrib
Old MacDonald Had an Apartment House	Barrett, J.*	Athen
Potato Talk	Rees, E.*	Rand
The Camel Who Took a Walk	Tworkov, J.	Dutt
George & Martha	Marshall, J.	HM
No Flying in the House	Brock, B.	Avon
The Sky Dog	Turkel, B.	Vik, Puff
The Strange Story of the Frog Who Became a Prince	Horwitz, E. L.	Dell
The Gingerbread Rabbit	Jarrell, R *	Cllr
The Tail Who Wagged the Dog	Kraus, R.*	Dutt
Fanona the Beautiful	Ross, J.	Holt
Half Magic	Eager, E.*	HBJ
Hailstones and Halibut Bones	O'Neill, M.	Dday
Star Girl	Winterfield, H.	Avon
Emma's Dilemma	LeRoy	Gem
Stoneflight	McHargue, G.	Avon
can i have a cookie (Family Circus Series)	Keane, B.	Fawc
Goodnight, Orange Monster	Lifton, B. J.	Athen
The Wercfox	Coatsworth, E.	Cllr
Goody Hall	Babbitt, N.	FS&G
The Day of the Ness	Norton, A. and Gilbert, M.	Dell
Sweetwater	Yep, L.*	Avon
The Gnome from Nome	Cosgrove, S.	Seren
Matthew Looney's Voyage to the Earth	Beatty, J.	Avon
Vampires, Werewolves & Other Stories	Hurwood, B. J.	SBS
Going for a Walk with a Line	MacAgy, D. E.	Dday

A Woggle of Witches	Adams, A.	Scrib
Charlie and the Chocolate Factory	Dahl, R. *	Knopf
Dragon, Dragon and Other Tales	Gardner, J.	Knopf
The Smartest Bear and His Brother Oliver	Bach, A.	Dell
The Boy Who Could Fly	Newman, R.	Avon
The Man Who Stole the Atlantic Ocean	Phillips, L.	Avon
The Velveteen Rabbit	Williams, M.	Avon
The Man Who Lost His Head	Bishop, C. H.	Puff
Little Prince	St. Exupery, A. De	HBJ
S.O.S. Bobmobile	Wahl, J.*	Dell
The Active-Enzyme Lemon-Freshened Junior High School Witch	Hildreick, E. W.	Dell
Doonesbury Series	Trudeau, G. B.*	Pop
Dorp Dead	Cunningham, J.	Avon
2001, A Space Odyssey	Clarke, A. C.*	Sig
Josephine Trilogy	Gripe, M.*	Dell
Star Treks (Series)	Blish, J.*	Ban
Season of Ponies	Snyder, Z. K.*	Athen
Magic Listening Cap	Uchida, Y.*	HBJ
The Wizard of Oz	Baum, L.	Rand, SBS
Moominland Midwinter	Jansson, T.	Avon
The World of Star Trek	Gerrold, D.	Bal
Elephi, the Cat with the High IQ	Stafford, J.	Dell
Six Million Dollar Man (Series)	Jahn, M.	Berk
The Hobbit	Tolkien, J. R. R.*	Bal
The Chronicles of Narnia	Lewis, C. S.*	Cllr
A Wrinkle in Time	L'Engle, M.*	Dell
Down a Dark Hall	Duncan, L.*	Sig
The Planet of Junior Brown	Hamilton, V.*	Cllr
Joshua, Son of None	Freedman, N.	Dell
The Little Girl Who Lives Down the Lane	Koenig, L.	Ban
The Weathermakers	Bova, B.*	Sig
The Last Ones	Cameron, I.*	Avon
Holding Wonder	Henderson, Z.*	Avon
House of Stairs	Sleator, W.	Avon
The People of the Ax	Williams, J.	Dell
The Galactic Rejects	Offutt, A.	Dell
The Alfred Hitchcock Series	Hitchcock, A. (ed.)*	Dell

Curses, Hexes and Spells	Cohen, D.	Lipp
Cat's Cradle	Vonnegut, K., Jr.*	Dell
Planet of the Apes	Boulle, P.*	Sig
Tarzan of the Apes	Burroughs, E. R.*	Bal
The War of the Worlds	Wells, H. G.*	Berk
The Best of the Planet Stories #1	Brackett, L.	Bal
The Adventures of Sherlock Holmes' Smarter Brother		Bal
Nerves	Del Rey, L.*	Bal
Dune	Herbert, F.*	Berk
The Crystal Cave	Stewart, M.*	Fawc
The Swarm	Herzog, A.*	Sig
The Player on the Other Side	Queen, E.	Bal
We Have Always Lived in the Castle	Jackson, S.*	Pop
Slave Ship	Pohl, F.*	Bal
Stranger in a Strange Land	Heinlein, R. A,*	Berk
A Separate Reality	Castaneda, C.*	Pkt
The Shockwave Rider	Brunner, J.	Bal
Ragtime	Doctorow, E. L.*	Ban

F. NATURE

Fish Is Fish	Lionni, L.*	Pant
ABC Science Experiments	Jilgrom, H.	Cllr
Six Foolish Fishermen	Elkin, B.*	SBS
Birds Eat and Eat and Eat	Gans, R.	Crow
Oxygen Keeps You Alive	Branley, F. M.*	Crow
Lonesome Little Colt	Anderson, C. W.	Cllr
Joey's Cat	Burch, R.*	Vik, Puff
The Secret Kitten	Mallett, A.	SBS
The Meanest Squirrel I Ever Met	Zion, G.*	Scrib

The Last Free Bird	Stone, A. H.	PH
Fat Cat	Kent, J.	SBS
Did You Ever See	Einsel, W.	SBS
Come Visit a Prairie Dog Town	Alston, E.	HBJ
Where Does the Butterfly Go When it Rains	Garelick, M.	SBS
Story About Ping	Flack, M.*	Puff
The Story of Ferdinand	Leaf, M.	Puff
The Tenth Good Thing About Barney	Viorst, J.*	Athen
Tooth Trip	McGuire, T.	Rand
Which Is Which	Russell, S. P.	PH
Science Experiments You Can Eat	Cobb, V.	Lipp
Bees, Bugs and Beetles	Rood, R.	SBS
Incredible Animals	Myers, J.	HPC
Abandoned	Griffiths, G. D.	Dell
Rabbit Hill	Lawson, R.	Dell
Animals Should Definitely Not Wear Clothing	Barrett, J.*	Athen
The Dog Who Thought He Was a Boy	Annett, C.	Sand
Meet Babar and His Family	DeBrunhoff, J.	Rand
Books of Horses	Balch, G.	SBS
Beasts, Brains and Behavior	Wily, J.	SBS
King of the Grizzlies	Seton, E. T.*	SBS
The True Story of Okee the Otter	Wisbeski, D.	Airmt
Brighty of the Grand Canyon	Henry, M.	RM
Charlie, the Lonesome Cougar	Van Cleefe, M.	SBS
Over in the Meadow	Langstaff, J.*	HBJ
Hemi: A Mule	Brenner, B.	Harp
Gentle Ben	Morey, W.	Avon
Black Beauty	Sewell, A.	G&D, Airmt, Peng, SBS
Lassie Come Home	Knight, E.	Dell
Room for Me and a Mountain Lion	Larrick, N.	Ban
A Pocket Guide to Trees	Platt, R.*	Pkt
That Quail, Robert	Stranger, M. A.	Fawc
White, White Still Water	Boxworth, J. A.	Harp

255

Big Mutt	Reese, J.	Airmt
Riff, Remember	Hall, L.	Avon
Ginger Pye	Estes, E.*	HBJ
Gifts of an Eagle	Durden, K.	Ban
Incident at Hawk's Hill	Eckert, A. W.	Dell
The Incredible Journey	Burnford, S.	Ban
Seal Morning	Farre, R.	SBS
Born Free	Adamson, J.*	Vint
Your Pet's Secret Language	Robbins, J.	Warn
Quail in the Family	Plummer, W. J.	Fawc
Cats: History, Care, Breeds	Metcalf, C.	Ban
Where the Red Fern Grows	Rawls, W.	Ban
One Day at Teton Marsh	Carrighar, S.*	Bal
In the Shadow of a Rainbow: The True Story of a Friendship Between Man and Wolf	Leslie, R. F.	Sig
A Dog Named Wolf	Munsterhjelm, E.	Dell
The Bog People	Glob, P. V.	Bal
America the Raped	Marine, G.	Avon
A Sand Country Almanac	Leopold, A.*	Bal
Rascal	North, S.*	Avon
The Closing Circle	Commoner, B.*	Ban
The Lives of a Cell: Notes of a Biology Watcher	Thomas, L.	Ban
Bigfoot	Slate, B., Berry, A.	Ban
Never Cry Wolf	Mowat, F.*	Dell
The Mother Earth News Handbook of Homemade Power	Shuttleworth, J.*	Ban
The Marvelous Mongolian	Aldridge, J.	Ban
How to Stay Alive in the Woods	Angier, B.*	Cllr
Snakes of the World	Stidworthy, J.	Ban
A Horse Called Bonnie	Johnson, P. and* Van Tuyl, B.	Sig
Where There Is Life	Sears, P. B.	Dell
My Side of the Mountain	George, J. C.	Dutt
Since Silent Spring	Graham, F., Jr.	Fawc
The Double Helix	Watson, J. D.*	Ment
The Wellsprings of Life	Asimov, I.*	Sig
To Live on Earth	Brubaker, S.	Ment
Silent Spring	Carson, R.*	Fawc

Our Vanishing Landscape	Sloane, E.	Bal
The Happy Dolphins	Carter, S., III*	Airmt
The Coming Age of Solar Energy	Halacy, D. S.	Avon
Golden Shadows, Flying Hooves	Schaller, G.*	Dell
Myth and Maneater, the Story of the Shark	Webster, D. K.	Dell
The Living Sea	Cousteau, J.*	Bal
Operating Manual for Spaceship Earth	Fuller, B.*	Pkt
Pilgrim at Tinker Creek	Dillard, A.	Ban
In the Shadow of Man	Van Lawick-Goodall, J.	Dell
Limbo of the Lost—Today	Spencer, J. W.	Ban
The Environmental Handbook	DeBell, G.	Bal
Direct Use of Sun's Energy	Farrington, D.	Bal
The Population Bomb	Ehrlich, Dr. P.*	Bal
Blue Meridian	Mathiessen, P.	Sig
The Moon Book	French, B.	Peng

G. PEERS

The Little Duck	Dunn, J.	Rand
Whistle for Willie	Keats, E. J.*	Puff
Dandelion	Freeman, D.*	Puff
Pell's New Suit	Diskow, E.	SBS
My Slippers are Red	Steiner, C.	Knopf
Evan's Corner	Hill, E. S.	Holt
No Room for the Baker	Recheis, K.	SBS
The Shy Little Girl	Krasilovsky, P.*	Sand
Ira Sleeps Over	Waber, B.*	HMS
The Hundred Dresses	Estes, E.	HBJ
Gabriella & Selena	Desbarats, P. and Grossman, N.	HBJ
Two is a Team	Beim, L. & J.	HBJ
I'll be You and You be Me	Krauss, R.*	BP
Three Friends	Fremlin, R.	Dell

258

The Room	Holland, R.	Dell
The Blanket Word	Arundel, H.*	Dell
They'll Never Make a Movie Starring Me	Back, A.	Dell
Fog	Lee, M.	Dell
The Soul Brothers and Sister Lou	Hunter, K.*	Avon
For All the Wrong Reasons	Neufeld, J.*	Sig
Run	Sleator, W.*	Avon
I Know What You Did Last Summer	Duncan, L.*	Airmt
Nobody Likes Trina	Whitney, P. A.	Sig
M. C. Higgins The Great	Hamilton, V.*	Dell
How Many Miles to Babylon?	Fox, P.	Airmt
An American Girl	Dizenzo, P.*	Avon
Please Don't Go	Woodford, P.	Avon
Rumble Fish	Hinton, S. E.*	Dell
Crack in the Sidewalk	Wolff, R.*	SBS
The Fog Comes on Little Pig Feet	Wells, R.*	Avon
Jeremy	Minahan, J.*	Ban
Ox Goes North	Ney, L.	Ban
I Was a 98-Pound Duckling	Van Leeuwen, J.*	Dell
Teacup Full of Roses	Mathis, S. B.*	Avon
Representing Superdoll	Peck, R.*	Avon
No More Trains to Tottenville	Campbell, H.*	Dell
The Troublemaker	McKay, R.*	Dell
It's Not What You Expect	Klein, N.*	Avon
Brian's Song	Blinn, W.	Ban
Is There A Life After Graduation, Henry Birnbaum?	Balducci, C.	Dell
Of Mice and Men	Steinbeck, J.*	Ban
The Chocolate War	Cormier, R.	Dell
The Magician	Stein, S.*	Dell
The Underside of the Leaf	Goffstein, M. B.	Dell
The Girls Of Huntington House	Elfman, B.	Ban
Looking Back: A Chronicle of Growing Up Old in the Sixties	Maynard, J.	Avon
Where Are You Going, Where Have You Been?	Oates, J. C.	Fawc
The Fires of Spring	Michener, J. A.*	Fawc
Memoirs of an Ex-Prom Queen	Shulman, A. K.	Ban

| Theophilus North | Wilder, T.* | Avon |
| Wee Pals (series) | Turner, M. | Sig |

H. SPORTS

Yoga for Children	Diskin, E.	Warn
Jim Thorpe	Fall, T.	Crow
Flat on My Face	First, J.	Avon
Casey at the Bat	Thayer, E.	PH
Sports Star: Jim "Catfish" Hunter	Burchard, S.*	HBJ
Pete's Home Run	Renick, M.	Scrib
Warm Up for Little League Baseball	Shirts, M.	Airmt
Cub Scout at Last!	Felsen, H.*	Scrib
Catch That Pass	Christopher, M.	Airmt
How To Play Baseball Better Than You Did Last Season	Kalb, J.	Cllr
Unsung Heroes of the Major Leagues	Berke, A.	Rand
Motorcycles	Schilling, P.	Ban
Wild Wheels	McKay, D.	Dell
Every Boy's Judo	Harrington, A.	Sig
Incredible Athletic Feats	Benagh. J.*	Ban
A Pony Called Lightning	Mason, M.	Cllr
Kung Fu: The Peaceful Way	Robinson, R.	Pyr
Kung Fu (series)	Lee, H.	Warn
Championship Teams of the NFL	Berger, P.	Rand
Amazing Baseball Teams	Wolf, D.	Rand
Arthur Ashe: Tennis Champion	Robinson, L. Jr.	Airmt
The Bears and I	Leslie, R.	Bal
Olga	Beecham, J.	Two-Con
Prairie Lady	Wagner, S.	SBS
Bikes	Henkel, S.	Ban
Tennis to Win	King, B.	Pkt
I Always Wanted to be Somebody	Gibson, A.	Dell
Breaking In	Lorimer, L., ed.	Dell

The Bad News Bears	Woodley, R.	Dell
Grand Prix Racing	William, P.*	SBS
Hang Tough, Paul Mather	Slote, A.	Avon
Guiness Sports Record Book	McWhirter,	Ban
	N. and R.	Ban
Wilt Chamberlain	Rudeen, K.*	Crow
Batting and Bunting	Allen, E.	SBS
Go Up for Glory	Russell, B.	Berk
Yoga for Young People	Kiss, M.	Airmt
Boy's Book of Biking	MacFarlan, A.	Airmt
Sunbonnet: Filly of the Year	Van Tuyl, B.	Sig
Young Olympic Champions	Gelman, S.*	SBS
Pro Basketball Champions	Vecsey, G.	SBS
Dr. J.: The Story of Julius Erving	Gergen, J.	SBS
The Quality of Courage	Mantle, M.	Ban
They Call Me Coach	Wooden, J.	Ban
Dogs: Selection, Care, Training	Boorer, W.	Ban
Horses and Ponies	Campbell, J.*	Ban
The 23rd Street Crusade	Carson, J.	SBS
The Contender	Lipsyte, R.	Ban.
The Illustrated Sports Record Book	Hollander, Z.	Sig
Me and the Spitter	Perry, G. with	Sig
	Sudyk, B.	
Instant Replay	Kramer, J.	Sig
Yoga (series)	Hittleman, R.*	Warn
Playing Pro Football to Win	Unitas, J. with	Sig
	Rosenthal, H.	
Clemente!	Wagenheim, K.	Airmt
Zanballer	Knudson, R.	Dell
Ball Four	Bouten, J.	Dell
Sailing Alone Around the World	Slocum, J.	Cllr
My Own Story	Ali, M. with	Bal
	Durham, R.	
The Legend Of Bruce Lee	Block, A.	Dell
Reggie: A Season with a Superstar	Jackson, R. with	PP
	Libby, B.	
I Am Third	Sayers, G.	Ban
Foul: The Connie Hawkins Story	Wolf, D.	Warn
The Legend of Dr. J.: The Story of Julius Erving	Bell, M.	Sig
The Rise and Fall and Rise of Modern Dance	McDonagh, D.	Ment

Airmt — Airmont Publishing Co., Inc., Thomas Bouregy & Co., Inc., 22 East 60th Street, New York, NY 10022

Apol — Apollo Editions, Inc., Dun-Donnelley Publishing Corp., 666 Fifth Avenue, New York, NY 10019

Arch — Archway Paperbacks (See Pocket Books)

Athen — Atheneum Publishers, 122 East 42nd Street, New York, NY 10017

Avon — Avon Books, The Hearst Corporation, 959 Eighth Avenue, New York, NY 10019

Bal — Ballantine Books, A Division of Random House, Inc., 201 East 50th Street, New York, NY 10022

Ban — Bantam Books, Inc., 666 Fifth Avenue, New York, NY 10019

Berk — Berkley Books, Inc., 200 Madison Avenue, New York, NY 10016

BP — Bookstore Press, 9 Housatonic Street, Lenox, Mass. 01240

Cllr — Collier Books, A Division of Macmillan Publishing Co., Inc., 866 Third Avenue, New York, NY 10022

Crow — Thomas Y. Crowell Co., Inc., Dun-Donnelley Publishing Corporation, 666 Fifth Avenue, New York, NY 10019

Dday — Doubleday & Company, Inc., Garden City, New York, NY 11530

Dell — Dell Publishing Co., Inc., 1 Dag Hammarskjold Plaza, 245 East 47th Street, New York, NY 10017

Dial — The Dial Press (See Dell Publishing Co., Inc.)

Dutt — Dutton Paperbacks, E. P. Dutton & Co., Inc., 201 Park Avenue South, New York, NY 10003

Fawc — Fawcett Publications, Inc., Fawcett Building, Fawcett Place, Greenwich CT 06830

FS&G — Farrar, Strauss & Giroux, Inc., 19 Union Square West, New York, NY 10003

G&D — Grossett & Dunlap, Inc., 51 Madison Avenue, New York, NY 10010

Gem	William Collins and World Publishing Co., Inc., 2080 West 117 Street, Cleveland, Ohio 44111
Harp	Harper and Row General Books, 10 East 53rd Street, New York, NY 10022
HM	Houghton Mifflin Company, 2 Park Street, Boston, MA 02107
Holt	Holt, Rinehart & Winston, Inc., 383 Madison Avenue, New York, NY 10017
HPC	Hart Publishing Co., Inc., 15 West 4th Street, New York, NY 10012
Knopf	Alfred A. Knopf, Inc. (See Random House, Inc.)
Lipp	J.B. Lippincott Company, East Washington Square, Philadelphia, PA 19105
Ment	Mentor Books. (See New American Library, Inc.)
NAL	New American Library, Inc., 1301 Avenue of the Americas, New York, NY 10019
Pant	Pantheon Books. (See Random House, Inc.)
Peng	Penguin (See Viking-Penguin, Inc.)
PH	Prentice-Hall, Inc., Englewood Cliffs, NJ 07632
Pkt	Pocket Books (A Division of Simon & Schuster, Inc.), 630 Fifth Avenue, New York, NY 10020
Plume	Plume Books (See New American Library, Inc.)
Pop	Popular Library Publishers. A Unit of CBS Publications, 600 Third Avenue, New York NY 10016
PP	Playboy Press (See Pocket Books)
Puff	Puffin. (See Viking-Penguin, Inc.)
Pyr	Pyramid Publications, 919 Third Avenue, New York, NY 10022
Rand	Random House, Inc., Alfred E. Knopf, Inc. and Pantheon Books, 201 East 50th Street, New York, NY 10022
RM	Rand McNally & Company, Trade Publishing Division, 8255 Central Park Avenue, Skokie, IL 60076
Sand	Sandpiper Books (See Houghton Mifflin Company)
SBS	Scholastic Book Services, 90 Sylvan Avenue, Englewood Cliffs, NJ 07632
Scrib	Charles Scribner's Sons, 597 Fifth Avenue, New York, NY 10017
Seren	Serendipity Press, Box 9123, Seattle, Wash. 98109
Sig	Signet Books (See New American Library, Inc.)
TwoCon	The Two Continents Publishing Group, Ltd., 30 East 42nd Street, New York, NY 10012

Vik	The Viking Press, Inc., 625 Madison Avenue, New York, NY 10022
VikPen	Viking-Penguin, Inc., 625 Madison Avenue, New York, New York 10022
Vint	Vintage Books (See Randon House, Inc.)
Warn	Warner Books, Book Order Department, Independent News Company, 75 Rockefeller Plaza, New York, NY 10019
WM	William Morrow & Co., Inc., Scott, Foresman & Co., 105 Madison Avenue, New York, NY 10016
WSP	Washington Square Press (See Pocket Books)

Chapter XII

TOWARD A PROFESSIONAL UNION

Daniel Fader

Many years ago I knew a boy named David who had convinced us all that he was the strongest boy in our class, the sixth grade at Mordecai Gist Elementary School in Baltimore, Maryland. Though another boy and I were nearly as big as he, we knew we were not as strong because he told us every day that we were not and could not hope to be.

Then, one fine spring afternoon, he and I walked to my home together though we did not live very close to each other. Down the long slope of Belle Avenue, from Garrison Boulevard to Dolfield Avenue we walked, and during each block of our journey he remembered to tell me or show me how strong he was. Across the street from my house, the trees greening and the turf fuzzy with thin spring grass, he did not forget to praise himself once more before we parted. And suddenly I understood what it meant to protest too much.

After more talk and more time for my courage to grow, we began to wrestle on the soft earth. It was I who said, "Let's wrestle," and it was he who thought I was crazy to say it. But by that time I almost knew what I would find: That he was not very strong and certainly not as strong as I was. I must have pinned his shoulders to the grass twenty times. I could happily have gone on wrestling and pinning him forever, but he said he had to go home.

A quarter of a century later I attended a conference whose

subject was the delivery of health care to the community. A mediocre opening paper, which received polite if perfunctory applause and no penetrating questions because it deserved none, was followed by such a brilliant second presentation that the debate it provoked was its presenter's best reward. The very good feeling it left in the large audience was not dissipated until part way through the third paper, when many of us realized we were experiencing the rare phenomenon of brilliant and stupid presentations back-to-back.

But if that phenomenon was rare, a rarer one awaited me. I had, after all, at my own professional meetings heard papers almost as good as the second one and almost as bad as the third. Perhaps I had even heard them given consecutively. But what I had never before witnessed was anything like the response of that audience to that dreadful third lecture: They murmured; they whispered; they talked loudly among themselves; *they booed the speaker.* And finally they arose in groups around the large auditorium to whistle and hiss that benighted lecturer off the platform and out of the auditorium. Long after the auditorium had cleared, I sat in a daze of admiration.

No, I do not admire the brutalization of anyone, however wrong. What I do admire is the honesty of response and certainty of self that allowed the members of that audience to work at conserving themselves. They understood that the speaker's bigotry and opinionated ignorance were, in that forum, an assault upon their profession and upon themselves—profession and self forming, in their view at that moment, an irreduceable whole. In that recognition, they are radically different from me and my kindergarten-through-graduate-school teaching colleagues in all of North America.

What is the most poignant word of our in-gatherings? What word occurs more often than any other in the titles which we use to describe our periodic gatherings for education, re-education, and occasional conviviality? Like my elementary school classmate who was not as strong as he claimed to be and perhaps secretly knew it, we protest our PROFESSIONAL condition so frequently and often so stridently that we raise persistent doubts in the minds of our two most considerable adversaries: ourselves, who know the secret truth, and the communities we serve, who do not even have to challenge us to wrestle because they know how weak we are.

Professional days; *professional* meetings; *professional* journals; *professional* contracts; *professional* conduct—the list is endless and endlessly embarrassing. The adjective "professional" preoccupies us just as Volpone's gold preoccupies him in Jonson's play which begins with Volpone's blasphemous salutation, "Good morning to the day; and next, my gold!/ Open the shrine that I may see my saint." We are no less blasphemous than Volpone, for we are as persistent in worshipful blind pursuit of our professionalism as he was of his gold. At the end, he loses all; where "all" is defined as "self-respect," so may we.

Not only do our protestations ring false and foolish, but our actions belie our words. When I witnessed many hundreds of medical people actively reject the unprofessional material delivered by that benighted lecturer, I realized that I had heard presentations nearly as bad at my own meetings but I had never heard such an appropriate response. The more I have thought about the persistent absence of deeply critical or outraged responses at our gatherings and in our journals, the more I have come to believe that our unending protestations of professionalism are symptomatic of a disease which may be equally fatal to our vocations and to our self-respect.

The fatal disease I refer to is the disabling absence of self-criticism. Meaningful, effective criticism is as remarkable by its absence in our profession as are responsive mechanisms for evaluating good and bad teaching. How else, but by the atrophy through disuse of the critical muscles, can we explain the weakness of our response to bad papers, bad lectures, and bad presentations in our Professional Journals or at our Professional Days and Meetings? Is it that we cannot recognize quality? I do not believe it. I believe instead that we are so inhibited by the covert agreement we have accepted together with our teaching credentials—do not criticize me or interfere in my classroom and I will repay the courtesy in kind—that we cannot afford to understand the near relationship among criticism, integrity, and performance. I believe that the absence of self-criticism within our profession renders us unprofessional, puts our integrity in question, and leaves our performance in doubt.

Once, when greener, I went to my department chairman to tell him of my recent experience as a replacement teacher. He had asked me to take one of Mr. A's classes for a week while that gentleman was flu-ridden. If he should need longer for recovery, I was told, I would be relieved at the beginning of the second week by the chairman himself or another colleague. But Mr. A. returned after a week and no one had to take further responsibility for his classes, which was good for Mr. A's colleagues but bad for his students.

I had met Mr. A's class four times during the week. In my free hour on Friday after the fourth meeting, a large delegation from the class came to see me in my office. Their question was as direct as it was naive: If they presented a petition "to somebody" would I be allowed to continue as their teacher? (Meant as a compliment, I think, was one boy's mumbled observation about Mr. A. being such a terrible teacher that *anybody* would be better.) After I had been told much more than I wanted to hear about Mr. A's abusive classroom habits and deadly dull teaching; after I had told them how pleased I was by their request but unhappy that no one could satisfy it; after I had contemplated my vulnerable (untenured) position—after all that, I went to my department chairman who gave me this truth to carry back to my teaching career:

"Oh, yes, Mr. A. Dreadful man. Dreadful teacher. Always has been, at least in the years I've known him. But of course he does do first-rate scholarship and he does have tenure. Don't get in his way. He can be very vindictive."

And Mr. A. has been hurting students ever since. Just as all his counterparts have done and will do in all the schools everywhere that are staffed by people like me and my former chairman, people who think of themselves as decent and caring human beings but who in fact have made themselves into monsters of inattention. We have built a part of our professional lives on the practical art of looking away. Are there very bad teachers in the department (division, faculty, school)? Ah, well, are there not, for example, good and bad doctors and lawyers in proportions equal to our own profession? The surprising answer to that popular evasion is *NO*, for we are unlike them in two crucial respects:

One, no matter how many of our students fail to recover from our ministrations or profit from our advice—almost no matter how many patients or cases we lose—we are guaranteed a full case-load and full calendar all the days of our teaching lives after our brief probation is done. And, two, unlike doctors or lawyers, we have no meaningful internal or external procedures of removal. No bar of peer opinion exists. No suit for malpractice is possible. Because effective criticism is nearly impossible, effective teaching has become more and more improbable. Effective teaching and meaningful criticism are as closely related as performance and self-respect.

Because we have so carefully insulated ourselves from internal and external criticism, we have become equal partners with our students and their families in the victimization of the innocent which more and more often passes for public education in North America. As are our students and the community of families which employs us to educate them, we are victim and victimizer alike. Perhaps the primary example of mutual suffering which the practices of separation and insulation have brought about, is the absurd doctrine of *in loco parentis* and the chief burden which accompanies it. Though it is habitual for us to disclaim in our time any part of the historical notion that we as teachers stand in place of parents during the school day, the fact is that we still act as though we were governed by that pernicious doctrine. No more or better evidence of this governance is needed than the existence of such a creature as Vice-Principal in Charge of Discipline.

Identified often by title and always by role, he exists wherever secondary education is found in the United States. He is both product and victim of the separation between school and community. Insomuch as he accepts his role as appropriate, he is a product; insomuch as he knows his role unplayable, he is a victim. For he is the teachers' delegate to

270

the impossible task of bringing discipline to those children and adolescents to and upon whom it is neither taught nor demanded at home. We who teach know how impossible the task is, for we had both to invent the position and then fill it with a person who would attempt what we could not perform. He is as much the visible evidence of our failure as our undisciplined students are evidence of failure in their families.

The sole important difference between these two apparently similar failures is that the family's responsibility is a reasonable extension of the child's begetting, while our responsibility as teachers is a reasonable extension of nothing except our fearful inability to know ourselves and to make ourselves known to the community. Even as one of our many mouths disclaims our role *in loco parentis*, another bespeaks our acceptance of the familial responsibility to teach self-discipline. We are all things to all people, including ourselves; diffuse at the edges, fractionated at the center, we have become known to the community as the expandable people. Tell us that we must take into our classrooms twice as many children as we can teach and anyone can manage— we will expand our infinitely expandable selves to accommodate (if not teach) those children. Are we demanding that our classes be significantly reduced in size so that children's hope for themselves (without which, nothing; nurtured by attention) may increase? We are not. Instead, we negotiate class size at double the number we know we can handle, then demand more pay and more sick leave and larger pensions and less lunchroom duty and . . . and we have traded our professional self-respect, without which professional identity is shamefaced, for better living conditions at the expense of working days so bad that many teachers can hardly bear to contemplate or discuss them.

Where lies our hope for ourselves? It lies, I think, in a new and radically different view which we must take of our own professionalism. Just as I argued earlier in this book for the resurgence of hope and humanity in our students that can arise from replacing ability grouping with a fellowship of care, so do I believe that a prognosis of hope for ourselves

271

can only be made if we turn the new professional institution in our midst towards new goals. Unionization seems to me inevitable at every level of American education; we who are giving our union its identity must shape it to our greatest needs.

To this point we have defined our greatest needs in terms understandable to everyone of us who has received minimal pay for maximal expectation from community, students, and self. Now many of us have discovered, as all of us will, our power through united negotiation to make great and lasting change in our material lives. Who can doubt the proved effectiveness of union in pursuit of equitable benefits and defined responsibilities? Having witnessed the power of collective bargaining coupled with implicit threat of withdrawn service, can we ever again deny to ourselves our capacity to shape important parts of our professional lives according to our own desires? Because such denial is no longer to ourselves believable, we must now bear both the privileges and consequences of growing self-control.

If unions do not become both advocates and instruments of meaningful *teaching evaluation*, then we have lost our last, best chance to establish our credibility as professionals in our own eyes as well as in the estimations of our students and our communities. If *tenure* is not made in part a function of continuing quality instead of wholly a fungus of longevity, then tenure has no hope of survival at all. Both evaluated teaching and dependent tenure are inevitable consequences of professional self-control. Without the manifest and assertive presence of both, we are not and cannot be professionals. Then, like David, antagonist of my youth, we will know ourselves to be of that pitiful company which does too little even as it doth protest too much.

Finally, in response to the naysayers who believe no human sufficient to judge another human being, especially themselves as teachers: Where, they ask (believing the question unanswerable), are the reasonable people who are willing to judge competence in teacher evaluation? Who will determine the quality of teaching that forms the basis for dependent, reassessable tenure? To the assertion implicit in the question—that we would be as firmly reluctant to judge our peers and colleagues as they would be to judge us—I answer with the strength that thousands of teachers have shown to me in answering the same question put to them: *Yes*, they have said and continue to say. *Yes!* It is not a job I seek but it is a job I will do. I am willing to judge my fellow teachers and to be judged in turn by them. I know the difference between good and bad teaching, and I am willing to judge and be judged by it.

If we do not seize the opportunity to judge ourselves, it will surely be seized from us. If we do not propose and act upon sensible standards of self-judgment, forming our own bar of peer opinion before which each of us must present ourselves on a periodic basis, then we will find ourselves judged by standards externally conceived and externally imposed. No better place exists to exhibit and emphasize our professionalism than the new organization called *union*, which must offer guarantees of our professional integrity in return for the benefits of income and good practice which have so long eluded us.

Appendix A

SAMPLE LESSONS FOR ACHIEVING READING OBJECTIVES WITH TRADEBOOKS

James Duggins and Tom Finn

A frequent excuse for using workbooks and reading textbooks rather than tradebooks is that students need to develop reading skills. These skills, so the argument runs, must be deliberately taught rather than trusted to inductive learning from wide reading.

We believe imaginative literature, because of its varied content and broad range of style, can easily be used to teach specific reading skills. The work of the teacher with such materials becomes that of a content analyst who reviews the works students read to determine which reading skills are best taught from those books. As a sample of this approach, we have chosen five books at different reading levels within the thematic category of "Family." Here are lesson plans to help achieve specific, cognitive reading objectives that can be taught with those books. Though many reading skills can also be taught with them (we have listed some), our practice differs substantially from that commonly seen in other materials because we use certain books and authors to develop certain skills, with the skill suggested particular to the work being read. The book chosen because it is enjoyed becomes a demonstration of the skill being taught rather than a dull exercise done for its own sake.

Grade 1–2   Theme: "Family"
Objective: Identify and Interpret Feelings
Books: *Titch,* Pat Hutchins, Cllr
                 Whose Mouse Are You?, Robert Kraus, Cllr

Preparation:
1. Appraise the reading level of the books and their appropriateness for your class. Although all these books are appropriate for many second grade children, some of the books will be easier for some classes than others.
2. Record the story, if possible, and put it in the listening center. Pictures of the scenes that portray feelings can be kept there on tag board with descriptive words.
3. Prepare hectofax dittoes of selected scenes depicting "feelings we like," and "feelings we do not like." These can be colored and arranged by the children.

Classroom Activities:
1. Read the story to the children.
2. Ask the children their ideas about how the characters feel as the story unfolds. At each juncture in the story ask children to predict what will happen next.
3. While reading to the children, ask questions intended to develop ideas about why things happened as they did.
4. Make lists of "feeling" words on the chalkboard, categorizing them under titles such as "Feelings we like" and "Feelings we do not like."

Other Objectives that Can Be Taught with These Books:
   Context Clues to Word Recognition
   Comprehension: Cause and Effect
   Comprehension: Inference

Alternate Books:
   Crowboy, Taro Yashima, Vik
   The Snowy Day, Ezra Jack Keats, Vik
   Whistle for Willie, Don Freeman, Vik

Grade 3–4   Theme: "Family"
Objective: Sequence
Book: *The Little Brute Family,* R. Hoban, Cllr

Preparation:
1. Appraise the reading level of the book and its appropriateness for your class. If you can get them "hooked" on this story of the "Little Brutes," they will easily move through all the books of Russell Hoban.
2. Have some of the better readers in your class record these stories in a listening center so that they can be followed by slower readers.
3. Prepare hectofax dittoes of selected scenes depicting "feelings we like," and "feelings we do not like." These can be colored and arranged by the children.

Classroom Activities:
1. Read the story to the children.
2. Ask the children their ideas about how the characters feel as the story unfolds. At each juncture in the story ask children to predict what will happen next.
3. While reading to the children, ask questions intended to develop ideas about why things happened as they did.
4. Ask children to arrange the events of the story (colored pictures) in the order in which they occurred. They can draw maps of the details, plans of the house, or identify objects in the Brutes' daily life.

Other Objectives Taught by This Book:
    Context Clues to Word Recognition
    Identifying and Interpreting Feelings
    Comprehension: Cause and Effect

Grade 5+   Theme: "Family"
Objective: Sequence
Book: *The Dollar Man,* Harry Mazer, Dell

1. The main character, Marcus, is a junior high school student and the book appeals to readers from fifth grade through high school. Senior high school readers, male and female, are often attracted to the story of a single female parent.

2. This novel convincingly portrays a single, unwed mother raising her son. A brief mention of this situation is enough to rouse reader interest. If *Mom, the Wolfman and Me* has been read by students, *The Dollar Man* is a natural follow-up.

3. The plot of the novel is classic in the sense that it is the story of a search. Marcus is searching both for his father and his acceptance of self. Sequence is a natural pattern in this novel, for there are no flashbacks and the plot is chronological. Students respond to questions about what they thought of Marcus at the opening of the book and how their views toward him altered as the story progressed.

4. The fantasy life of Marcus is an important element of the novel. A discussion of why the world of make-believe is often an escape for people with problems, can lead to insights from students. Older readers can look back on their own junior high school years and discuss Marcus' situation as one they have witnessed or experienced.

5. The theme of "family" is well developed as Marcus becomes more and more determined to discover who his father is. The contrast between Marcus' life and that of his friend, Bernie, provides opportunities for comparison and contrast of family patterns. Marcus' discovery of his father in the last two chapters should provoke student reaction to the meaning of "parent."

6. The novel ends as Marcus gains insights about himself and his mother. Students may wish to project, in discussion or writing, how Marcus' high school life will develop or how his relationship to his mother and peers will be altered because of his encounter with his father. The theme of adolescent peer loyalty and its consequences is also strong, and writing or talking of this should be fruitful. *The*

Human Comedy, by William Saroyan; *The Cool World,* by Warren Miller; and *Dinky Hocker Shoots Smack!* by M. E. Kerr, are additional novels to foster comparison and contrast.

Other Objectives That Can Be Taught with This Book:
   Recalling Details
   Characterization
   Predicting Outcomes
   Forming Judgments
   Understanding Characters' Emotions

Grade 7+	Theme: "Family"
Objective:	Sequence
Book:	*Farewell to Manzanar,* Jeanne Wakatsuki Houston and James D. Houston, Ban

1. Readers from seventh grade up are likely to find this book of considerable interest. Precocious younger readers will also appreciate it. The topic of World War II is popular among secondary students, and this reminiscence of a young Japanese American is part of the untold history of the period.

2. Teachers using this autobiography with a large group will find that a discussion begun by questioning them about what they know of World War II can lead into a discussion of what took place in America during the war. If they lack knowledge of the internment of Japanese Americans, the teacher can supply or recommend sources for background information. Thereafter could follow a discussion of what it might have been like to be placed in an internment camp. Selected readings from pp. 13–16 convey the feelings of leaving home and entering the internment camp and can provoke personal engagement on the parts of some students. Those who have read *The Diary of Anne Frank,* or *Summer of My German Soldier,* will be able to make natural connections to the Houstons' story.

3. You may wish to begin with the authors' "Foreword," but it may best be appreciated after completing the book. Their section called "A Chronology" is also of more interest to many after reading the body of the autobiography. Since a number of Japanese words are used, students should be aware of "Terms Used in This Book" and told that footnotes will explain other terms as they read. The book covers in chronological order the events from December 7, 1941, to 1951. Because Chapter 7 is presented in a different form, some students may need help to understand how it fits into the narrative; a comment on the use of italics in this chapter and in chapters ten and eighteen should help clarify their change of style and purpose. Before students read Section III, a comprehensive discussion of the book to that point would be beneficial. Though the book's sequence is changed to a flashback in the last five pages, its meaning and purpose should be understandable to most readers.

4. While the book is a chronological account of Jeannie's formative years in very unsual surroundings, it is also the history of her family. What happens to her father, mother, and brothers is very important in any discussion of the story and will help students recall the sequence of events. The moves the family makes from 1941 through 1951 may also provide a key to events in the family's life.

5. After completing the book, students may wish to discuss how the experience of Manzanar affected various members of the family. The father's reactions progress in stages that may trigger other details of the story. Jeannie's whole life was changed by the experience; questions of how and why can lead students to a recounting of when events took place that caused her to behave as she did after leaving Manzanar.

6. After reading the body of the book, a first or second reading of "Foreword," and "A Chronology" should make them more meaningful to the reader. Ask

students to explain how each of the chronological events affected the life of the entire Wakatsuki family. Ask them for specific examples of what kept the family together during these trying times.

7. As a concluding activity, have students comment on what they think happened to Jeannie from the time she was crowned queen (1951) until she wrote this book in 1973. They may also wish to consider how they would react to spending time in a place like Manzanar under similar conditions.

Alternative Objectives:
   Recalling Detail
   Inference
   Comparison and Contrast
   Understanding and Interpreting Human Motivations

Grade 8++   Theme: "Family"
Objective: Sequence
Book: *If Beale Street Could Talk,* James Baldwin, Sig

1. The reading level of the book is about seventh grade, but the subject matter and language may be more appropriate for senior high students. Teachers should read the book before placing it in the classroom library.

2. If the book is to be made available for all students, present it in a book talk. Even a very general idea of Fonny and Tish's situation will arouse interest. The opening pages, pages 3 to 14, read aloud, form a powerful introduction. If the book is recommended only to individual students, a brief comment on the story line should be enough motivation.

3. Baldwin's technique of using flashbacks is sophisticated but not difficult. On page 11 Tish begins to think back to when she first met Fonny. This is a form of recalling the past, but on page 14 her thinking takes the form of a true flashback. After students have read to page 32, a discussion of time

and event might be both useful and necessary. The reader is given clues to narrative change by a wider spacing between paragraphs. Point these out to students as clues to changes in time (see page 11).

4. Another important writing technique is the use of *point of view*. Tish tells the story, and students can be asked why Baldwin tells the story from her point of view rather than Fonny's? When the novel opens, Tish is two months pregnant; at its closing, she delivers a child. The pregnancy cycle and the changes in Tish's body are good references for helping students piece together the flashbacks that provide the details of Fonny and Tish's life together and the story of Fonny's arrest and imprisonment. The flashbacks also provide so much information about the families of the two lovers that discussions of the differences and similarities between the two families would be profitable.

5. After completing the book, discuss how the reader finds out about Fonny's arrest and what the two families do to get him out of jail. How do the two fathers react and help the young lovers? What part do the mothers and sisters play in helping Tish and Fonny? In these discussions, questions about how and when the reader learns these facts should help to clarify the use of flashback.

6. In considering the theme of family, students may discover that role-playing various family members in extended scenes from the novel can provide insights into their characters and the various meanings of the book. Do students consider Tish and Fonny a "family" and why? This question can be very helpful to self-discovery for many students.

7. As a concluding activity, ask students to discuss the scene where Tish tells Fonny his trial has been postponed and she says, "It is not that he gives up hope, but that he ceases clinging to it." (pp. 273-234) What does this tell us about Fonny and the future of the two lovers? Will Fonny get out of jail? What kind of life can he and Tish hope for? To provide

further understanding of the novel's ending, discuss why Baldwin calls Part Two "Zion." Students may wish to write the continuing story of Fonny and Tish or may try to write their own ending to the novel.

Alternative Objectives:
Comparison and Contrast
Understanding and Interpteting Human Motivations
Recalling Details
Predicting Outcomes

Appendix B

FOR FURTHER READING

Adventuring with Books, Twenty-four Hundred Titles for Preschool—Grade 8, Root, Shelton L., ed., Citation Press, New York, 1973.

Arizona English Bulletin (Entire issue on adolescent literature), April, 1976, Donelson, Kenneth L., ed., University of Arizona, Tempe, Arizona.

Books for You (Senior High Booklist), NCTE, Urbana, Illinois, 1976

Carillo, Lawrence W., *Teaching Reading, A Handbook,* St. Martin's Press, New York, 1976.

Curley, Marie T., "The Buckram Syndrome," *The Public Library Reporter, # 13,* American Library Association, Chicago, Illinois, 1968.

Drama in Your Classroom, Tiedt, Iris M., ed., NCTE, Urbana, Illinois, 1974.

Duggins, James, *Teaching Reading for Human Values in High School,* Charles E. Merrill, Columbus, Ohio, 1972.

Edwards, Margaret A., *The Fair Garden and the Swarm of Beasts, The Library and the Young Adult,* Hawthorn Books, New York, 1969.

Elkins, Deborah, *Teaching Literature, Designs for Cognitive Development,* Charles E. Merrill, Columbus, Ohio, 1976.

Fader, Daniel, *The Naked Children,* Bantam, New York, 1972.

Goodman, Kenneth S., *Miscue Analysis,* NCTE, Urbana, Illinois, 1973.

Hackett, Vicki L., *Games for Teaching Literature,* J. Weston Walch, Portland, Maine, 1975.

Hawkins, Thom, *Benjamin: Reading and Beyond,* Charles E. Merrill, Columbus, Ohio, 1972.

High Interest—Easy Reading, for Junior and Senior High School Students, White, Marian E., ed., Citation Press, New York, 1972.

Hurwitz, Abraham B. and Goddard, Arthur, *Games to Improve Your Child's English,* Simon and Schuster, New York, 1969.

Moffett, James, and Wagner, Betty Jane, *Student Centered Language Arts and Reading Handbook, Second Edition,* Houghton-Mifflin, Boston, Mass., 1977.

Peterscn, Clarence, *The Bantam Story, Thirty Years of Paperback Publishing,* Bantam, New York, 1975.

Reading Ladders for Human Relations, Fifth Edition, Reid, Virginia M., ed., NCTE, Urbana, Illinois, 1972.

Rosenblatt, Louise, *Literature as Exploration, Revised Edition,* Noble and Noble, Inc., New York, 1967.

Russell, David H., *The Dynamics of Reading,* Ruddell, Robert B., ed., Ginn-Blaisdell, Boston, Mass., 1970.

Smith, E. Brooks, and Goodman, Kenneth S., and Meredith, Robert, *Language and Thinking in School, Second Edition,* Holt, Rinehart, and Winston, New York, 1976.

Smith, Lillian H., *The Unreluctant Years,* Viking, New York, 1975.

Stanek, Lou W., *Censorship, A Teacher's Guide,* Dell, New York, 1976.

Trela, Thaddeus N., *Fourteen Remedial Reading Methods,* Fearon, Belmont, California, 1967.

Your Reading, Booklist for Junior High Students, Walker, Jerry L., ed., NCTE, Urbana, Illinois, 1975.

Appendix C

THE RIGHT TO READ

An open letter to the citizens of our country from the National Council of Teachers of English:

"The worthy fruit of an academic culture is an open mind...."

Charles W. Eliot, "First Inaugural Address," Harvard University, October 19, 1869.

"Where suspicion fills the air and holds scholars in line for fear of their jobs, there can be no exercise of the free intellect.... A problem can no longer be pursued with impunity to its edges. Fear stalks the classroom. The teacher is no longer a stimulant to adventurous thinking; she becomes instead a pipe line for safe and sound information. A deadening dogma takes the place of free inquiry. Instruction tends to become sterile; pursuit of knowledge is discouraged; discussion often leaves off where it should begin."

Justice William O. Douglas, United States Supreme Court: Adler v. Board of Education, 1952.

The right to read, like all rights guaranteed or implied within our constitutional tradition, can be used wisely or foolishly. In many ways, education is an effort to improve the quality of choices open to man. But to deny the freedom of choice in fear that it may be unwisely used is to destroy the freedom itself. For this reason, we respect the right of individuals to be selective in their own reading. But for the same reason, we oppose efforts of individuals or groups to limit the freedom of choice of others or to impose their own standards or tastes upon the community at large.

The right of any individual not just to read but to read whatever he wants to read is basic to a democratic society.

This right is based on an assumption that the educated and reading man possesses judgment and understanding and can be trusted with the determination of his own actions. In effect, the reading man is freed from the bonds of discovering all things and all facts and all truths through his own direct experiences, for his reading allows him to meet people, debate philosophies, and experience events far beyond the narrow confines of his own existence.

In selecting books for reading by young people, English teachers consider the contribution which each work may make to the education of the reader, its aesthetic value, its honesty, its readability for a particular group of students, and its appeal to adolescents. English teachers, however, may use different works for different purposes. The criteria for choosing a work to be read by an entire class are somewhat different from the criteria for choosing works to be read by small groups. . . . And the criteria for suggesting books to individuals or for recommending something worth reading for a student who casually stops by after class are different from selecting material for a class or group. But the teacher selects books; he does not censor them. Selection implies that a teacher is free to choose this or that work, depending upon the purpose to be achieved and the student or class in question, but a book selected this year may be ignored next year, and the reverse. Censorship implies that certain works are not open to selection, this year or any year.

Many works contain isolated elements to which some individuals or groups may object. The literary artist seeks truth, as he is able to see and feel it. As a seeker of truth, he must necessarily challenge at times the common beliefs or values of a society; he must analyze and comment on people's actions and values and the frequent discrepancy between what they purport to live by and what they do live by. In seeking to discover meaning behind reality, the artist strives to achieve a work which is honest. Moreover, the value and impact of any literary work must be examined as a whole and not in part—the impact of the entire work being more important than the words, phrases, or incidents out of which it is made.

Wallace Stevens once wrote, "Literature is the better part

of life. To this it seems inevitably necessary to add, provided life is the better part of literature." Students and parents have the right to demand that education today keep students in touch with the reality of the world outside the classroom. Much of classic literature asks questions as valid and significant today as when the literature first appeared, questions like "What is the nature of humanity?" "Why do people praise individuality and practice conformity?" "What do people need for a good life?" and "What is the nature of the good person?" But youth is the age of revolt, and the times today show much of the world in revolt. To pretend otherwise is to ignore a reality made clear to young people and adults alike on television and radio, in newspapers and magazines. English teachers must be free to employ books, classic or contemporary, which do not lie to the young about the perilous but wondrous times we live in, books which talk of the fears, hopes, joys, and frustrations people experience, books about people not only as they are but as they can be. English teachers forced through the pressures of censorship to use only safe or antiseptic works are placed in the morally and intellectually untenable position of lying to their students about the nature and condition of mankind.

The teacher must exercise care to select or recommend works for class reading and group discussion which will not embarass students in discussions with their peers. . . .

What a young reader gets from any book depends both on the selection and on the reader himself. A teacher should choose books with an awareness of the student's interests, his reading ability, his mental and emotional maturity, and the values he may derive from the reading. A wide knowledge of many works, common sense, and professional dedication to students and to literature will guide the teacher in making his selections. The community that entrusts students to the care of an English teacher should also trust that teacher to exercise professional judgment in selecting or recommending books.

The Threat to Education

Censorship leaves students with an inadequate and distorted picture of the ideals, values, and problems of their culture. Writers may often be the spokesmen of their culture, or they may stand to the side attempting to describe and evaluate that culture. Yet, partly because of censorship or the fear of censorship, many writers are ignored or inadequately represented in the public schools, and many are represented in anthologies not by their best work but by their "safest" or "least offensive" work.

The censorship pressures receiving the greatest publicity are those of small groups who protest the use of a limited number of books with some "objectionable" realistic elements.... The most obvious and immediate victims are often found among our best and most creative English teachers, those who have ventured outside the narrow boundaries of conventional texts. Ultimately, however, the real victims are the students, denied the freedom to explore ideas and pursue truth wherever and however they wish....

Many well-meaning people wish to restrict reading materials in schools to books that do not mention certain aspects of life they find offensive: drugs, profanity, Black Power, anti-war marches, smoking, sex, racial unrest, rock music, politics, pregnancy, school dropouts, peace rallies, drinking, Chicano protests, or divorce. Although he may personally abhor one or more of these facets of modern life, the English teacher has the responsibility to encourage students to read about and reflect on many aspects, good and bad, of their own society and of other cultures.

The English Teacher's Purposes and Responsibilities

The purpose of education remains what it has always been in a free society: to develop a free and reasoning human being who can think for himself, who understands his own and, to some extent, other cultures, who lives compassionately and cooperatively with his fellow man, who respects both himself and others, who has developed self-discipline and self-motivation and exercises both, who can laugh at a world which often seems mad, and who can successfully develop survival strategies for existence in that world....

Aware of the vital role of literature in the education of mankind, the English teacher has unique responsibilities to his students and to adults in the community. To his students, he is responsible for knowing many books from many cultures, for demonstrating a personal commitment to the search for truth through wide reading and continual critical questioning of his own values and beliefs, for respecting the unique qualities and potential of each student, for studying many cultures and societies and their values, and for exhibiting the qualities of the educated man. To adults, he is responsible for communicating information about his literature program; for explaining, not defending, what books he uses with what students, for what reasons, and with what results; and for communicating the necessity of free inquiry and the search for truth in a democratic society and the dangers of censorship and repression.

The Community's Responsibility

American citizens who care about the improvement of education are urged to join students, teachers, librarians, administrators, boards of education, and professional and scholarly organizations in support of the students' right to read. Only widespread and informed support in every community can assure that—

enough citizens are interested in the development and maintenance of a superior school system to guarantee its achievement;

malicious gossip, ignorant rumors, and deceptive letters to the editor will not be circulated without challenge and correction;

newspapers will be convinced that the public sincerely desires objective school news reporting free from slanting or editorial comment which destroys confidence in and support for schools;

the community will not permit its resources and energies to be dissipated in conflicts created by special interest groups striving to advance their ideologies or biases; and

faith in democratic traditions and processes will be maintained.

Appendix D

EDUCATIONAL PAPERBACK
ASSOCIATION

In May of 1975, a group of paperback wholesalers from throughout the country held an exploratory meeting to discuss some of their common problems in selling and supplying the educational market. They discussed promotional activities, exhibits, sales programs, order fulfillment, single copy orders, stock, catalogues, bookfairs, federal programs, school bookstores, and supplemental services to schools. The discussions were so useful to the participants that they voted to form themselves into a permanent organization called the Educational Paperback Association (EPA), which all paperback wholesalers and publishers with a special commitment to the educational and library paperback book market would be invited to join.

We believe that the existence of such an organization as EPA should be widely known to teachers and school administrators primarily because its wholesaler membership is composed of distributors with a genuine commitment to fulfilling school orders as swiftly, accurately, and inexpensively as possible. We recommend to our readers the following list of thirty wholesalers from fifteen states and four Canadian provinces, as well as ten publishers with an unusual interest in educational paperbacks.

CALIFORNIA

Milligan News Company
150 North Autumn
San Jose, California 95110
(408) 286-7604
  Pat Milligan
  Jim Barton

Cal-West Periodicals, Inc.
2400 Filbert St.
Oakland, California 94607
(415) 444-3570
  Mike Magee

Drown News Agency
15172 Golden West Circle
Westminster, California
92683
(714) 892-7766
  John Jennison

COLORADO

Columbine Distributing
Company, Inc.
1671 Valtec Lane
Boulder, Colorado 80302
(303) 449-1973
  Emil Clausen
  Bob Putman

CONNECTICUT

H.P. Kopplemann, Inc.
140 Van Block Avenue
Hartford, Connecticut
06101

(203) 549-6210
  Allan Hartley

FLORIDA

Florida Educational Paperbacks, Inc.
4905 Rio Vista Avenue
Tampa, Florida 33614
(813) 886-2969
  John & Sue Michel

ILLINOIS

Champaign-Urbana News
Agency
103 North Second
Champaign, Illinois 61820
(217) 352-8006
  Jeff & Craig Hays

Egypt News, Inc.
414 East Broadway
Johnston City, Illinois
62951
(618) 983-8010
  Bob Stocks

Alfonsi News & Book Ser-
vice
Airlawn Street
Taylorville, Illinois 62568
(217) 824-9871
  Gene Alfonsi
  Sally Bender

MAINE

Portland News Company
270 Western Avenue
Portland, Maine 04104
(207) 774-2633
  Debbie Molander

MASSACHUSETTS

Holyoke News Company
720 Main Street
Holyoke, Massachusetts
01040
(413) 534-4537
  Marty Zanger
  Sally Zanger

Samuel Black Company
100 Memorial Avenue
West Springfield, Massa-
chusetts 01089
(413) 733-3178
  Jason Berger

MICHIGAN

Southern Michigan News
Company
7240 Jackson Road
Ann Arbor, Michigan 48103
(313) 665-3754
  Bill Soutar

Ludington News Company,
Inc.
1600 East Grand Boulevard
Detroit, Michigan 48211
(313) 925-7600
  Jerry Ludington

  Sandy Topolski
  Julie Marshall
  George Fisher

Suits News Company
5601 Enterprise
Lansing, Michigan 48910
(517) 393-1740
  Alan Suits
  Thad Suits
  Sam Hughes

Michiana News Service
2232 South 11th Street
Niles, Michigan 49120
(616) 684-3013
  Ted Majarek
  Robert Sones
  Jim King
  Cynthia Kulesia

NEW HAMPSHIRE

Dover News Inc.
35 Fourth Street
Dover, New Hampshire 0382
(603) 742-1562
  Doug Bates

NEW YORK

Southern Tier News Com-
pany, Inc.
3465 Oakwood Avenue
Elmira Heights, New York
14903
(607) 734-7108
  Marvin H. Rubin

OHIO

Central News Company
111 East Voris
Akron, Ohio 44311
(216) 535-6101
  Jim Looman

Klein News Company
1771 East 30th Street
Cleveland, Ohio 44114
(216) 623-0370
  Sharon Saffitz

OREGON

F.C. Himber & Sons, Inc.
1380 West 2nd Avenue
Eugene, Oregon 97402
(503) 686-8001
  Bill Golliher

Bay News Agency
3155 N.W. Yeon Avenue
Portland, Oregon 97210
(503) 228-0251
  Bob Betzold

PENNSYLVANIA

Altoona News Agency
808 Green Street
Altoona, Pennsylvania
16601
(814) 944-3593
  Roy Newborn
  Barbra Newborn

Valley Distributors, Inc.
2947 Felton Road

Norristown, Pennsylvania
19403
(215) 279-7650
  Sid Handler

Mid-Penn Magazine Agency, Inc.
100 Eck Circle
Williamsport, Pennsylvania
17701
(717) 323-8471
  Alan Demel
  Patricia Triaca

TEXAS

Trinity News Company
2412 N.E. Parkway
Fort Worth, Texas 76104
(817) 624-4151
  E. Lynn Bartlett

WASHINGTON

Riches & Adams, Inc.
1555 West Galer Street
Seattle, Washington 98119
(206) 284-7617
  Genevieve Lofgren
  Bob Lofgren

WISCONSIN

Interstate Periodical Distributing
201 East Badger Road
Madison, Wisconsin 53701
(608) 271-3600
  Ed Crossman
  Bruce Sherbow

EPA WHOLESALER MEMBERS—CANADA

BRITISH COLUMBIA

Vancouver Magazine Services
3455 Gardner Court
Vancouver, British Columbia
(604) 298-3221
 Jim Grubb

NOVA SCOTIA

H.H. Marshall, Ltd.
3731 Mackintosh Street
Halifax, Nova Scotia
(902) 454-8381
 Cynthia Ferguson

ONTARIO

Academic Book Caravans
Box 768
Hamilton, Ontario
(416) 387-0690
 Don Geraghty

Metro-Toronto News Company
120 Sinnott Road
Scarborough, Ontario
(416) 755-1166
 David Lappin

EPA PUBLISHER (ASSOCIATE) MEMBERS

Avon Books
959 8th Avenue
New York, New York 10019
(212) 262-4126
 Cathy Lobel

Ballantine Books
201 East 50th Street
New York, New York 10022
(212) 572-2473
 Gillian Jolis

Dell Publishing
1 Dag Hammarskjold Plaza
New York, New York 10017
(212) 832-7300
 Paul O'Donnell
 Betsy Gould

Houghton Mifflin Company
2 Park Street
Boston, Massachusetts
02107

(617) 725-5000
  Toni Lopopolo
  Tom Consolino

New American Library, Inc.
120 Woodbine Street
Bergenfield, New Jersey
(201) 387-0600
  Adele Satz

Pocket Books, Inc.
1 West 39th Street
New York, New York 10018
(212) 245-6400
  Dominic Salvatore

Popular Library
600 Third Avenue
New York, New York 10016
(212) 661-4200
  Michael Israel

Scholastic Magazines
50 West 44th Street
New York, New York 10036
(212) 867-7700
  Richard Mitchell

Select Magazines, Inc.
229 Park Avenue South
New York, New York 10003
(212) 677-6464
  Susan Occhipinti

Viking-Penguin, Inc.
625 Madison Avenue
New York, New York 10022
(212) 755-4330
  Marilyn Abel

International Periodical
Distributors Association
350 Madison Avenue
New York, New York 10017
(212) 986-8150
  Don Spring